Seven Deadliest Unified Communications Attacks

Syngress Seven Deadliest Attacks Series

Seven Deadliest Microsoft Attacks
ISBN: 978-1-59749-551-6
Rob Kraus

Seven Deadliest Network Attacks
ISBN: 978-1-59749-549-3
Stacy Prowell

Seven Deadliest Social Network Attacks
ISBN: 978-1-59749-545-5
Carl Timm

Seven Deadliest Unified Communications Attacks
ISBN: 978-1-59749-547-9
Dan York

Seven Deadliest USB Attacks
ISBN: 978-1-59749-553-0
Brian Anderson

Seven Deadliest Web Application Attacks
ISBN: 978-1-59749-543-1
Mike Shema

Seven Deadliest Wireless Technologies Attacks
ISBN: 978-1-59749-541-7
Brad Haines

Visit **www.syngress.com** for more information on these titles and other resources.

Seven Deadliest Unified Communications Attacks

Dan York

Technical Editor **Dustin D. Trammell**

ELSEVIER

AMSTERDAM • BOSTON • HEIDELBERG • LONDON
NEW YORK • OXFORD • PARIS • SAN DIEGO
SAN FRANCISCO • SINGAPORE • SYDNEY • TOKYO
Syngress is an imprint of Elsevier

SYNGRESS®

Syngress is an imprint of Elsevier.
30 Corporate Drive, Suite 400, Burlington, MA 01803, USA

This book is printed on acid-free paper.

Notices
Knowledge and best practice in this field are constantly changing. As new research and experience broaden our understanding, changes in research methods, professional practices, or medical treatment may become necessary.

Practitioners and researchers must always rely on their own experience and knowledge in evaluating and using any information, methods, compounds, or experiments described herein. In using such information or methods, they should be mindful of their own safety and the safety of others, including parties for whom they have a professional responsibility.

To the fullest extent of the law, neither the Publisher nor the authors, contributors, or editors assume any liability for any injury or damage to persons or property as a matter of products liability, negligence or otherwise, or from any use or operation of any methods, products, instructions, or ideas contained in the material herein.

Library of Congress Cataloging-in-Publication Data
Application submitted

British Library Cataloguing-in-Publication Data
A catalogue record for this book is available from the British Library.

ISBN: 978-1-59749-547-9

10 11 12 13   5 4 3 2 1

Elsevier Inc., the author(s), and any person or firm involved in the writing, editing, or production (collectively "Makers") of this book ("the Work") do not guarantee or warrant the results to be obtained from the Work.

For information on rights, translations, and bulk sales, contact Matt Pedersen, Commercial Sales Director and Rights; e-mail: m.pedersen@elsevier.com

For information on all Syngress publications,
visit our Web site at www.syngress.com

Typeset by: diacriTech, Chennai, India

Working together to grow
libraries in developing countries

www.elsevier.com | www.bookaid.org | www.sabre.org

ELSEVIER   BOOK AID
             International   Sabre Foundation

*For my daughters Chloe and Cassie, as their generation will inherit
the security choices we make today.*

Contents

A preview chapter from *Seven Deadliest USB Attacks* can be found after the index.

Acknowledgments

No book of this size could be done in the tight time frame it was done without a great amount of help. First and foremost, I need to thank my wife Lori who, despite being an artist with absolutely *zero* interest in the subject matter, read each and every page and provided excellent feedback about how the book flowed. Her razor-sharp editing skills definitely made this a more readable book. I could not have done this book, too, without her taking care of everything else going on in our lives. Signing up to write a book in a compressed time frame right before the holidays was not the smartest thing to do. Thanks, Lori – and maybe one of these years, I'll actually move out of writing purely tech books…

I'm incredibly grateful to my technical editor, Dustin Trammell, who took a great amount of time and care to make sure that the text was technically accurate. He provided solid criticism with solutions and contributed some outstanding ideas about how to make the book stronger. Many thanks, too, to Andy Zmolek, a friend from the VoIPSA circles, who not only first pointed Syngress to me as a potential author but also later provided copious detailed notes and feedback on the chapters. Thanks, as well, to Matthew Cater and Rachel Roumeliotis from Syngress for both approaching me to write this book and then doing all they did to make it a reality.

Thanks, too, to Randy Resnick of the VoIP Users Conference for his many comments and encouragement on the overall text, to Scott Beer of Ingate Systems for feedback on the SIP trunking chapter, and to Martyn Davies, Adam Kalsey, and Alan Percy for their comments. I also have to thank my Blue Box podcast cohost and fellow VoIPSA board member Jonathan Zar, as well as the entire Blue Box community, for all the discussions and dialogue since October 2005 that laid the foundation for this book. I need to thank, as well, the many, many people in the IETF Real-time Applications and Infrastructure (RAI) area, who are the real heroes here, as they continue to slave away in the tedious and not very glamorous world of trying to create standards and other mechanisms to make communications more secure.

I want to give a special thanks to Voxeo CEO Jonathan Taylor and President Anne Bowman, who undoubtedly thought I was crazy but didn't object to me pursuing this book, and to my outstanding Voxeo Conversations team who put up with a tired and sometimes grumpy manager and did their best to not comment on the dark circles under my eyes. (The negative side of using a UC system with video!)

Finally, I want to thank all of the security professionals, developers, and system administrators out there who are working each day to make our communications systems more secure. This book comes out of the many conversations I've had with so many of you through the Blue Box podcast, the VOIPSA blog, the VOIPSEC mailing list, and at the many conference presentations I've given on VoIP and UC security. Thank you for asking me tough questions and for encouraging me to keep on telling the story – may this book help in some small way to keep those conversations going.

About the Author

Dan York, CISSP, is the Best Practices Chair and member of the Board of Directors of the Voice over IP Security Alliance (VoIPSA), as well as the producer of "Blue Box: The VoIP Security Podcast" where since October 2005 he and co-host Jonathan Zar have discussed VoIP security news and interviewed people involved in the field. Dan is employed as the Director of Conversations at Voxeo Corporation heading up the company's communication through both traditional and new or social media. Earlier, Dan served in Voxeo's Office of the CTO focused on analyzing or evaluating emerging technology, participating in industry standards bodies, and addressing VoIP security issues. Prior to Voxeo, Dan worked at Mitel Networks in Ottawa, Ontario, where he chaired Mitel's Product Security Team coordinating efforts of a cross-functional team to respond publicly to security vulnerability reports and to ensure that Mitel VoIP and Unified Communications products were as secure as possible.

Since the mid-1980s, Dan has been working with online communication technologies and helping businesses and organizations understand how to use and participate in those new media. Dan frequently presents at conferences on security and communications topics, has authored multiple books on Linux and networking, and writes extensively online at sites such as www.voipsa.org/blog and www.disruptivetelephony.com.

Dan lives with his family in Keene, NH, where he works remotely using Unified Communications systems. More information about Dan can be found at www.danyork.com.

About the Technical Editor

Dustin D. Trammell is the Founder of the Computer Academic Underground and cofounder of the Austin Hackers Association (AHA!). He has over a decade of experience in various areas of information security including vulnerability assessment, penetration testing, secure network architecture, vulnerability research and exploit development, and security research in specific areas related to network protocols, network applications, steganography, and VoIP.

Over the years, Dustin has been involved with many security community projects such as design and development of Sender Policy Framework (SPF) for e-mail (RFC 4408) and contributing as a core developer for the Metasploit Project. Dustin has also released numerous security tools such as the infamous PageIt! mass-paging application, the hcraft HTTP exploit-crafting framework, and the SteganRTP VoIP steganography tool.

He regularly releases vulnerability and exploit advisories, speaks at security-related events and conferences, and is on the Technical Advisory Board of the VoIPSA.

Throughout Dustin's career, he has performed security research and development focused on attack vectors and exploitation methods for BreakingPoint Systems, VoIP security research for TippingPoint, and founded the VIPER Lab VoIP vulnerability research group at Sipera Systems. Before Sipera, Dustin was a Security Research Scientist for Citadel Security Software (acquired by McAfee) responsible for vulnerability analysis, research, and remediation within the scope of the Linux, Solaris, AIX, and HP/UX platforms.

Introduction

WHAT THIS BOOK IS ABOUT

Let's begin with a quick glimpse into a typical day at a company:

There you are at your desk, wanting to talk with your colleague Steve in another office about a new project you need his help on. You turn to your laptop, switch to a software program, and look at Steve's presence info. The little bubble next to Steve's name is green, indicating he is there and available. Next to his name is also a status message that says "In the office today."

Rather than calling Steve immediately, you send him an instant message (IM) with the text, "Hi. Can I call you?" He replies, "Sure." You hit the **Call** button. The softphone on your laptop gets connected to the phone on his desk and you're talking. He asks if you want to do video, and since you do, you both hit a **Video** button and you're suddenly looking at each other. While explaining the project to him, you send him a PowerPoint slide deck through the file transfer part of your software clients. Steve mentions that the project sounds like something he worked on before and pastes the URL to his older project in your IM chat window. As the call goes on, you decide you want to show him a demo of the project and proceed to launch a screen sharing session.

Steve asks you some more questions, to which you say you'll have to get back to him after the call. You both talk for a while more and then you end your call. You go back to your notes, dig up the answers to the questions Steve asked, and write them up in your IM chat session. He responds by thanking you and saying he's looking forward to helping.

A fantasy, you say?

No, it's how millions of people communicate on a daily basis today. The many people out there, perhaps including you, now have access to unified communications (UC) systems.

If you are reading this book, this kind of communication session may already be normal to you. Or this could be the vision you are being sold by a UC vendor. Regardless, let's think for a moment about what the components of this "call" were:

- Presence information showing me Steve's status
- IM text chat before, during, and after the session
- Voice communication
- Video communication
- File transfer
- Screen sharing
- Seamless movement between and among the different modes of communication

Many different communication channels – yet from a user point of view, it was all just a simple and seamless experience. You could have also added into the scenario conferencing in a third person or interacting with a "bot" or automated agent to retrieve information. There are a myriad of possibilities.

The reality is that behind all the magic, there are potentially a great number of different tools and platforms, conceivably provided by a great variety of different vendors. To provide a UC solution like this, your company might be using products and services from "communications" companies like Cisco,[A] Avaya,[B] Alcatel-Lucent,[C] Mitel,[D] and more; your company might be using software from traditional technology companies like Microsoft or IBM; perhaps from business systems companies like Oracle and SAP; perhaps open-source or internally created solutions; your company might be using a newer entrant into the market like Skype; or – you might be using all of the above. Many vendors and many channels.

Adding to the fun, your communications systems *might* be all located in one central place, but more likely are scattered in different locations and data centers as part of a massively distributed network. Your systems might interconnect to hosted services out "in the cloud" or send traffic across the public Internet. They may interact with phones on desktops and also software on mobile smartphones. And, of course, it is all running over the standard IP data network that every other software, device, and service uses.

Amidst all that chaos, the question is: How in the world do you *secure* such a communications infrastructure?

That is what this book is all about.

[A]www.cisco.com
[B]www.avaya.com
[C]www.alcatel-lucent.com
[D]www.mitel.com

WHAT THIS BOOK IS NOT ABOUT

It may come as a surprise, but this book is NOT just about "VoIP Security," per se. Voice over IP (VoIP) is certainly one of the communication channels used in UC, but it is not the only one. Indeed, in these days voice may not even be the primary channel.

You will certainly learn about VoIP security, particularly in a couple of chapters, but that's not the overall focus. If you want to dig deep into the details of VoIP security, there are a number of great books out there written by some outstanding security professionals. They can take you down to the packet level if you want.

This book aims to take a slightly different view to look at the *intersection* of the various communication technologies that make up what we call UC today. VoIP is one of those technologies, as is IM, as is presence, and as are other collaboration technologies.

DEFINING UNIFIED COMMUNICATIONS

So then, what exactly *is* this thing called UC?

Analyst Blair Pleasant with UC Strategies promotes this rather formal definition of UC[1]:

> *UC is communications integrated to optimize business processes. UC integrates the necessary and appropriate real-time and non-real-time communications with business processes and requirements based on presence capabilities, presenting a consistent unified user interface and user experience across multiple devices and media types. Using rules and policies, UC supports the enterprise to manage various types of communications across multiple devices and applications, while integrating with back-office applications, systems and business processes, with the goal of improving business agility and results, leading to increased revenues, decreased costs and improved customer service.*

Her definition focuses on the theme of *integration*, which again is what differentiates UC from simply VoIP. Blair goes on to list the components that are often found in UC systems[2]:

- Call control and multimodal communications: this may or may not be an IP-PBX;
- Presence: desktop, telephony, device presence, as well as rules engine to manage access to presence information;
- Messaging: instant messaging, e-mail, voice mail, unified messaging, and video messaging;
- Conferencing: audio, Web, and video;
- Collaboration tools: whiteboarding, document sharing, and so on;
- Mobility and mobile access;
- Business process integration (sometimes called *Communication Enabled Business Processes* [CEBP]);
- Telephony integration: PBX/IP-PBX gateways to connect to the UC voice communications elements;

- Many forms of clients and endpoints: telephones, SIP phones, softphones, wireless phones and mobile devices, soft clients (including Web and voice portals);
- Speech-recognition servers.

Your UC systems may contain some or *all* of those different components. Your systems may also include additional components like the following:

- Directories and directory servers, which are often the source of the contact list users have;
- Database servers, which are providing the underlying data store;
- Application servers, which are providing additional functionality into the communications sessions.

This last point about applications highlights an intriguing aspect of UC where presence systems, in particular, enable automated notification and communication to reach you in the optimal way. For instance, a calendar system integrated with UC can use your presence and availability information to determine the best way to contact you with a reminder. This might be through IM or through an automated call, but it can build off your presence information and how *you* want to be contacted.

Very rapidly you could see *UC* becoming an all-encompassing term, which is a significant challenge.

For the purpose of our discussions here in this book, a "typical" UC system is thought of as being comprised of the following:

- A control channel, server, or service that is providing the overall session control;
- A unified client in the form of software running on employees' desks;
- Presence information about each employee;
- One or more real-time communication channels, including typically
  - Voice
  - IM
  - Video
- Connectivity to the larger external communication network, perhaps both the public switched telephone network (PSTN) and the public IM networks, as well as the general public Internet. Your system may obviously be different but the principles will be similar.

NOTE

It is perhaps not surprising that every vendor may have a slightly different definition of UC. Some vendors slapped UC onto every product vaguely connected with telephony. Some even went a few years back and renamed all their products to have UC in the actual product names.

It is also not surprising that recently some vendors had second thoughts about this UC branding, and so you are starting to see UC get downplayed or replaced with other terms such as *collaboration* or *unified communications and collaboration*.

ABOUT THE UNIFIED COMMUNICATIONS MARKET

One note about the overall UC market: because the term *UC* is so all-encompassing, the "UC market" has a vast number of players all engaged in a hypercompetitive battle to convince enterprises that *they* are the ones who can truly provide the rich collaboration that enterprises are seeking. Some of the major players in the UC space include:

- **Telephony/telecommunications companies** – The big players in the traditional IP telephony space including Cisco, Avaya, Siemens and the "tels" – Nortel (now part of Avaya), Alcatel-Lucent, Mitel, ShoreTel, and so on. They come at it with a voice background and believe they can provide the whole solution.
- **Back-office infrastructure companies** – Microsoft and IBM pretty much own the enterprise back-office server infrastructure, and it is no surprise that they are coming on very strong with Microsoft Office Communications Server and IBM Lotus Sametime. They have the IM and collaboration side down pat, and see voice as just another channel.
- **Business systems companies** – It might not be immediately intuitive, but big companies like Oracle and SAP already provide collaboration software on the business process and customer relationship management side, so adding the communication elements is not a huge step for them.
- **Cloud-based companies** – The ease of launching companies "in the cloud" has brought a wealth of startups that offer flexible collaboration options at attractive prices as well as increasing competition between companies providing "cloud computing" platforms. Google, in particular, continues to expand its range of cloud-based services and has recently made significant improvements to Google Voice and also purchased the SIP-based Gizmo VoIP service. While not directly in UC, you could easily see them continuing to move in that direction.
- **Consumer-focused companies** – There is a range of companies that started out focusing more on consumers but are now moving to have business and enterprise offerings. Skype is most notable here, offering a rich collaboration experience and claiming that 35% of its usage is now business related. Facebook is another company providing some collaboration elements and seeming to want to grow to include more. As consumers use these collaboration services for their own personal usage, they begin to find ways to use them in business settings as well.
- **Open source** – The number of open-source options for communications continues to grow, offering options for companies that want to "roll their own" solutions and have the technical savvy to do so. Digium is certainly the market leader in this space with their Asterisk PBX and associated ecosystem of partners, but other systems like FreeSWITCH and sipXecs are also out there.

And on any given day, *more* players are entering the space. UC is not so much about any certain set of vendors as it is more about a wide landscape of infrastructure and integration.

TELLING THE STORY

So, what are the elements of the security story that will be woven across the next seven chapters? It may help, first, to understand the structure of each chapter. For each of the topics, the chapter covers:

- An introduction to the threat with some example of the problem
- The anatomy of the threat: how can someone attack your system?
- The dangers of the threat: what are the potential results of an attack?
- The future outlook for the threat: what will the future hold? Will the threat grow larger or smaller?
- Specific strategies about how to defend your system against the threat

Along the way, I have tried to give links to resources in addition to providing other information that will help you learn more about the specific threat

It may also help you if you understand that I tend to look at security through the lens of the "CIA triad," namely:

- **Confidentiality** – Ensures that information is only accessible to the appropriate people. For example, ensuring that information about a call is known only to the caller, the recipient and authorized entities or applications between the caller and recipient.
- **Integrity** – Ensures that information is not *modified* in transit or in storage. For example, ensuring that the message the recipient receives is *identical* to the message the sender sent.
- **Availability** – Ensures that the systems, infrastructure, and endpoints are all *available* and that a communication session can occur. For example, ensuring that a denial-of-service (DoS) attack will not seriously impact communication.

Throughout the book, you will often see that when I am discussing threats, I refer to how they will impact these three factors.

Our story begins with Chapter 1, "The Unified Communications Ecosystem," where we will talk about the single biggest security challenge of UC systems. The challenge is that with UC, communications infrastructure is no longer isolated to its own servers and systems but rather is interlinked with a vast number of other systems. Your communications system is no longer a separate box on a wall but instead is software running on a server somewhere on your data network and connected to all sorts of other services. The surface area that can be attacked has become incredibly large.

In Chapter 2, "Insecure Endpoints," we'll take a look at the device on your desk formerly known as a *phone* and ask questions like: do you *really* need to run an ssh server on that phone? Do you include it in your patch plan? We'll talk about what attacks are out there. We'll also discuss one super simple step to secure your endpoints that is so often missed.

We'll next address a threat that is very easily understood in Chapter 3, "Eavesdropping and Modification." We'll explore how basic network security tools can intercept unsecured voice and IM traffic. We'll also talk about some of the, um, "interesting" things that can be done to *modify* communications over an IP network without the knowledge of the originator of the call, and we'll cover some of the tools that are out there to make this all scriptable.

With Chapter 4, "Control Channel Attacks: Fuzzing, DoS, SPIT, and Toll Fraud," we'll discuss about the plumbing of UC infrastructure. Amazingly, we'll work speedboats and fancy cars into the chapter, and then talk about how you can avoid being the one whose company is funding those toys. DoS attacks and protocol fuzzing may not be overly interesting, but they can be quite deadly, and toll fraud can be hugely expensive. We'll also touch on Spam for Internet Telephony (SPIT) because, well, it makes for really great headlines and someday it just might be a problem.

Since UC systems aren't terribly helpful unless you can communicate with people outside of your system, Chapter 5 looks at "SIP Trunking and PSTN Interconnection" and the really bad things that can happen if you don't secure the connection from your premise out to your gateway to the PSTN (also known as the *traditional phone network* we're used to).

Chapter 6, "Identity, Spoofing, and Vishing," identifies the challenges with identity in the age of text-based protocols like SIP and how easily they can be manipulated. We'll look at some nasty tricks scammers are playing on people with copying IVR trees, touch on social engineering, and talk about some of the emerging ways to address strong identity.

Finally, with Chapter 7, "The End of Geography," we explore what it means when IP networks remove the traditional physical barriers around offices. Your UC system can now be massively distributed and decentralized across many offices, as well as the public Internet. You can federate with other companies, or with public IM networks. You can push some of your UC functionality out "into the cloud" or make use of application services running in the cloud. How can you secure these interconnections? And, can you trust the cloud to be there when you need it? We'll look at the security issues and the questions you need to ask when considering cloud-based or hosted systems.

All in all, it should be a fun journey through this brave new world of UC and how we can realize the benefits of UC while also providing an adequate layer of security.

AND SO IT BEGINS

Before we get started, though, one final note: any book like this is by its nature already aging by the time it ships. So to help keep it up to date, you can head on over to "www.7ducattacks.com," where I will provide updates to the information in the book, links to some audio interviews about the topics, links to tools, and of course any errata. You can also comment on the book there or send me any comments and feedback you may have.

You can also find more of my writing and audio on security-related topics at

- www.blueboxpodcast.com
- www.voipsa.org/blog
- www.disruptivetelephony.com

And, of course, I'm on Twitter as twitter.com/danyork.
With that, let's begin...

Endnotes

1. www.ucstrategies.com/unified-communications-strategies-views/will-the-real-definition-of-unified-communications-please-stand-up.aspx
2. Ibid.

The Unified Communications Ecosystem

1

INFORMATION IN THIS CHAPTER

* Anatomy of Attacks against the UC Ecosystem
* Dangers Associated with the UC Ecosystem
* Future of Attacks against the UC Ecosystem
* How to Defend Your UC Ecosystem

In June 2007, security researcher Carl Livitt announced the discovery of a vulnerability in AsteriDex,[A] an address book application for the open source Asterisk private branch exchange (PBX) that would let an unauthenticated attacker execute arbitrary commands on the Asterisk management console. These commands could be operating system commands that would be executed in the context of the account executing the Asterisk PBX application. Proof-of-concept exploit code was provided, which showed both writing text to a random file and also downloading code to the exploited server so that the attacker could gain shell access to the system.

A few months later in August 2007, Digium issued a security advisory[B] indicating that if Asterisk was configured to use Internet Message Access Protocol (IMAP) for voice-mail storage, an attacker could send an e-mail with a malformed multipurpose Internet mail extensions body to a user and when the user next listened to his or her voice mail by phone, Asterisk would crash. Not just for that one user, but for all users. All a remote attacker would need to do would be to send a bogus e-mail message to employees at companies using Asterisk, and then sit back and wait for the system to crash. That's it. Quick denial-of-service (DoS).

A year and a bit later in October 2008, VoIPshield Systems researchers discovered a DoS vulnerability in Cisco's Unity unified messaging product where an attacker could send a malformed *messaging application programming interface* command to a Microsoft Exchange Server and cause the Cisco Unity system to stop responding.[C]

[A]www.packetstormsecurity.org/0707-exploits/asteridex-exec.txt
[B]http://downloads.asterisk.org/pub/security/AST-2007-022.html
[C]www.cisco.com/warp/public/707/cisco-sr-20081008-unity.shtml

Cisco and Microsoft investigated the issue and Microsoft released security bulletin MS09-003[D] in February 2009 to fix the issue.

An address book application letting you execute arbitrary commands on your PBX management console? An e-mail message crashing your PBX? A connection to an application program interface (API) on a Microsoft mail system causing a Cisco messaging product to stop responding?

Welcome to the interconnected security nightmare of unified communications (UC). The challenge is that with UC, communications infrastructure is no longer isolated to its own servers and systems. Instead, it is interlinked with a vast number of other disparate systems.

> **WARNING**
>
> While Asterisk, Cisco, and Microsoft systems are referenced here, you should not take that to mean that those systems are more vulnerable than others. They tend to just be more open about the security vulnerabilities they have, as well as the corresponding fixes. Other vendors may have just as many vulnerabilities, but just may not be as open with the information.

ANATOMY OF ATTACKS AGAINST THE UC ECOSYSTEM

Back in the days of "traditional" telephony, your security concerns were fairly limited. As shown in Figure 1.1, you generally needed to focus on

- physical access to the PBX switch itself and its console
- physical wiring
- voice-mail passwords
- class of service
- public switched telephone network (PSTN) gateways.

FIGURE 1.1

Traditional Communication Security Was Fairly Straightforward

---

[D]www.microsoft.com/technet/security/bulletin/ms09-003.mspx

Security typically involved making sure the PBX was in a secured location and that wiring cabinets were locked so that someone with a lineman's handset and alligator clips couldn't just listen in to your calls. You established the appropriate "class-of-service" settings for each extension so that each extension had only the appropriate dialing privileges necessary. You made sure people were using good voice-mail passwords so that someone couldn't come in and reprogram outbound dialing on an extension to get free long-distance calls. You have set up appropriate controls and/or monitoring on the outbound PSTN connections, which were typically directly inside the PBX itself. Take these precautions and generally you were set. Plus, all the phones were on their own dedicated wires, so there was generally no shared infrastructure like there is in Internet Protocol (IP) networks.

EPIC FAIL

One of the attacks that is still one of the most common ways for attackers to ring up free long-distance calls at the expense of some unwitting company is to attack voice-mail systems and make use of elevated privileges. For example, some PBXs have a feature where someone calling into the voice-mail system and authenticating can then choose an option and enter in another code to gain access to outbound dial tone from the PBX. The caller can then enter any phone number and be connected.

While this may have once sounded like a great idea so that traveling employees could call back into the company, enter a code, and then make long-distance or international calls from the company's PBX, there is also a huge opportunity here for exploitation by an attacker who can figure out the access code. All he or she needs to do is (1) determine the PIN to access a voice-mail box and (2) determine the PIN/code needed to make outbound calls, if one is even required. With that information, the attacker can now make endless long-distance or international calls at the PBX owner's expense. Many attackers may, of course, sell this information to others so that they, too, can make free calls.

This feature goes by multiple names, but it is often called *direct inward system access* or *DISA*. If you're smart, you'll make sure that this is disabled from any system you administer.

Also check for the capability of a voice-mail user to configure the forwarding of their extension to an external number. This is another way for attackers to dial into a company, enter an extension, and then be connected to a remote or international number.

These are extremely serious ways that attackers could easily run up tens of thousands (or more!) of dollars in fraudulent charges on your company's account. Oh, and just because you are using an IP-PBX now doesn't mean this capability isn't present... it may be there – it may even be on by default. Check now!

Today, however, in our massively interconnected world of IP communications, the security of your communications infrastructure is much more complex. As shown in Figure 1.2, you don't only have to worry about your PBX and wiring, you also have to worry about e-mail servers, Web servers, business systems, desktop PCs.... Oh, and of course, the underlying network infrastructure! All those "phones" are

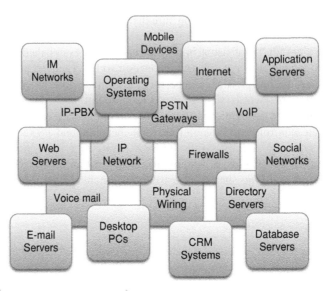

FIGURE 1.2

The Interconnected Communication Infrastructure of Today

now little computers (or softphones[E] running on computers) spread out all over the computer network. The PSTN gateways are probably not directly in the PBX any more – in fact, they may not even be on premises any more but may instead be out across the public Internet via Session Initiation Protocol (SIP) trunks.

Add in multichannel communication where you have an instant messaging (IM) infrastructure that might be Microsoft Office Communications Server, IBM Sametime, or some other commercial or open source solution. Tie it into central directories like Active Directory or Lightweight Directory Access Protocol (LDAP)-based systems. Sprinkle in the latest whiz-bang dashboards that upper management wants. Then, add in all the Web services APIs that the Web team wants to use to enable "click-to-call" from your main Web site. Next, add the other APIs the business systems team wants so that you can know the presence of your suppliers through federated IM and be able to initiate IM sessions or calls to them… then toss in the ability for traveling and remote employees to be able to securely connect in across the public Internet as if they were in the office… plus this… plus that…

You've got yourself a mess.

Even worse, in many companies no one single person or team may be accountable for the "communications infrastructure." Instead, someone (you?) owns the UC software and services, but they run on servers maintained by a server team, connecting

---

[E]A "softphone" is a software program running on a computer that can be used instead of a traditional "hardphone" that sits on a desk. Typically, a person would use a headset connected to the computer to call people over the phone system. From the phone system's point of view, the softphone is simply another phone connected to the system, just like all of the traditional hardphones.

over a network maintained by the network team, interacting with e-mail servers run by the e-mail team and Web servers run by the Web team... and then, of course, with the firewall team zealously guarding the edge of the network where it touches the Internet.

A lot of different pieces and players. A lot of different people to interact with to make sure everything is secure. And, of course, a lot of potential finger-pointing when something goes wrong.

The strength of UC is that it has enormous potential in strengthening the collaboration between employees, enriching the connections between a distributed workforce, and generally making employees more productive and through that potentially increasing a company's revenue and profit. The weakness of UC, though, is that these advantages come at the price of increased complexity, and as anyone involved in security knows, complexity is the enemy of security.

You are no longer talking about a small set of isolated solutions; instead, you have a large ecosystem of interconnected systems and services.

DANGERS ASSOCIATED WITH THE UC ECOSYSTEM

So let's take a moment to talk about the dangers inherent in this large ecosystem of systems and services. There are obviously many dangers, and we'll be diving into more detail on many of the threats throughout the rest of the book. However, the biggest overall categories of threats are DoS, toll fraud, and exposure of information.

DoS/Availability

Probably the single biggest threat to the overall UC ecosystem is the issue of *availability*. With all the different components connected to each other over the IP network, how do you ensure that the systems can in fact communicate with each other? DoS attacks aren't necessarily interesting to talk about, but they are probably much more of a threat to the UC systems than many other attacks.

DoS attacks are only part of the availability picture, too. What happens when a zillion people inside your company all start downloading the YouTube clip that's a viral video? Or if they are all watching the live-streaming of some major political event? Is your network set up correctly to prioritize your communications traffic?

NOTE

While we are discussing just a "DoS" attack here, your UC system, particularly its public-facing components connected to the Internet, could of course be subjected to a "distributed denial-of-service" (DDoS) attack as well. In such an attack, a large number of computers out on the Internet will begin attacking your systems from all over the Internet, making it extremely difficult to identify and block the source of the attacks. Typically, the computers participating in a DDoS attack are compromised (or zombie); computers that have been infected with malicious code are known as a *bot*. These computers together are operating as part of a "botnet" that is being controlled by an attacker and is targeted at your exposed systems.

Toll Fraud

Toll fraud is perhaps even less important to discuss than DoS attacks, but yet it can incur very real – and very large – costs to your company. This is really the one area of UC security where the financial risk is the greatest. As mentioned, some of the concerns here are the traditional ones like voice-mail system configuration, but in the brave new interconnected world of UC, we have to seriously think about the call control and the signaling pathways between our different components.

Is it possible that a disgruntled employee could figure out a way to make free calls? And then pass that information along to someone on the outside? Is it possible for someone remotely to be able to connect to your system as if they were a remote extension? Or can they connect directly to your SIP service provider and make calls to the PSTN using your account? Are all these signaling channels locked down and secured? Are you logging and monitoring appropriate connections?

Exposure of Information

This is easily the area people can best understand. The most tangible example is eavesdropping on voice or IM communication. If you send that information out across a network unprotected, there is certainly the chance that someone could intercept that communications stream and learn what you are doing. Now, this could be across the public Internet with some third-party learning information about the internal workings of your company – or it could be an internal employee learning information he or she shouldn't learn. (Such as, say, the fact that the company is being bought next week and half the staff will be let go!)

In an interconnected UC environment, though, there are other ways to learn information beyond just the communication streams. Signaling data, be it for calls and IM or for indication of presence (whether a person is available for communication or not), can be shared between systems across the internal network. Business systems can share out information about customers or vendors in ways that can be seen by others. APIs that let information be accessed can have weak (or no) authentication.

There is also the more subtle issue of exposure of aggregate data where pattern recognition can identify interesting trends. For instance, call detail records could be sent in the clear from a call server to a logging server or exposed on the call server through some type of easy-to-use API. The records for an individual call may not mean much, but over time patterns might emerge. Going back to our previous example, someone might notice a large number of calls between the CEO's extension and the phone number for a law firm associated with a company that is suspected to want to acquire your company. Patterns may emerge that give away confidential information.

How are you securing the transport of signaling and media between UC components? What authentication systems are in use? Who has access to what information? How are the APIs secured? What kind of information can you gain from them? How is communication handled with remote employees across the public Internet?

There are many more dangers in UC systems, of course, but these are really the largest concerns when you look at the overall ecosystem.

TIP

In 2005, the Voice over IP Security Alliance created the "VoIP Security Threat Taxonomy" to provide a vendor-neutral view into the threats to Voice over IP (VoIP) systems and services. The taxonomy document is available as a PDF download from www.voipsa.org/ Activities/taxonomy.php. While it is obviously specific to the VoIP part of UC, it provides some solid background information that will help in your understanding of the overall threats to UC.

FUTURE OF ATTACKS AGAINST THE UC ECOSYSTEM

The future of UC systems looks incredibly bright. Each month brings more new and better ways to enhance collaboration within an enterprise. While we don't know if the name "UC" will be with us in the long term, the idea that there are better ways for employees to collaborate most certainly will be.

Regardless of what it may be called, it will only get more complex and potentially insecure as communications systems get woven into back-office systems, APIs get more robust, and UC systems get more federated and interconnected.

Let's take a look at several different areas of growth.

Social Software and Services

As people increasingly integrate "social" tools, such as Twitter and Facebook, into their daily lives and use those tools for business communication, they will want those tools integrated where appropriate into their communications systems. As an example, in late 2009, Siemens demonstrated how their UC system could incorporate presence updates from Twitter. The idea reflects the fact that employees traveling probably won't immediately go and update their presence status within their UC system when they land at some airport – but many of them will update Twitter immediately once they land. Why not incorporate that information from an employee's tweet into their status in the UC system?

Companies, vendors, and employees are increasingly going to be looking at these types of integrations. For you as a security professional, there are a host of security issues here: understanding the APIs to communicate to the social services, understanding the security of the transport from your UC system to the social service (and whether that matters, given that much of the information may be public, anyway), understanding how you deal with compliance issues if you are in an industry where you need to be concerned about such topics, and just having yet another service out on the public Internet that you have to be concerned about.

Public Versus Private Information

There is also a more subtle security concern with integration of social tools. Generally, when people are using social services like Twitter and Facebook, they are blurring the boundaries between their personal and work lives and increasingly between information that they would have made public and information that they would have previously kept private. As UC systems seek to have integration with social tools, that data from social tools will be pulled into corporate systems. How do you ensure the privacy of data once it hits your enterprise system?

For example, a small percentage of people on Twitter make their updates private and you have to be approved by them before you can see their Twitter stream. If one of these people is an employee and your UC system starts following them (and is approved by the person), who should have access to that information within the UC system? Everyone? People on a specific team? People the person approves?

Similar questions could arise about Facebook information. If you haven't accepted someone as a "friend" on Facebook, should they be able to see your information in the corporate UC system?

There are a whole host of thorny issues here. As security professionals, it may or may not necessarily be our role to come up with guidelines or policies here, but you can expect to be asked at some point. If you get a chance during the evaluation of new integration services, it might be smart to inject these questions up front so that people do think a bit about them before jumping into the new service. (And yes, this may be highly unlikely, but we can only hope they will.)

Federation

One of the big buzzwords in enterprise communications right now is "federation" – the ability to exchange information between trusted systems that are federated together. I'll discuss this concept in detail more in Chapter 7, "The End of Geography," but it's worth mentioning here.

The reality is that very few large companies are entirely homogenous with regard to their communication infrastructure. As companies purchase other companies, they inherit the communication systems of that acquired company. Sometimes, it is easy to swap it out for what the main company uses, but often, there is either too great a cost or too much of a disruption to make the change quickly. The result is that one part of the company is running Microsoft OCS while another part is running IBM Sametime and yet another part is using an open source Jabber/XMPP solution. One set of offices have Cisco IP-PBXs while another set of offices have Avaya solutions, another set has Mitel equipment, and a few offices are using Asterisk.

People are generally looking for one or more of these types of information to be shared:

- **Presence** You want to see someone's presence information. You want to know if they are online and available. Can you IM or call them?
- **IM** Once you know their presence, you want to be able to IM them, regardless of what system they are on.

- **Voice/Video** You want to be able to initiate a voice or video call with them directly from your endpoint to theirs. From a company cost-savings point of view, the company may want to do this kind of federation so that a call, say via SIP, goes across the IP network from your system to the recipient without ever touching the PSTN and incurring costs there.
- **Collaboration** You want to be able to easily share files with the person, or do a "Whiteboard" session, or share your screen.

Naturally, you want all of this to be seamless to the end user – and of course secured since it may involve confidential company information.

So far what you've seen here has all been *intradomain* federation, that is, it's all within the network of the same company, as shown in Figure 1.3. However, companies today also want to engage in *interdomain* federation where the connections occur between companies, as shown in Figure 1.4.

Say you are in a consulting company that wants to have this rich collaboration with clients and you want to federate with your clients' systems. But how does the company securely ensure that you see only the appropriate client information? How do you ensure on your end that information from a client is only seen by appropriate personnel on your side?

Or say that you want to have this kind of federation with your suppliers so that directly in your business systems you can see the presence status of your account representative at the supplier and can initiate an IM or call with that account representative?

Or what if you want to engage more with your customers via IM and want to federate with the public IM networks (For example, Yahoo! Messenger, Microsoft Windows Live Messenger, AIM, GoogleTalk, and so on.). How do you securely connect to those public IM networks and ensure they only see appropriate information?

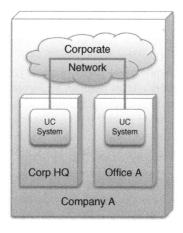

FIGURE 1.3

Intradomain Federation between Branch Offices

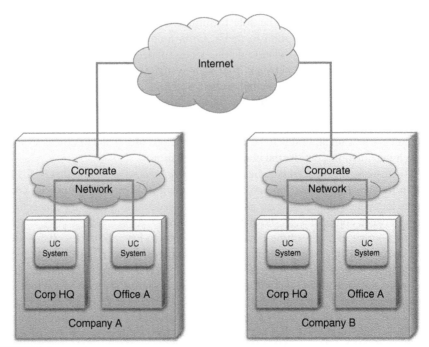

FIGURE 1.4

Interdomain Federation between Companies

There are a host of issues here, some of which we'll touch on in more detail in Chapter 7, "The End of Geography." The net result, though, is that you are going to need to understand options for how you securely federate your system to the many other systems out there – both within your own company and externally.

Mashups and APIs

As the ecosystem of interconnected applications and services expands, APIs play a key role in linking the applications together. Sadly, though, it seems like with each new component in a UC ecosystem, vendors feel a need to create yet another new and different API. Very often, these APIs run on new ports on the servers, which means yet another port for you to scan and potentially open up on routers if the components are separated on your network. It also means yet another port to engage with security testing.

There is a great need for standardization in this area; but while we wait for the glacial pace of standards, we have to look at each new API and determine the security risks.

Customers and vendors are also increasingly looking to enable *mashups* to occur: small, lightweight interaction between two or more services typically over a Hypertext Transfer Protocol (HTTP) connection. For instance, a customer relationship management application may want to graph your customer data against Google

Maps. Or someone may want to access an external service to pull up geo-location information about an incoming phone number.

From a security point of view, many of these services are running out on the public Internet. Is the information you are mashing up with the external service confidential in nature? If so, how is the transport being secured? What kind of privacy protection does the service claim to have? and so on.

With an ever-increasing number of publicly-accessible APIs out on the Internet, you can be sure that some enterprising employees are going to want to connect your data to those services. How you do that securely without compromising the security of your overall UC ecosystem will definitely be one of your challenges.

It's All about the Cloud

Along with all those external services, the reality is that today it is increasingly all about "the Cloud." With the insane amounts of network bandwidth we have today, we can now realize the dreams we had years before of massively distributed networks with functionality split between on-premise systems and hosted systems that live somewhere "out in the cloud." There are some amazing benefits and capabilities you can have here, but also a whole host of security challenges.

We're going to spend much of Chapter 7, "The End of Geography," diving into greater detail on this topic, but for now, it's just worth noting that the future UC ecosystems will undoubtedly have major components that are based out in the cloud.

Bright Shiny Objects

Finally, you should note that vendors in the UC space definitely have a seriously bad case of the "bright shiny object" syndrome. Because it is such a hypercompetitive space and, as was mentioned in the introduction to this chapter, has so many different players, there does seem to be a heavy interest by vendors in attempting to differentiate by chasing whatever bright shiny object is currently the obsession of the early adopters of technology. This object may be some new service (for example, Twitter) or new device (for example, iPhone).

Today, judging from keynote speeches by UC vendors at recent industry conferences, vendors are seeking to make their apps more social and integrate in Twitter, Facebook, and other such services. Next year, they may all be talking about how they can interoperate with Google Wave, shown in Figure 1.5, or perhaps even include an embedded Wave server directly in their solutions.

The point is really that whether we like it or not, UC vendors are going to be chasing these bright shiny objects and trying to figure out how they can add them into their collaboration offerings. As a security professional, if you want to stay current with what vendors are offering, you, too, may need to allocate some of your time to chasing those bright shiny objects in the collaboration space and understand what the security impacts may be. The good news is that if you do so, you'll at least be able to respond somewhat intelligently when someone in your organization

FIGURE 1.5

Google Wave Provides a New Way to Collaborate

forwards you a link about your UC vendor adding in features connected to whatever the latest rage is.

HOW TO DEFEND YOUR UC ECOSYSTEM

At the end of the day, your best strategy for defending your brave new world of UC is really to

- identify all the ecosystem components
- develop security plans for all components
- test the whole system.

It sounds simple, but admittedly it is not. Let's examine each point.

Strategy #1: Identify All Ecosystem Components

This sounds like it should be simple, right? But if you go back to Figure 1.2, can you name all the components that make up your UC infrastructure?

Consider that a typical system probably includes most of the following, and that some of these functions may be consolidated on one server while other functions may be distributed to other parts of the network:

- Call servers for voice
- Video servers

- Conferencing servers for voice or video conferencing (and perhaps one for each)
- Voice-mail servers
- Interactive voice response and auto-attendant servers
- Gateways to the PSTN, which may be external through SIP service providers
- IM servers
- Presence servers
- E-mail servers
- Web servers
- Collaboration servers for file, data, presentation, or screensharing
- "Hardphones" on employee desks (typically "IP phones" today)
- "Softphones" on employee computers and laptops
- Other "software clients" that provide collaboration functionality
- Directory servers, such as Active Directory, LDAP, and so on
- Database servers
- Firewalls
- Firewall traversal solutions
- Software for mobile phones, particularly "smartphones"

You also have to understand the underlying network infrastructure, including

- Local area network infrastructure, that is, Ethernet switches.
- Routers and their associated access control lists.
- Internet-related infrastructure, such as DNS servers, proxy servers, and so on.
- Power supplies, including backup power sources.
- Patch-management processes for the operating systems deployed.

It's no easy task and can easily morph into a gigantic process that could consume many hours of time.

Your best plan may be to start like this

1. Identify the software and the hardware used for, say, basic telephony.
2. Ask yourself the question:
   - *What other products and services does this depend upon in order to remain in operation?*
3. For each identified component, repeat step 2.
4. Once you have completed the identification process for that one set of software and hardware, ask yourself the question:
   - *Are there other collaboration services that are not linked into the first set of software and hardware?*
   - *If so, repeat steps 2 and 3 for each of those services.*
5. Buy yourself a beer or other beverage when you finally have mapped out all the intricate connections.

Now you should have a list of the different components and essentially a map of which components are connected to which other components.

Strategy #2: Develop Security Plans for All Components

Next, you need to figure out the security profile of each piece of the overall puzzle. For each of the components in your list, you need to come up with a list of answers to questions about the security of that component. The list of questions will obviously vary based on your own situation, but here's a list to start you out on building yours:

1. What is the component? Hardware? Software? A service?
2. Is it owned by your company? Or is it an external service?
3. Who specifically has responsibility for the component? Is it a specific person or a group?
4. What is the contact information for that person?
5. Do you have backup contact information for someone else if that person is not available?
6. Where is the component physically located? What data center? What server?
7. If the component is software on a server:
   a. What operating system and version?
   b. Is the operating system up-to-date with security patches?
   c. If not, are there reasons it has not been updated? What is the plan to get it updated?
   d. What are the patch management plans for the server?
   e. Who has administrative access to the server?
   f. What kind of logging is done by the software and who has access to those logs?
   g. Is there a plan for upgrades to the software? What is it?
   h. Where are the license keys or any other information needed to reinstall the software should that ever be necessary?
   i. What are the backup plans? Has a restore been tried recently?
8. If the component is hardware:
   a. What is the vendor contact information?
   b. Who is the contact person on your end for the vendor? Does the vendor know to whom to send any information about the product, such as the existence of new upgrades or fixes?
   c. If there is a warranty for the product, what is it? When does it expire? Who knows about it?
   d. Are there any systems in place to alert you to hardware failures?
   e. What operating system is running inside the device?
   f. All of the questions in #7 above related to software.
9. If the component is an external service:
   a. What is the vendor contact information?
   b. Who is the contact person on your end for the vendor? Does the vendor know to whom to send any information about the product, such as the existence of new upgrades or fixes?
   c. What kind of service level agreements are in place? Who knows about them?

d. What do you have to do to get support from the vendor?

e. Is there a place on the Internet to get information about the current status of the service?

10. Is there currently any kind of routine security scanning of the component? If so, who has access to the results? Do the results trigger any actions? If so, what and by whom?

11. Is the component a single point of failure?

a. If so, what is the plan should that component fail to get the system back in operation?

b. If not, what are the redundant systems in place? Are they manually or automatically activated?

12. What kind of information is handled by the component? What are the security risks associated with that information?

Etcetera, etcetera, etcetera...You get the idea. Your list may be much simpler than this one or it may be quite longer. The key questions to me are the first ones – What is the component? Who is in charge of it? How can you reach them if there is a problem?

As people within the company come to rely on the new UC infrastructure, they will have little tolerance for downtime. Who are you going to call?

Further, as you try to understand the overall security risks to your UC infrastructure, you need to understand where the weak points are and use that understanding to develop your plans to improve the security of the system.

Strategy #3: Engage in Holistic Ecosystem Testing

After you have identified and understood all the components of your UC system and have gathered security information about the various components, you need to devise a plan to test the security of the system to be sure it is really as secure as you think it is.

The challenge you face is that you really need to test the whole UC system, not isolated components.

If you go back to the examples at the very beginning of the chapter, you could see someone testing the security of the AsteriDex application alone and separate from the security of the Asterisk PBX. It may have passed fine. The person testing may have checked the security of the Asterisk PBX and found it fine, too. Similarly, most IMAP mail servers may undergo security testing, but this particular vulnerability was only an issue when the IMAP mail server was used in conjunction with Asterisk.

That's the key. The vulnerabilities may not be there in the stand-alone system testing. They may only be found when you test the applications and services together.

Doing so may be a bit of a challenge, of course. In the ideal world, you might have your own test lab with a copy of the software that is deployed in the production environment. You can then hammer it with your suite of security tests without having any impact on the real network. However, in reality, your company may not be able to afford to pay for a complete duplicate setup. You may have to test on the real production network. If so, you may need to find an odd time when a potential disruption may not impact business.

It may be a challenge, but if you can figure out how to test the whole system with all of its various components, you'll be much more certain about the security of your overall UC environment.

SUMMARY

In the modified words of a former US President, "It's the ecosystem, stupid." That's what it all comes down to. The great benefit of UC is that it provides unprecedented levels of communication and collaboration both within an enterprise and also between an enterprise and trusted partners. The downside is that there is an added level of complexity within the communications infrastructure that you as a security professional must address.

Your communications system is no longer the province of a single vendor who came in, screwed a PBX to the wall, and wired up phones to every desk. There is no longer "one throat to choke." Instead you have an interconnected network of systems and services, each with potentially its own owner, its own upgrade schedules, its own vulnerabilities…and then the larger issue of the new vulnerabilities created when systems are combined.

The complexity will only get greater as even more vendors join the UC space and as UC continues to encompass even more communication modalities and systems.

You have to understand what you currently have deployed, what the security risk is associated with the system, and who will fix it (and how and when) if something goes wrong.

It's the ecosystem, stupid… now let's start diving into some of the components.

Insecure Endpoints

INFORMATION IN THIS CHAPTER

- Anatomy of Attacks against UC Endpoints
- Dangers of Attacks on Endpoints
- The Future of Attacks against UC Endpoints
- How to Defend Your Endpoints

In November 2008, security researchers at Voice over Internet Protocol (VoIP) Shield Systems issued an advisory[A] stating that Microsoft Office Communicator could stop responding if it received an instant messaging (IM) with a very large number of emoticons. Yes, if someone sent you a message with too many smiley faces, your unified communications (UC) client would stop responding, stop accepting phone calls, and even switch to showing you as offline.

Earlier in June 2008, security researchers at France Telecom/Orange discovered[B] that it was possible for an attacker to send a malformed Real-time Transport Protocol (RTP) (audio) packet to a Cisco 7960G or Cisco 7940G IP phone and cause that phone to reboot, thus disconnecting any calls in progress and effectively creating a denial of service for the time that the IP phone took to reboot.

That same month, an advisory[C] was issued about a vulnerability in AOL Instant Messenger (AIM) client where a remote attacker could send a malformed RTCP packet during a video call and cause malicious code to be executed on the victim's computer.

Going back a bit to the ShmooCon conference in January 2006, Shawn Merdinger, a security researcher for TippingPoint at that time, outlined in his presentation[D] the systematic research he had performed on 11 Wi-Fi IP phones and the wide range of security vulnerabilities found in those phones. Almost all of them had services running on

---

[A]http://web.nvd.nist.gov/view/vuln/detail?vulnId=CVE-2008-5181
[B]http://web.nvd.nist.gov/view/vuln/detail?vulnId=CVE-2008-4444
[C]www.zerodayinitiative.com/advisories/ZDI-08-097/
[D]www.blueboxpodcast.com/files/shmoocon_preso_voip_wifi_phone_merdinger.pdf

17

undocumented ports. In several instances, this provided full administrative control over the phone merely by telnetting to the specific port. No log-in credentials were required, and the attacker could change the phone configuration, reboot the system, and more.

More recently, in August 2009, security researcher Walter Sprenger with Compass Security announced[E] that the authentication mechanisms of a series of snom IP phones could be bypassed by sending a modified HTTP request to the phone. The phone has a built-in Web interface for phone management, and administrators are encouraged to enable authentication and use strong passwords. However, this particular vulnerability allowed an attacker to completely bypass the authentication mechanism and obtain full administrative access to the snom IP phone. Once connected, the attacker could listen to conversations, initiate outgoing phone calls, and view and modify the configuration for the phone.

TIP

To see recent vulnerabilities related to UC, go to the Web site of the US National Vulnerability Database (NVD) and search on terms such as *VoIP*, *SIP*, and *IM*. The search interface is at http://web.nvd.nist.gov/view/vuln/search

---

The list could go on and on. The reality is that in today's UC systems, the "endpoints" are no longer "dumb" phones. The piece of plastic sitting on your desk looking like a phone is in fact a little computer, and in the world of UC, we are not only talking about phones but also IM clients and softphones. With increased complexity comes additional security concerns.

NOTE

Throughout the book, the term *endpoint* is used to refer to the hardware device or software program a person uses to interact with a UC system because it could be a hardphone, a softphone, an IM client, a dedicated "UC client" software, or any other potential software applications or hardware devices. The reality, though, is that the security issues are basically the same, regardless of the actual form of the hardware device or software application the person is using. For this reason, the simple term *endpoint* is used.

ANATOMY OF ATTACKS AGAINST UC ENDPOINTS

Let's now take a look at a number of common attacks against UC endpoints and some specific examples.

General DoS Attacks

First, there are some very simple, rudimentary attacks that may also be very effective at knocking UC endpoints off the network.

[E]www.csnc.ch/misc/files/advisories/cve-2009-1048.txt

Packet Flooding

A very basic attack is to simply flood a network with an extremely high volume of packets. This may cause performance of the UC endpoints to degrade significantly. Many tools for "packet flooding" still exist, ranging from a simple "*ping -f*" on a UNIX system to specific tools targeted at generating insane volumes of traffic.

Session Initiation Protocol–Specific Commands

One of the simplest attacks is to write a short script that sends the Session Initiation Protocol (SIP) command *BYE* to every IP address in a range. Devices receiving this *BYE* command would simply hang up any active calls. Thankfully, over time, vendors got smarter about not accepting just any *BYE* command, so this attack has become less effective. However, other variations on this attack still exist.

Finding Endpoints to Attack

Beyond the really basic attacks, an attacker needs to find UC endpoints that can be attacked, identify what those endpoints are, and then proceed to attack those endpoints.

Enumerating Endpoints

If an attacker has access to your internal network, perhaps through an unsecured Wi-Fi wireless network or a compromised device on the network edge, he or she can use a network-scanning tool such as "nmap"[F] to scan your network. For example, if your UC system is SIP-based, you can scan the network for any device with services listening on port 5060, the default SIP port, as shown in this command sample:

```
bash-3.2# nmap -p 5060 --open 172.20.12.0/24
Starting Nmap 5.00 ( http://nmap.org ) at 2009-11-27 16:06 EST
Interesting ports on pc-00135.example.local (172.20.12.135):
PORT     STATE SERVICE
5060/tcp open sip
MAC Address: 08:00:0F:19:A0:FE (Mitel)
Interesting ports on pc-00143.example.local (172.20.12.143):
PORT     STATE SERVICE
5060/tcp open sip
MAC Address: 00:04:F2:17:12:80 (Polycom)
```

You'll notice that the nmap identified each of the examples as, in this case, Mitel and Polycom IP phones. Other variations of nmap commands could further probe and identify, for instance, other services running on the endpoints. There are also tools that are specifically focused at finding SIP endpoints such as the *svmap* tool that is a part of the *SIPVicious* tool suite.[G]

[F]http://nmap.org/
[G]http://code.google.com/p/sipvicious/

Once the attacker has identified UC endpoints, he or she can then move on to attacking each endpoint with specific attacks outlined in the next sections. There are, of course, tools that automate this process by scanning an IP address range, identifying the device found at each target IP address and then attempting to compromise that device. A list of some of the scanning and enumeration tools targeted at VoIP can be found in the VoIP Scanning and Enumeration Tools section of the VoIPSA VoIP Security Tools List available at www.voipsa.org/Resources/tools.php#VoIP Scanning and Enumeration Tools.

Utilizing Search Engines

Another way for an attacker to identify target UC endpoints is to simply do a Google search on certain unique phrases that appear in URLs associated with the administration interface for the endpoint. This will find any of those particular endpoints that are directly connected to the Internet or whatever network the attacker is scanning. For example, Figure 2.1 shows the results of a Google search on 'inurl:"NetworkConfiguration" cisco,' a phrase used in the URL for various Cisco IP phones.

Now that the attacker has identified the endpoints, he or she can move on to trying specific techniques to compromise them. Given that the specific lists of phrases to be used in this kind of search can be found on the public Internet, this is yet another reason not to directly connect your endpoint to the Internet.

FIGURE 2.1

Using Google to Find Cisco IP Phones on the Internet

Default Passwords

Default passwords continue to be probably the single biggest problem with UC endpoints, particularly for hardware endpoints like IP phones. One reason for this is the desire by IP phone vendors to make it as easy as possible for large companies to rapidly configure and deploy large numbers of IP phones. Using a default username and password makes it simple for system administrators to quickly configure the phones. Likewise, some enterprise IT departments find default usernames or passwords to be convenient for shipping IP phones out to remote workers. Ship the phone, send the user the default username and password, and also send the configuration information that needs to be entered. Simple and easy.

There is, though, a very fundamental problem:

Default passwords often do NOT get changed!

Far too often, the devices are simply deployed with the default username and password left exactly as it was shipped from the factory. Sometimes, too, the vendor has not even remotely tried to make the default password hard to guess. Security researcher Shawn Merdinger found that the Hitachi WIP-5000 Wi-Fi handset had a hard-coded administrator log-in of "0000" on the phone keypad. Another classic case was the 2007 security advisory where the Vonage VoIP Telephone Adapter was deployed and directly connected to the Internet with an administrative username of "user" and a password of "user".[H]

While you might not necessarily think of Vonage's adapter as a "UC device," a simple glance at the list of default passwords (see Figure 2.2) such as that maintained by Sergio Castro for SIP devices at www.infosegura.net/passwords.htm will show you that a significant number of the major UC vendors have similar weak passwords. The VoIP Wiki at www.voip-info.org/ also has pages devoted to many of the IP phones out there that include default passwords. You can also simply do a Google search on the phrase "default password list" to find a significant number of sites providing default passwords to a wide range of devices, systems, and software.

Naturally, tools exist to help make this task easier. One example is *sipflanker*,[I] a tool that will scan a range of IP addresses, identify the devices with Web administration interfaces, and then attempt to log in to that device using various default usernames and passwords.

The greatest danger of this attack is simply that the attacker doesn't need to do anything more. They have full administrative access and can typically do anything they want to the compromised device.

Hidden Accounts

Right up there with default passwords is the whole issue of having "hidden" accounts for administrator access. A great example was the Phillips VOIP481 wireless handset for VoIP, which was one of the first to have a Skype client contained entirely in the

[H]http://web.nvd.nist.gov/view/vuln/detail?vulnId=CVE-2007-3047
[I]http://code.google.com/p/sipflanker/

>PASSWORDS FOR SIP DEVICES

If you have passwords to contribute, or are searching for a specific one, contact me: sergio<at>infosegura.net

SIP DEVICE	USERNAME(S)	PASSWORDS(S)
Asterisk	maint	password
Asterisk (Flash Operator Panel)	(none)	passw0rd
Cisco IP Phone	(none)	1234
Cisco ATA	admin	(none)
Cisco Call Manager	admin	admin
Cisco IP Conference Station	End User	7936
Polycom Sound Point IP Phone	Polycom	456
Polycom Soundstation IP	administrator	**#
Polycom	Polycom	Splp
Microsoft Response Point	(none)	admin
Avaya SIP phone	admin	barney
Netgear	admin	password
Linksys	(none)	admin
Snom	(none)	0000
Dlink	user	user
Dlink	(none)	12345
D-link	(none)	(none)
Aastra	admin	22222
Grandstream	(none)	admin
Cortelco	root	1234
Mitel	admin	5215

FIGURE 2.2

A Publicly Available List of Default Passwords for UC Devices

handset. Security researcher Luca Carettoni disclosed in early 2008[J] that, among a number of vulnerabilities, there was a hidden administrator account with the username of "service" and the password of "service." Similarly, researcher Shawn Merdinger found that the UTStarcom F1000 wireless handset had an undocumented Telnet port with a username of "target" and password of, well, "password" that gave root access to the VxWorks shell.

Sometimes these accounts are created to serve as a "back door" for service technicians to be able to easily service the device or to serve as a way to recover the main administrator password if it is forgotten. Sometimes they seem to have been simply left during the development stage. Regardless, they need to be found and, if possible, disabled or have their password changed. Security through obscurity is not a true solution, and before long, someone will publish the information in an advisory on the Internet.

[J]www.securenetwork.it/ricerca/advisory/download/SN-2008-01.txt

Undocumented Services

Similar to hidden accounts, many if not most UC endpoints do not completely document all the services running as part of the endpoint. In his ShmooCon 2006 presentation cited at the beginning of the chapter, security researcher Shawn Merdinger tested 11 different Wi-Fi handsets and found that all the 11 devices had undocumented ports open. In multiple cases, Merdinger was able to connect to an undocumented port and obtain administrative access to the device.

Web Exploits

Most of the attacks mentioned so far have been relatively simple. However, if you consider each of those UC hardware endpoints is a little computer with a Web server inside, you realize that like all Web servers, it may have security vulnerabilities that can be exploited by an attacker willing to put in some time to figure out how to abuse the Web interface. Consider the following examples:

- The Phillips VOIP481 wireless handset mentioned previously also contained a vulnerability, where the Web server performed no input validation on the URL it was receiving.[K] Researchers found that you could use the "../" character sequence indicating a higher level directory to traverse the directory structure of the phone's file system and uncover various files on the system. For instance, sending the Web server the command "*GET /../../../../../../../../../ etc/passwd HTTP/1.0*" would retrieve the "passwd" file with the system usernames in it.
- The Web interface on certain snom phones allowed an attacker to obtain full administrative access to the IP phone without any username or password if the attacker modified the HTTP "Host" header being sent to the server so that it appeared as if the request was coming from the device itself.[L]
- A Polycom IP phone was found to reboot if it received a long URL sent to the Web server.[M]

More examples are out there. The point is that attackers can try "standard" attacks against Web servers on your UC endpoint. Note, too, that many of the fancier hardware endpoints also include a Web browser to display information on the endpoint screen. These browsers, naturally, can be subjected to the typical types of attacks that can be performed against generic Web browsers.

Protocol Fuzzing

A slightly more complex attack involves the concept of "fuzzing" or intentional fault injection. Fuzzing is essentially modifying or manipulating a protocol beyond its intended use or valid format to cause some unintended effect on the target endpoint.

[K]www.securenetwork.it/ricerca/advisory/download/SN-2008-01.txt
[L]http://web.nvd.nist.gov/view/vuln/detail?vulnId=CVE-2009-1048
[M]http://web.nvd.nist.gov/view/vuln/detail?vulnId=CVE-2006-5233

We will discuss fuzzing in more detail in Chapter 4, "Control Channel Attacks: Fuzzing, DoS, SPIT, and Toll Fraud," but for now consider an example of a vulnerability that was found via fuzzing: Siemens IP phones were found to disconnect calls and reboot on receiving a specially crafted SIP packet.[N] A simple exploit script was circulated publicly on mailing lists.[O]

EPIC FAIL

The ZoIPer softphone was found to crash if an attacker sent a SIP INVITE request with a specific header being empty.[P]

Similar types of attacks against the SIP and signaling protocols and other media exist for other vendor endpoints.

Local Files

Finally, a note on local files. You need to understand what information may be stored locally by your UC endpoint. If it is a software endpoint, does it store log files or chat sessions in a particular place on your computer? Are those log files encrypted or just in plain text? If they are stored in the clear, how likely is it that an attacker could access them? All the transport security in the world will not matter if an attacker can simply read the chat transcripts of the local disk.

TIP

Finally, a curious aspect of UC systems is the possibility to create a self-inflicted DoS attack in the event of a power outage or other similar event that takes the system offline. As the power returns, all the IP phones boot up and start attempting to register with the call server. In a large enterprise, this could be literally thousands of phones trying simultaneously to connect, and this could cause connection problems with your UC system. If you are responsible for a large UC implementation, think about the effect of a power outage and what will happen when the power comes back on.

DANGERS OF ATTACKS ON ENDPOINTS

In the introduction of this chapter, as well as the preceding section "Anatomy of Attacks against UC Endpoints," you saw many dangers with attacks on endpoints. Let's take a look at several of the major dangers in more detail.

[N]http://web.nvd.nist.gov/view/vuln/detail?vulnId=CVE-2008-7065
[O]www.securityfocus.com/archive/1/archive/1/498599/100/0/threaded
[P]http://web.nvd.nist.gov/view/vuln/detail?vulnId=CVE-2009-3704

Denial of Service or Availability

By far, the greatest danger to individual endpoints is denial of service. The simplest way for an attacker to cause problems may be just to take the endpoint offline. This could be through one of the attacks mentioned in the preceding section "Anatomy of Attacks against UC Endpoints." It could be an attack that saturates the network with too much traffic.

It could also be a more subtle attack, for instance, that deregisters the endpoint from an SIP server so that the person can make outbound connections but cannot receive incoming connections. Or an attack that modifies the user's presence to the rest of the UC system so that they appear to be "Not available" or "Busy" when in fact they are there and are able to be a part of a communication session.

Any of these types of attacks could lead to a loss of revenue for the person or the company. Imagine if it were a sales person whose UC client showed him or her as not available when potential customers were calling in. There could be a loss of reputation or good will within the company. Your coworkers might not be too pleased with you if you weren't taking their phone calls (because you didn't know you were receiving them) or your presence was always showing up as "Away," even though they knew you were in the building.

This latter example also shows another more subtle danger of DoS attacks, that is, damage to the reputation of the UC system. If people believe that presence, for instance, is frequently wrong, they will come to distrust the entire UC system and speak poorly of the system to their coworkers and others. If a part of your goal is to support the usage of the UC system, such negative perception will not help with that.

Toll Fraud

As mentioned in Chapter 1, "The Unified Communications Ecosystem," toll fraud continues to be the most financially damaging danger. With endpoints, the danger here is primarily that they could be used to make outgoing phone calls, as mentioned in the 2009 attack against snom IP phones discussed in the introduction of this chapter. If an attacker can gain access to the administrative interface for the IP phone, he or she can potentially cause serious harm.

For example, consider a case where an attacker gains access to the administrative interface on an SIP device on, say, extension 1234. The attacker sets the call forwarding it to a premium service phone number or to an international number. The attacker then distributes your company's toll free number and the extension number (for free or for profit) to people he or she knows. Those people then call to your company, enter the extension, and get connected to the external service. They are in fact costing your company twice as they are incurring costs on the inbound toll free number, as well as the outbound calls to external services. These types of attacks could rack up serious amounts of charges on your company's systems.

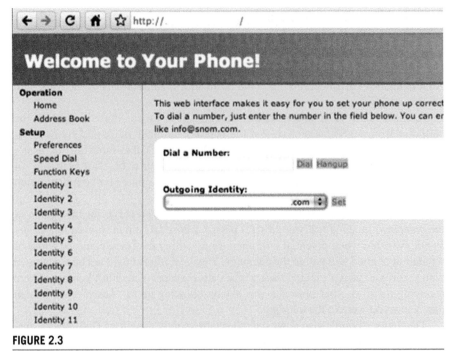

FIGURE 2.3

The snom IP Phone User Interface Allows Outbound Dialing

Another example is shown in Figure 2.3, where an attacker has gained access to the administrative interface of a snom IP phone, conceivably across the public Internet through Google searches. The attacker can now place an outbound call from this phone. Now, in this case, the snom phone will ring as the call is being made, so there isn't necessarily the large toll fraud case outlined above, but the attacker could enter a premium number and incur some cost. At the very least, the attacker could severely annoy the owner of the phone because the owner would think a call is coming in when, in fact, the phone is ringing as part of connecting to the outbound call.

Eavesdropping or Exposure of Information

Recall the attack against snom IP phones mentioned in the introduction of this chapter. An attacker who successfully compromised an IP phone had the ability to listen to any calls originating from or terminating at the endpoint. Likewise, an attacker who inserted a keyboard logger onto a computer could potentially read every IM message composed by a user of that computer. In Chapter 3, "Eavesdropping and Modification," we will discuss this in more detail. For now, it is mostly important to note that this can be one of the dangers of not protecting your endpoints enough.

> **WARNING**
>
> Do not forget to investigate how data is stored on a local system or any intermediary system. If, for instance, all log files of IM chat sessions are stored in clear, unencrypted text on a local computer where multiple people have access to the computer, the fact that the IM client encrypts sessions between the computers and the server does not fully protect those sessions. The session transcripts could still be read locally by anyone with access to the local computer.

Annoyance

The final danger worth pointing out is the annoyance factor. If you do not protect your endpoints properly, it is relatively straightforward for an attacker to create attacks that annoy your end users. Such attacks could come in various forms such as ones that

- repeatedly initiates a call to a person on a random interval and with what appears to be a valid Caller ID, but which then has no one on the other end
- randomly hangs up on various people connected to your UC system
- deletes every fourth or fifth IM message sent
- inserts or replaces words in IM messages
- transfers calls to a given extension to some other random extension
- modifies users' presence messages to show incorrect data.

By themselves, the attacks may be relatively insignificant, but they impact the reputation of the UC system, and will lead to distrust of the system and a negative attitude that is shared with others. They also, of course, could cause very real customer dissatisfaction and revenue loss.

THE FUTURE OF ATTACKS AGAINST UC ENDPOINTS

Originally, phones were dumb pieces of plastic with buttons on them that sent signals back to a central switch. As this chapter has documented, the device, formerly known as a *phone* has evolved into an actual computer sitting on a desk in the shape of a phone. As the UC market continues to expand, endpoints are getting smarter, moving increasingly into software, and becoming more mobile. Let's look in more detail at several of the trends.

More Powerful Endpoints

IP phones have benefited greatly from the ever-increasing capabilities of computer hardware in general, including faster microprocessors, larger memory capacity, and greater network bandwidth. A single IP phone shipping in 2010 has far more computing capacity than most of the early PBXs. This trend will only continue. IP phones are adding color displays with full-blown Web browsers. Some are adding embedded cameras so that you can stream videos directly to the person you are calling. With both greater computing capability locally and greater network bandwidth, IP phone vendors are seeking to use that capacity to provide even greater communication options to users. Part of this is natural evolution and part of this is also an effort of the device manufacturers to differentiate their products and retain relevance in a market where, as noted in the next section, people are increasingly looking for better software options.

From a security point of view, this evolution only *increases* the amount of concern that must be given to the security of IP endpoints. As vendors and users add more applications to the endpoints, there are more services that can potentially be attacked. There is also more interaction among the applications within the device itself. With the embedded Web browsers, for instance, you now need to be concerned about all the cross-site scripting attacks and many other Web security issues outlined in books such as *Seven Deadliest Web Application Attacks* (ISBN: 978-1-59749-543-1, Syngress). Complexity is the enemy of security, and with the evolution in hardware, IP endpoints are only growing increasingly more complex.

Migration into Software

While the hardware is getting more capabilities, you are also seeing an interesting shift into increased usage of software-based clients such as softphones. For many years, various industry analysts and vendors have been advocating that communication would move to softphones, and for many of those years, it seemed to be happening at a glacial pace or hardly at all. Today, though, people are in fact moving increasingly to using softphones, driven by several factors:

- **UC systems** The multimodal communication experience of UC is driven typically by a software UC client. As users become increasingly accustomed to using that software client, the need for a hardware device becomes less.
- **Embedded Web cams and the rise of video** People have been declaring the era of the videophone for decades, but as embedded Web cams have become nearly ubiquitous in new laptop models, people are in fact starting to use video as a part of regular communication. As the video is used by the UC client on the laptop, it provides yet another reason why people will focus on using the software client instead of the phone they may have on their desk.
- **Increased IM usage at the expense of voice** Many organizations using UC find that they are more heavily utilizing IM for communication and as that occurs, voice becomes less utilized; as a result, people are willing to use a softphone for the times when they need voice.
- **Voice improvements negating headset need** Historically, the use of softphones has required the use of a headset, which often made for a less-desirable user experience. People either had to constantly wear their headset or had to find their headset to talk when a call came in. If the headset was not connected to the computer, you might not be able to make or receive calls at all until you connected the headset. Today, improvements in echo cancellation and other aspects of voice

software have made it where some computer users no longer need to use a headset for most situations. As these improvements continue, it becomes easier for users to simply start talking to their computer while making or receiving calls.

- **Wideband audio** Similarly, softphones are enabling people to experience "wideband" audio (sometimes called "*HD audio*"), where they have a much richer audio experience than they are able to have with traditional telephony. While this is also possible with "hard" endpoints, it is standard in softphones like Skype. Once users start to experience the feeling of almost being right in the room with someone, it is difficult to go back to the traditional audio experience.

- **Consumer experiences** Increasingly, consumers are getting the experience of using voice over software clients. With Skype, the focus is around voice, but the other main IM services, such as AIM, Microsoft's Windows Live Messenger, and Yahoo! Messenger, have all allowed voice as well. Similarly, many of the "Web 2.0" and social networking services let consumers use voice from directly within their Web browser, typically by way of a Flash application.

There are a host of other reasons, but the end result is that we're seeing an increased acceptance and even desire for software-based endpoints. Will the phone on the desk ever go away? Probably not from all desks, but certainly from many, as users migrate to either using software endpoints or, as noted in the section below on "Mobility," using their mobile phones for more enterprise interaction.

From a security point of view, the shift to software endpoints is a mixture of good and bad news. On the good news side, software clients can be easier to upgrade or patch than hardware endpoints. Software clients can also be integrated into other existing security policies and tools.

On the bad news side, software clients are well… *software*. They are programs running on commodity operating systems with all of the inherent issues that come with being a software program. Are there potential buffer overflows in the code? Does every field in an entry form do appropriate checking so that an attacker can't insert malicious code? A software client just offers a whole new range of points that an attacker can target.

Commodity Operating Systems

With the increasing shift to software endpoints, more communication is occurring on top of "commodity operating systems" such as Microsoft Windows, Linux, and Mac OS X. On the security side, you obviously have to pay attention to the security updates for those operating systems.

Beyond the software endpoints, though, an interesting migration is happening within the world of hardware endpoints as well. Historically, because of the limited processing power available, many of the traditional IP phone vendors used dedicated embedded operating systems such as VxWorks from Wind River.[Q] From a security point of view, there was an actual *advantage* that each vendor essentially created

---

[Q]www.windriver.com

their own embedded operating system version, and so the devices were not subject to the more common and larger-scale security concerns in commodity operating systems. For example, the devices were not running the Web servers found in Windows or Linux, so the typical attacks against those Web servers did not impact the devices. There was, of course, the *disadvantage* that the range of software solutions in the embedded device was typically limited and was not always clear how much security exposure the applications were subjected to. The limited processing power of hardware endpoints also often made them much more susceptible to resource exhaustion-based DoS attacks. The patch or update process was also not as clear as it would be for, say, Linux or Microsoft Windows.

Today, with the increased processing capabilities in hardware endpoints, many of these endpoints are now running embedded versions of commodity operating systems like Linux and Windows. The good news about this is that the devices can now run software such as the Apache Web server that is heavily used in the wider market and has been subjected to solid security review. It is also an operating system that you and your colleagues may be more familiar with and know the right security questions to ask. The bad news is that the devices are running that commonly used software. Many of the same concerns you have about securing Microsoft Windows or Linux on a desktop or server level are also true at the embedded device level.

This trend is continuing, though, and you should expect to see an increasing number of the hardware endpoints used in UC systems using embedded versions of commodity operating systems.

Heterogeneous Deployments

In the past, when you bought your "phone system" from a vendor, you bought the entire system from that one single vendor only. You bought the PBX, the phones, the operator consoles, the monitoring software and everything. In fact, you had to buy it all from one vendor because the products all used various proprietary protocols and other techniques to lock you in to a single-vendor solution.

Today, while many companies might still choose to buy from a single vendor for the sake of convenience, the reality is that in the era of interoperable protocol standards like SIP, the companies are no longer required to buy from the same vendor. You can purchase an IP-PBX and IP phones from Avaya, for instance, and then later add SIP-based IP phones to the system from, say, Cisco or snom. There is, in fact, an entire industry of vendors creating inexpensive SIP phones that can be added to SIP-based systems. Given the options, many companies are looking around at their options and purchasing SIP phones from other vendors. If the power and intelligence of the UC system is in the software client and the hardware device can be any device that works with the system, then there is little incentive for a company not to try out products from other vendors.

However, for you trying to secure the UC infrastructure, this newly heterogeneous environment poses some challenges. As outlined in the introduction of this chapter and in the section "Anatomy of Attacks against UC Endpoints," the level of security concern by the different endpoint vendors varies widely. With each new endpoint introduced into your network, you need to review the security of that endpoint, understand the exposed services on that endpoint, understand what patch plan may or may not exist, and figure out how you secure the connections to that endpoint. Each new product and vendor means more that you need to do to ensure the overall security.

Given the ever-increasing competition and commoditization in just about every market out there, you can expect to see companies increasingly capitalizing on the increasing interoperability between UC systems and endpoints, and purchasing more and different endpoints.

Mobility

Undoubtedly, some of those endpoints connected to your UC system will be mobile endpoints. People want to be able to interact with their communication system from wherever they are and whenever they want. They want mobility. An interesting trend is that many people within companies want to use their own mobile phones. A large part of this, of course, is driven by the ubiquitous and personal nature of mobile phones. We carry our mobile phone everywhere, all the time. We, therefore, want those to be the devices we use to communicate with other people.

There is also the factor that as people use UC systems more and more, they want their mobile experience to be the richer communication and collaboration experience possible on their desktop or laptop. They want presence information and IM services. The IP-PBXs and other systems before UC have provided wireless handsets, typically operating over Wi-Fi or DECT, but those were just "phones." People want more of the UC experience. You also must add in the growing consumer usage of "smartphones," such as the Apple iPhone, that are setting expectations of what should be possible.

From a security point of view, there are multiple concerns here. First is the very basic issue of having *mobile* endpoints. How do you secure the communication to that endpoint? How do you make sure it is available? What do you do when someone loses a mobile phone? All these are questions you have to now deal with. There are some fundamental trust issues that now confront you. If you make enterprise dialing capabilities available to a mobile endpoint, for instance, how do you prevent someone from borrowing that mobile phone and making large numbers of calls? You have to think through how you secure both the mobile endpoints and the services to which they connect within your enterprise.

The second concern is the issue of making communication possible to *employee mobile phones*. Now, obviously, if your company provides everyone with a mobile phone (or everyone who may need access to the UC system), you have to understand the security ramifications of extending communication out to those specific endpoints. If the company doesn't provide mobile phones or wants to extend the communication out to other mobile devices, you need to understand the security profile of each of those devices and how, or *if*, you can extend UC capabilities out to those devices.

Regardless of what devices are being used, the reality is that companies and individuals will increasingly be asking for mobile access to your UC systems.

Massively Distributed Endpoints

As will be discussed in Chapter 7, "The End of Geography," one of the strengths of a UC system is that you can now deploy an endpoint basically anywhere in the world where you can obtain an IP address. This strength is also a weakness from a security point of view. And this trend will only continue. Expect to be asked to connect UC endpoints from all over the public and private networks.

HOW TO DEFEND YOUR ENDPOINTS

When formulating a plan to defend your UC endpoints against attackers, you may find it helpful to think in terms of a five-step plan:

1. Identify all of the connected endpoints.
2. Change default passwords.
3. Disable unnecessary services.
4. Ensure endpoints are included in patch management plans.
5. Apply extra hardening to Internet-connected endpoints.

Strategy #1: Identify All Connected Endpoints

Your first challenge is to *identify* all the endpoints connected to your UC system. This may sound rather straightforward, but in practice, it may be a bit more challenging. Consider this – one of the benefits of many SIP-based systems is that one extension can ring multiple endpoints. For example, if you called someone in your research department at extension 2001, it might ring at all of the following:

- an IP phone on the researcher's desk in his or her office
- an IP phone in the research lab
- an IP phone in the researcher's home office
- a softphone running on the researcher's laptop
- a softphone running on the researcher's mobile phone
- a traditional (non-IP) phone connected through the IP-PBX
- a regular mobile phone number belonging to an assistant
- an automated application that may wait a few rings and then pick up to assist in locating the person.

These eight separate endpoints are associated with one extension. Gone are the days when you could think of one extension equaling one phone. Today you may have one, two, five, or more devices registering to the same extension, as shown in Figure 2.4.

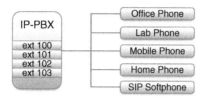

FIGURE 2.4

IP-PBXs Allow Multiple Devices Connected to a Single Extension

Nmap Output	Ports / Hosts	Topology	Host Details	Scans

	Port	Protocol	State	Service	Version
◉	80	tcp	open	http	Polycom SoundPoint VoIP phone http config
◉	5060	tcp	open	sip	Polycom SoundPoint 501 2.1.0.2708

FIGURE 2.5

Zenmap Identifying a Polycom IP Phone

The first stop is to examine the logs or configuration data for your UC system. If it is an SIP-based system, there will be a component of the system called a *Registrar* server that will be accepting registrations from endpoints. That Registrar server should be able to either provide a list of currently connected endpoints or at the very least a log of all devices that have registered. You will now have IP addresses or domain name system hostnames that you can use to find the endpoints.

Another mechanism is to use network security tools to enumerate all the endpoints on your network. As discussed earlier in the "Anatomy of Attacks against UC Endpoints," one approach you can use is to scan your network with "nmap" or another similar tool.

Once you have the list of potential endpoints, you need to go through the process of finding out exactly what kind of device each endpoint is. Now, the scanning software you use may help with this and attempt identification of the endpoint during the scanning process. As an example, Figure 2.5 shows the Zenmap tool (a graphical interface to nmap) identifying an endpoint as a Polycom SoundPoint IP phone.

In an ideal world, your company may have some type of network inventory software running that keeps track of what is connected to the network and can assist you in identifying the endpoints.

TIP

A list of VoIP scanning and enumeration tools can be found on the VOIPSA Tools page at www.voipsa.org/Resources/tools.php

Once you know the number of endpoints you have to deal with and what those endpoints are, it is time to examine each one individually to see what you can do to harden that endpoint.

Strategy #2: Change Default Passwords!

The single biggest step you can take to secure your IP phone endpoints is to *change default passwords!* To make it easy for you to rapidly configure and deploy handsets, many manufacturers ship their IP phones with a default username and password. By connecting to the management Web interface inside of the IP phone and entering this username and password, you gain full administrative control over the phone. You have the ability to change configuration settings, peruse log files, but very often also *make phone calls!*

As mentioned earlier in the section "Default Passwords," the problem is that those default usernames and passwords are widely available on the public Internet! If you simply go to Google.com and do a search on "default password list," you will see many sites that list default passwords for a range of different types of network devices, including IP phones, PBXs, and more. For IP phones in particular, you can go to the VoIP Info Wiki at www.voip-info.org/ and search for the default password for your IP phone.

Depending upon the size of your installation, the process of going through and changing every single default password may be laborious and time consuming, but you will greatly reduce the possible options for an attacker.

WARNING

As important as it is to *change* default passwords, it is equally important to *record* the new passwords in some manner that they are easily recoverable if necessary. It won't help you if someone changes all the default passwords, and then he or she is not available when you need to access the phone Web-management interface. You need some system that securely tracks all of the passwords you are using.

Strategy #3: Turn off Unnecessary Services

As mentioned in the introduction of this chapter, many of the IP phones ship with a range of services enabled on them. Many of those services may be unnecessary and can or *should* be disabled. What you need to do for each endpoint is as follows:

1. Ask the IP phone vendor directly what operating system is running inside the IP phone and what steps the vendor has taken to use a minimal operating system load with the least number of necessary packages and services installed.
2. Scan the endpoint with a tool like "nmap" to determine what ports on the endpoint have services listening on them.
3. Determine what service is (or *should* be) running on each identified port either by using a tool like nmap or by comparing those port numbers to a list such as the

Internet Assigned Number Authority (IANA) Port Number list at www.iana.org/ assignments/port-numbers. Note that the vendors may be using their own software running on unassigned ports that they have chosen to use, or even on ports that have been assigned by IANA to other, different services.

4. Examine vendor documentation or online information to understand *why* a particular service is running on the endpoint. Break down your list of services into "necessary," "questionable," and "unnecessary." For instance, a service running on port 5060 for the SIP protocol is definitely *necessary* for an IP phone if your UC system uses SIP for signaling. A Telnet server running on port 23 is probably *not* necessary. Perform a risk assessment for each service, asking yourself what an attacker could do if he or she gained access to that particular service.

5. Figure out *how* you can disable unnecessary services and do so. With luck, you may simply be able to log in to the Web configuration menu for the IP phone and disable the services there directly. However, you may have to access some other configuration option. Unfortunately, as security researcher Shawn Merdinger found out in his research for ShmooCon in 2006, some vendors provide no way for you to disable services. You may be stuck with the device as it is.

NOTE

Because some vendors may run unnecessary services on the phones and provide you no way to disable them, the ideal situation is whether you can obtain an evaluation IP phone and perform a security scan on the device *before* your company has purchased a large quantity of the devices. Ask your vendor and see whether you can make passing the security scan part of the purchasing process.

If you can't disable services, you have to go back to your risk assessment and determine whether some of the exposed services do represent a serious threat. If so, you may need to look at other options such as using router access control lists to restrict traffic to those particular ports.

Strategy #4: Develop Patch Plans for All Endpoints

Another defense strategy is to ensure that you have plans in place to address future software updates or patches for each of your endpoints.

For your software endpoints, such as softphones or IM clients, this may be a relatively simple and easy system to set up. The software may have an update mechanism built directly into it to check for updates and install them. If so, you just need to ensure that this autoupdate function is enabled for each instance of the software. Alternatively, you may need to (or *choose* to) use a centralized software update tool to push new updates out to all the software clients. Regardless, with software clients, setting up an update process is typically a very straightforward process.

For hardware endpoints, though, it can be a much more challenging exercise. To start with, the hardware device itself may not have any easy way to check for updates.

You may need to obtain this information from the product's vendor. To do that, you may need to join a vendor partner program, sign up for a mailing list, or just periodically check a Web page. Each vendor has a different way of notifying customers of software updates. When communicating with the vendor, try to learn what their patch and security process is for the endpoints you are using and also how the vendor's patch process may fit into whatever patch management process you have within your organization. Also, be sure to find out how long the vendor will commit to providing security updates to your device and when the "end of support" date may be for your endpoints.

Once you have obtained the software update for the hardware device, your next challenge may be installing the software on the device or, more precisely, on *all* your devices. What you do not necessarily want to be doing is going around to each and every one of your devices and upgrade the process on specific devices. You may have to do that, but ideally there will be some way to centrally push out updates to a range of your hardware devices.

Note that some hardware endpoints download and install their software from a central server every time they boot up. This can make the software update process very simple as new software loads simply need to be loaded into the central server and the IP phones need to be power-cycled. The negative side of this approach is that this central server can be an attractive target for an attacker because he or she can potentially compromise the software loads and thereby compromise all your phones. Alternatively, an attacker might set up a rogue download server and attempt to trick the IP phones into downloading software from the rogue server instead of the correct central server.

Ask your vendor whether the IP phones download their software from a central server and, if so, what the vendor has done to prevent an attacker from compromising the system.

> **WARNING**
>
> It perhaps goes without saying, but you definitely should have a couple of devices available for which you can *test* the upgrade or update process before you start upgrading devices in your production network.

Beyond the specific software used for your software or hardware devices, you also have to be concerned about the operating systems used for the endpoints and whether that operating system is fully patched. For the software clients, they will obviously be running on commodity operating systems like Microsoft Windows, Linux, or Apple's Mac OS X where the update process is straightforward. For the hardware devices, though, they will typically be running an "embedded" operating system. Many times this will be a version of embedded Linux, but it could also be a different or a proprietary operating system. Ideally, the vendor should provide patches for the underlying operating system, as well as for the vendor's software, but you need to ask questions to be sure of this.

Strategy #5: Understand How to Update and Secure Remote Endpoints

If you have endpoints that are remote, you naturally need to take extra precautions to ensure that those devices are secured, particularly if they turn out to be directly connected to the Internet. In general, there are two categories of remote endpoints of high concern:

- traveling remote workers, typically using a softphone and UC client on a laptop
- fixed remote worker phones, typically home-office extensions.

As will be discussed in Chapter 7, "The End of Geography," the best way to support these remote endpoints is to have some type of secure gateway on the edge of your network to interact with these remote endpoints. Similarly, at a remote location, it is best to have these endpoints behind some kind of firewall or other security device so that they are not *directly* connected to the Internet. However, there have been instances where someone is just trying to get something to work, and so they set their commodity home router to simply port-forward SIP traffic through to their IP phone. This effectively winds up putting the IP phone directly onto the public Internet.

For the *traveling remote workers* or *road warriors* who spend their weeks flying all over the world to meet with customers, partners, and so on, you will have no idea what kind of networks they will be connected to and what they will need to do to connect back to your system. Typically, these folks are already equipped with virtual private network (VPN) software, which sets up a secure, encrypted communication tunnel back to the corporate network. Your UC software can simply ride across that tunnel back into the corporate network. The good news for you is that these teleworkers generally use software clients on laptops so that the process of ensuring the software is up to date and may be relatively straightforward. They may just need to connect to a specific internal Web site across the VPN, or may be able to obtain the download from some other internal server.

The *fixed remote worker endpoints* may prove a bit more challenging on two fronts: the security of the Internet connection and the ease of providing updates to the remote endpoint.

On the issue of the Internet connection, the main concern is the security of the home router, gateway, or firewall that connects the home network to the public Internet. If you are able to specify exactly what home gateway or router people are required to use, you will be able to choose a device that can be securely configured. However, in many environments, home-office workers may already have a home router that they have purchased, use it, and do not wish to change it. Engineers at home offices may have custom-built gateway servers that they use for their development work. You may simply have to work with what is already deployed out there in the field.

What you ideally want to have in each remote location is a home router that lets the UC signaling and media securely through the firewall portion of the router to the remote endpoint. What you do *not* want is a device where you have to set up "port forwarding" on the firewall that exposes ports on the UC endpoint directly out onto the public Internet. If you do this, an attacker scanning the home router will see the open port that actually connects to the UC endpoint and can then target the UC endpoint directly through the open port to see whether it can be compromised.

The second challenge with fixed teleworker endpoints is getting software or firmware updates out to the devices and then installing it. In many cases, you may be dealing with a UC software client that is running on a home PC or laptop and then separately a stand-alone "hard" IP phone of some description. The UC software client will probably not be the challenge. As mentioned earlier, regarding the traveling teleworker, software clients are relatively easy to update. They can be configured to automatically check, pull updates from a site, or have updates locally installed. Depending upon the size of the UC software client and the capacity of your e-mail system, you may even be able to simply e-mail out an update to remote office users. (This is not recommended, but it could be *possible*.)

The IP phone device is a different matter. When considering what IP phone or other device to deploy remotely, you must take into consideration how you are going to update that phone remotely. For instance, some IP phones have the ability to download software updates from a Web site. Do yours have this capability? If so, how are you making the software updates available? Are they stored on a publicly accessible Web server? If so, the remote IP phone simply needs to be configured with the URL of the update server and it can download the updates from there.

If you are not putting updates out on a publicly accessible Web server, how will remote users be able to download those updates? Will they have to connect via a VPN? If so, how will the IP phone know to connect across the VPN? Will the user have to download the software update and then install it from a local server? If so, will this be easy for them to do?

Your challenge will be to make this simple, easy, and ideally automatic. If it is not automated, you need to have a plan for alerting the remote employees about an update for the remote IP phone.

The key aspect for both traveling teleworkers and fixed teleworker endpoints is that you need to understand the following:

1. Where they are located (or whose laptop they are on).
2. What kind of security exposure they are.
3. What is the plan to keep them up to date with new software.

With these three steps in mind, you can minimize the risks associated with remote endpoints and have a plan to update remote endpoints to address risks that may arise.

SUMMARY

In the world of UC, securing the endpoints can be a challenging endeavor. On the one hand, UC systems increasingly have software endpoints running on commodity operating systems and are subject to all the challenges that exist with it. On the other hand, the device on your desk, formerly known as a *phone*, has morphed into a full-blown little computer, complete with a Web server, user accounts, administrator access, and so on. Add to that the fact that it is all running over an IP network with all the security issues that come with it. It can be a challenge, but by taking some simple steps and remembering the basics of IT security, you can go a long way in reducing your risk.

Next, in Chapter 3, "Eavesdropping and Modification," we're going to dive into some very tangible attacks against IP phones and other endpoints.

Eavesdropping and Modification

3

INFORMATION IN THIS CHAPTER

- Anatomy of Eavesdropping and Modification Attacks
- Dangers of Eavesdropping and Modification Attacks
- The Future of Eavesdropping and Modification Attacks
- How to Defend against Eavesdropping and Modification Attacks

Imagine that somewhere within your IT organization you have someone with too much time on his or her hands or who has issues with the way current management is running things…or hates his job…or dislikes her boss…Whatever the reason may be, he or she is in a position with access to the core Internet Protocol (IP) network running through your organization. Let's give this person a name and call him Joe. One day, when working with Wireshark, the network protocol analyzer, Joe, notices the menu item **Telephony | VoIP Calls**. In trying it out, he discovers that…ta da… he can listen to any call going to and from the IP-PBX. Naturally, he starts figuring out how to listen in to the more interesting calls, and in particular to target calls to and from the CEO. Once he is able to isolate these calls, he automates his setup a bit. He finds a number of other tools and writes a script so that any calls to or from the CEO are saved to disk and converted into MP3 files. He then downloads those files onto his iPod and can listen to corporate conversations on his daily commute to and from work. Alternatively, he could install freely available speech-to-text software to get transcripts of all of those calls.

As Joe does this, he also discovers that again using Wireshark, he can easily see the instant messaging (IM) conversations of his colleagues. So he starts watching those conversations as well.

In the course of doing this, Joe discovers that the company is going to be sold to a larger company known for aggressive layoffs after an acquisition. Figuring that his job is going to be axed, Joe starts doing all he can to sabotage the chances for the acquisition to be successful. First, he begins executing some of the denial-of-service attacks you learned about in Chapter 2, "Insecure Endpoints." When calls come in to the CEO from certain lawyers, the calls are disconnected. He also randomly disconnects other calls that are going on throughout the company.

Because he fears he'll be easily found out, Joe starts to get a bit more sophisticated in his attacks. He sets up a script that strategically drops any IM messages that include certain keywords. He also tries his hand at modifying IM messages and replacing words like "buy" with "sell." It's not terribly effective, but it does create a degree of confusion.

Joe also finds some tools on the Internet that let him mix in different backgrounds to audio streams using the Real-time Transport Protocol (RTP). With this tool, he's able to have a bit more "fun." When Joe's scripts alert him that the CEO is on a call with the acquisition lawyers, Joe can mix the sound of people arguing into the outgoing RTP stream. To Joe, the fun part about this particular attack is that the CEO has no idea the attack is going on. It's only in the *outbound* stream to the lawyers. They hear the arguing and ask the CEO what is going on. The CEO has no idea what they are talking about.

In the end, you can imagine that Joe probably got caught – but not before causing a good degree of confusion and annoyance – and maybe sabotaging the acquisition as well.

Does this all sound like fiction or a Hollywood movie? Unfortunately, it's a very real possibility *if an attacker can get to the right point in your network.* Voice, video, and IM – the cornerstones of unified communications (UCs) – can be both observed and modified by an attacker with access to the correct point in the network. Let's look at this in more detail.

ANATOMY OF EAVESDROPPING AND MODIFICATION ATTACKS

For an attacker to make these attacks, he or she has to get between the endpoints and then use various tools to pull off the attacks. You need to understand one important distinction between eavesdropping attacks and modification attacks.

Eavesdropping attacks are far easier and can be passive; that is, a piece of software can simply be sitting somewhere in the network path and capturing all the relevant network traffic for later analysis. In fact, the attacker does not need to have any ongoing connection to the software at all. He or she can insert the software onto a compromised device, perhaps by direct insertion or perhaps by a virus or other malware, and then come back some time later to retrieve any data that is found or trigger the software to send the data at some determined time. The point is that you may have no idea that the software is there monitoring and capturing all your traffic. It's a very simple and straightforward attack on the confidentiality of your system if the attacker can get between the endpoints.

Modification attacks have the same need as eavesdropping attacks to get to the right point in the network, but they also have a timing requirement. The attacks are only useful if you can modify the communications stream while the communication is taking place. The attacker also has to insert his or her software in the network path in a true man-in-the-middle (MiTM) attack where he or she is able to not just observe packets, but actually receive the packets, modify them, and send them on.

The classic example is if you were able to get between someone calling their financial broker and when the person said to "buy 10,000 shares," you were able to change what the person said to "sell 10,000 shares." Such attacks are possible, but they require not only being able to get to the right point in the network but also to be able to time the attack exactly. With voice or video, this could be rather difficult. With text-based mediums like IM, it's obviously a bit easier because the attacker has text that can be scanned and modified.

Modification attacks could be performed by code that is inserted and left behind, particularly if the target media is text-based like IM, but other tools out there do require the active participation of the attacker to get the timing just right.

Let's look at mechanisms to get between the two endpoints and then at a couple of specific attacks.

> **NOTE**
>
> If you go back to the "CIA triad" referenced in the introduction to the chapter, modification attacks are against the integrity of a communications system: the information received by the recipient is not the same information that was sent by the sender.

Getting between the Endpoints

The attacks outlined in the introduction to the chapter work by taking advantage of the way many UC systems separate *signaling* (also often referred to as *call control*) from *media*. As shown in Figure 3.1, the signaling for a session in a Session Initiation Protocol (SIP)-based system may take a different network path from the media sent between the endpoints.

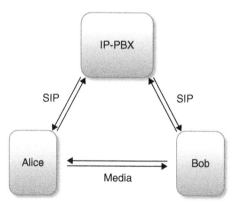

FIGURE 3.1

With SIP, Signaling and Media Take Different Paths

With SIP, the person initiating the voice, video, or IM session sends an initial message (called a SIP INVITE) from their endpoint to the recipient. The INVITE may pass through one or more SIP proxy servers until it reaches the recipient's endpoint, as shown in Figure 3.2. The endpoints then send further SIP packets to negotiate what type of media will be sent between the endpoints, the addresses (IP or host) to which the media will be sent, and any other options related to the session.

Once the media session has been negotiated, the endpoints start sending media to each other. For voice or video sessions, the media will be sent as RTP (defined in RFC 3550[A]) packets. For IM, the media will be sent as Message Session Relay Protocol (MSRP, defined in RFC 4975[B]) packets. Depending upon the network infrastructure, the endpoints may or may not stream the media directly from endpoint to endpoint. There may also be media servers or session border controllers (SBCs) or other devices between the two endpoints.

NOTE

For voice and video, SIP has become the primary industry-standard signaling protocol for communication between endpoints. For IM, though, SIP and its "SIMPLE" derivative is just one of the two major open standards for IM. The other major protocol, the Extensible Messaging and Presence Protocol (XMPP), also known as the *Jabber Protocol*, has a different model where the session initiation and messaging are sent from the XMPP client to a XMPP server and from there on through other servers to the recipient endpoint. Unlike SIP/SIMPLE, XMPP does not have separate channels for signaling and media. All the IM traffic occurs within the XMPP stream itself. However, the XMPP community has been developing Jingle,[C] a framework for using XMPP for multimedia traffic such as voice and video. Jingle typically adopts a similar model to that of the SIP space, where the signaling goes over XMPP and the media (typically RTP) goes directly from endpoint to endpoint (and potentially through media servers).

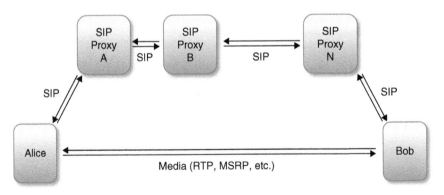

FIGURE 3.2

SIP Traffic May Pass through Multiple Proxy Servers

[A]http://tools.ietf.org/html/rfc3550
[B]http://tools.ietf.org/html/rfc4975
[C]http://xmpp.org/tech/jingle.shtml

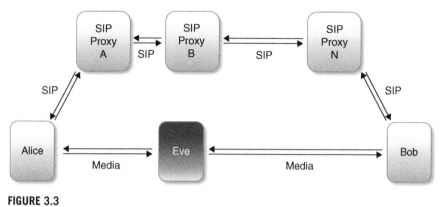

FIGURE 3.3

An Attacker, Eve, Needs to Get Somewhere between the Two Endpoints

The trick, then, is for the attacker to get himself or herself between the two endpoints in either the signaling or the media streams, as shown in Figure 3.3.

The attacker can potentially observe and modify network traffic if he or she can

- get in the *network path* between the two endpoints
- get between two of the *servers* or *proxies* involved with sending the traffic between the endpoints
- get on the same *network segment* as one of the endpoints
- compromise the *local system* of either endpoint.

Let's look at each of these in a bit more detail.

Get in the Network Path

The reality is that the picture in Figure 3.2 is a lot more complicated than is shown in the simple diagram. For communication across a wide area network (WAN) or across the public Internet, the picture may look a lot more like Figure 3.4, with many network points between two endpoints. As the media traffic traverses the network, it has to pass through any number of network routers, each one of which is a potential point where an attacker could be able to insert code to observe and/or modify media traffic. The media stream may also pass through one or more *media proxies* that are designed to pass the media from one network segment to another.

If an attacker can compromise a router or other device such as a firewall, SBC, or media server, he or she can then observe all the traffic flowing through the network device. In the Pena/Moore Voice over Internet Protocol (VoIP) fraud case to be discussed in Chapter 4, "Control Channel Attacks: Fuzzing, DoS, SPIT, and Toll Fraud," Pena and Moore were able to compromise a large number of network devices simply by logging in with default usernames and passwords. Such devices also have vulnerabilities discovered over time and if they are left unpatched, attackers can exploit publicly known vulnerabilities to compromise network devices and obtain a higher level of access to those devices.

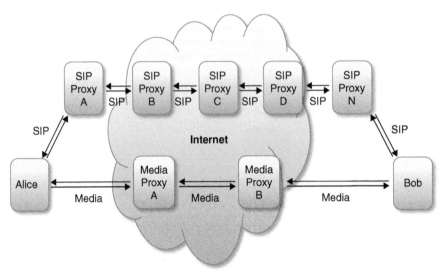

FIGURE 3.4

The Network Path between Two Endpoints May Be Very Complex

> **WARNING**
>
> Remember that the security of your UC system relies on the security of the underlying IP network. Have all the devices on the edge of your network been checked for vulnerabilities lately? Do you have them included in patch management plans to be sure they are up-to-date with any available patches? How strong are the passwords for the admin accounts on network devices? How often are your networks checked for rogue wireless access points and modems? Are your employees trained to identify and report social engineering attacks?

The challenge is of course how to find the path between two endpoints, particularly when the very design of the Internet is to allow multiple paths for traffic to flow. It's not impossible to do, but it's also not trivial. However, as traffic flows between the endpoints across larger and larger networks, and particularly the public Internet, the number of network points between the endpoints continues to expand and the possible points of compromise expand. If your UC system has endpoints that are out across the public Internet, for instance, you then have to worry about the security of every possible Internet service provider (ISP) between your corporate UC system and the remote endpoint. (And the reality is that you can't know about the security of every ISP and therefore need to use one of the solutions discussed in the section "How to Defend against Eavesdropping and Modification Attacks" at the end of this chapter.)

Get between Two Servers or Proxies

One mechanism for an attacker to try to get into the path is to try to get between two of the servers involved with the communication. Now, as mentioned previously, the media may stream directly from one endpoint to the other in a completely "peer-to-peer" fashion. However, even in a peer-to-peer arrangement, the media may still pass through a network device such as a SBC that sits on the edge of a network and acts as a proxy to send the traffic out onto a public network. In most IM networks, Skype being perhaps the only major exception, all the traffic is routed from server-to-server. Your IM client connects to its local server and IM traffic goes to that local server, and then from that server to another server, and then on until it reaches the destination network.

An attacker may be able to identify these "servers" by the amount of traffic flowing out of them and then target those servers – or the path between those servers – as where a compromise needs to occur.

Get on the Local Network Segment

If an attacker can obtain access to the local network segment where one of the endpoints is located, he or she can potentially sniff the network for the media traffic and intercept and/or modify the traffic. A classic case where this can happen is with an unsecured Wi-Fi network where an attacker can use any of the many available wireless packet sniffing tools to see the traffic on the Wi-Fi network. This could be a "rogue" Wi-Fi network at your corporate location or it could be the Wi-Fi café where a remote employee is working.

The attack vector could also be an unsecured Ethernet port in a lobby or conference room, but this requires physical access to the ports (versus being out in the parking lot with Wi-Fi) and is probably less likely. More probable than either the Wi-Fi or Ethernet attack may be an attacker compromising a computer on the local subnet, perhaps by way of malware (virus, malware, bot, and so on).

Compromise the Local System of Either Endpoint

Another avenue for an attacker is to compromise the security of the local system serving as either endpoint of the connection. For instance, if the attacker can convince you to download some malware or otherwise have your system infected, he or she can get their software installed directly on the system initiating communications sessions. The attacker can now log all communication locally and potentially record all audio or video sessions and then send them to an external server at some point.

Note that this approach has the added benefit for an attacker that it may be possible to defeat encryption mechanisms by simply recording the audio from the local system before it enters an outbound encrypted stream. In January 2008, there was a widely publicized case where a division of the German government was reported to be considering[D] such an approach specifically to be able to tap into communications made over the Skype network.

[D]http://skypejournal.com/blog/2008/01/the_bavarian_intercept_proves.html

Using Wireshark to Capture Voice

As mentioned in the introduction to this chapter, Wireshark,[E] the industry-standard free network protocol analyzer that is widely used for network administration (and was previously known as *Ethereal*), has some solid capabilities with regard to capturing and interpreting VoIP Calls. As shown in Figure 3.5, the latest version 1.2.4 of Wireshark has a **Telephony** menu in it with a range of options.

If you select **VoIP Calls** from the **Telephony** menu, you will see a list of what calls Wireshark found in the packets it captured, as shown in Figure 3.6. From

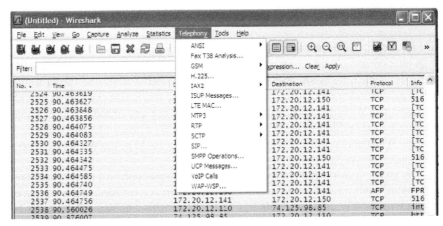

FIGURE 3.5

Wireshark Includes a Telephony Menu

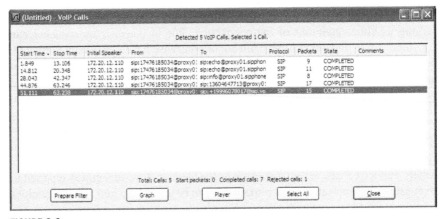

FIGURE 3.6

Wireshark Shows You All of Your VoIP Calls

[E]You can download Wireshark for free for Microsoft Windows, Linux/UNIX, or Apple Mac OS X at www.wireshark.org/

here, you have a couple of options. If you select any one of the calls and click the **Graph** button, you get a great chart such as the one in Figure 3.7 that shows the actual flow of SIP and RTP messages during the course of this particular call. This is actually a great way to learn about how network traffic flows in a SIP-based system.

Back in the **VoIP Calls** window, if you select a call and press the **Player** button and then **Decode** on the next screen, you will then see an audio player similar to Figure 3.8 and have the ability to listen to either side of the conversation. Just click into one of the two audio streams and press the **Play** button to get started.

When you enter the **RTP Player** in Wireshark, you may need to check the **Use RTP timestamp** check box to have your audio correctly interpreted. After you check the box, you'll need to press the **Decode** button after which you should see your audio in the player window. Note also that the RTP Player does not support all possible audio formats, so it may not always work for audio you have captured.

Wireshark also has the ability to save audio streams to files for later listening, although the path to do so is not exactly intuitive. If you select an **RTP packet** in the capture window, you can select the menus **Telephony | RTP | Stream Analysis**…. If you don't have an RTP packet selected, you can select the menus **Telephony | RTP | Select All Streams**,

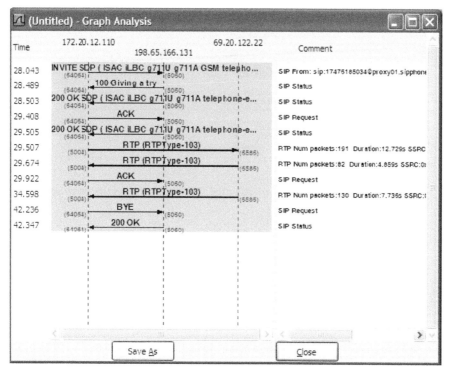

FIGURE 3.7

Wireshark Can Easily Show You the Messages in the Flow of a Call

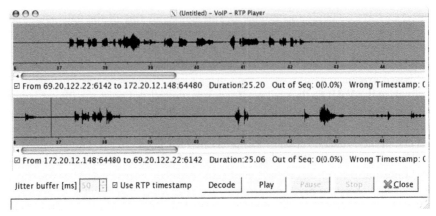

FIGURE 3.8

Wireshark's Audio Player Lets You Listen to Captured Conversations

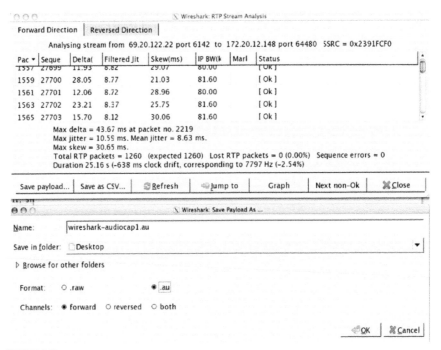

FIGURE 3.9

Wireshark Lets You Save RTP Audio Payloads to Files on Disk

choose a stream, and press the **Analyze** button. In both cases, you will then wind up in an analysis window resembling the top portion of Figure 3.9. By clicking the **Save payload**... button, you will bring up a screen like that on the bottom of Figure 3.9 that will let you save the RTP audio payload out as an audio file.

Note that there are other tools out there that make this process easier, but Wireshark does have the basic functionality.

EPIC FAIL

A college installed a shiny new IP-PBX on its campus and installed IP phone endpoints in each of the student rooms in a residence hall. It wasn't long before some enterprising (or bored) student discovered that all the residence hall phones were on the same local network and with an easy tool like Wireshark, the students could start listening to any phone calls made over the IP phone network! Oops. Needless to say, the college quickly tried to figure out how to enable encryption on its network.

Using Wireshark to Capture IM Traffic

Wireshark can, of course, be used to capture and analyze IM traffic, as well as voice. The major difference is that there is not an entire menu in the Wireshark tool devoted to IM as there is for telephony. With a little bit of understanding what protocols are used by the various services, you can find the relevant traffic within your Wireshark captures. Figure 3.10 shows a capture of Yahoo!Messenger traffic where

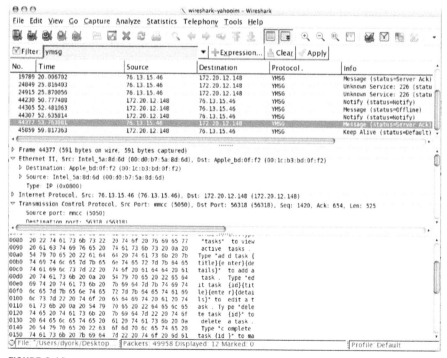

FIGURE 3.10

Wireshark Can Show IM Traffic Such as Yahoo!Messenger

Table 3.1 IM services and Wireshark display filters	
IM service	**Wireshark display filter**
AOL Instant Messenger	aim
Internet Relay Chat	irc
Jabber/XMPP/GoogleTalk	jabber
Microsoft MSN Messenger/Windows Live Messenger	msnms
SIMPLE	sip
Yahoo!Messenger	ymsg

the message of the text is readable. You can see at the top of the Wireshark window that the display filter has been set to *ymsg* so that only Yahoo!Messenger messages are displayed. Table 3.1 shows the text you can use as a display filter for common IM protocols.

Notice that "SIMPLE," the SIP-based protocol for IM mentioned earlier in the chat, has only "sip" as the display filter. Because SIMPLE is based on SIP, you actually want to filter on SIP and then look through for the SIMPLE messages. Alternatively, you could also filter on *msrp*, the MSRP protocol, which is basically the IM equivalent of how RTP is used for audio.

Now as you explore the different IM conversations you capture, you may find that a number of them are unreadable. For instance, you may see in MSN or Jabber conversations who or where the participants are in an exchange, but the actual body of the exchange is not readable. This is because the IM clients being used are in fact encrypting the messages between the IM clients and the IM servers. Many of the current products ship with encryption on by default and while it is always possible for a user to turn the encryption *off*, odds are that they won't. It may also just be part of the UC system. For instance, Microsoft in their Office Communication Server uses Transport Layer Security (TLS) encryption to secure the transport of its SIMPLE-based communication.

NOTE

The Skype exception – You may have noticed that there has been no discussion on how to intercept Skype IM, voice, or video calls. The truth is that it is an extremely difficult task to accomplish. Skype does encrypt all of its signaling, voice, video, and IM, and while the security community may strongly dislike the lack of peer review of Skype's encryption protocol, the fact is that it does protect the transport of communication over Skype. The only real attack scenario identified thus far is to attempt to compromise local systems and install some type of monitoring system. Security researchers continue to probe for Skype's weaknesses, but in the meantime that is why Skype is missing from these tables and sections.

Capturing Audio, Video, and IM using Other Tools

There are, of course, many other tools beyond Wireshark that let you capture voice, video, and IM conversations. Wireshark has been demonstrated here primarily because it should be familiar to most network administrators and also because it is cross-platform (Windows, Linux/UNIX, and Mac OS X), and therefore easy for you to download and experiment with. Let us, though, take a quick tour of some of the other tools available.

- **UCSniff** (http://ucsniff.sourceforge.net/) A newer tool for Windows or Linux, from Jason Ostrom and Arjun Sambamoorthy at Sipera's Viper Labs, can find and record both voice and video conversations and save them to a file for later listening. It supports a wide range of codecs, real-time monitoring, MiTM attacks, virtual local area network hopping, and more. It integrates a number of existing tools into one easy-to-use package.
- **VideoSnarf** (http://ucsniff.sourceforge.net/videosnarf.html) Another tool from the Sipera Viper Labs team that provides a subset of the UCSniff functionality and focuses only on extracting H.264 video streams from the RTP streams.
- **Cain & Abel** (http://www.oxid.it/cain.html) It is primarily a password recovery tool for Windows, and it also includes the ability to record VoIP audio conversations to files for later listening.
- **Oreka** (http://oreka.sourceforge.net/) An open-source call recording solution for Windows or Linux that monitors RTP streams on the network and captures them into audio files and then presents a Web interface allowing you to access the recordings. The project claims that it has been tested to work with a number of common IP-PBX and other similar VoIP systems.
- **VoIPong** (http://www.enderunix.org/voipong) An older program (circa 2005) that identifies VoIP Calls that are G.711 encoded and dumps them to WAV files for listening.
- **Vomit** (http://vomit.xtdnet.nl/) One of the earliest tools, "Voice over Misconfigured Internet Telephones" will retrieve a Cisco IP phone conversation from a tcpdump-formatted packet capture and convert it to a WAV file for listening.

There are certainly other tools out there as well, but these are some of the more common ones you will see discussed in security-related articles and information.

Modification Attacks

In an attack that modifies the media stream, the attacker's software injects itself in between the sender and the recipient in a true MiTM attack, as shown earlier in Figure 3.3. Whether the media is voice, video, or IM text, the idea is the same. The attacker sets the software up so that it relays the media stream unmodified for almost all the packets and then modifies the individual packets critical to the attack. Given that the senders and recipients would not see any modification until the attack, the software could sit in the network for weeks, months, or even years until it is activated for the attack.

Ettercap

There are several different programs out there for performing network MiTM attacks, but perhaps the best known is Ettercap.[F] Ettercap uses "ARP poisoning" (also called *ARP spoofing*) to make other computers on a local network believe that it is a different computer. A full discussion of Address Resolution Protocol (ARP) attacks is a bit beyond the scope of this book, but the basic idea is that on a local network segment, network traffic needs to be reduced from IP addresses down to the actual Ethernet addresses assigned to network interface cards. ARP is the protocol used to provide this IP address to MAC address mapping.

Let's look at a simplified example. Computer A with IP address 192.168.1.100 wants to send a message to Computer B with IP address 192.168.1.107. Because they both reside on the same local network segment and no routing needs to be performed, Computer A sends out a broadcast ARP message on the local network asking for the MAC address of 192.168.1.107. Computer B responds back that its MAC address is 11:22:33:44:55:66 and now Computer A can start sending Ethernet frames directly to Computer B. This is basically how ARP works and is shown in Figure 3.11. The other element here is that Computer A will *cache* the MAC address for Computer B in its local ARP cache so that it doesn't have to issue an ARP for every frame it needs to send. Computer A will maintain the address for Computer B in its ARP cache for a certain period of time and then will send out a new ARP packet to make sure the address is the same.

What Ettercap does is send out fake ARP messages that point an IP address to the attacker's computer. In our example, let's say that Ettercap is running on Computer E. When Ettercap is launched, it may send out an ARP response indicating that 192.168.1.107 (and any other IP addresses) now point to Computer E's address

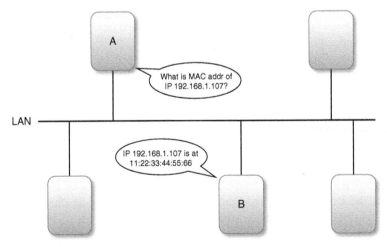

FIGURE 3.11

Two Computers Using ARP to Find MAC Addresses

[F]http://ettercap.sourceforge.net/

of 66:55:44:33:22:11. Computer A, seeing this ARP packet, would update its local ARP cache to now start streaming packets for "Computer B" to 66:55:44:33:22:11. Similarly, Computer E would send a fake ARP packet to Computer B so that it would update its local ARP cache for Computer A's address to point to Computer E. The end result is that Computer A thinks Computer E is Computer B, and Computer B thinks Computer E is Computer A. This attack is shown in Figure 3.12.

Now that the attacker is between the two computers, he or she can observe the traffic flowing between the two points on the network and also modify the traffic. Ettercap supports *filters* that allow for the modification of network traffic. The software includes a filter creator and a number of prebuilt filters you can use. The basic idea is to create a filter that detects a certain pattern in the network packet flow and then substitutes some other data for that pattern.

RTP InsertSound and RTP MixSound

For their book "Hacking Exposed VoIP: Voice over IP Security Secrets and Solutions" (ISBN: 978-0-07-226364-0), Mark Collier and David Endler created a number of tools for security professionals on their Web site (www.hackingvoip.com) including two worth mentioning here. *RTP InsertSound* is a tool that can insert audio into a RTP stream by tricking the receiving endpoint into accepting the attacker's RTP packets instead of the legitimate RTP packets. If you go back to the attack described in the beginning of the section "Anatomy of Eavesdropping and Modification Attacks" where the word "buy" was replaced with the word "sell," RTP InsertSound could be used to attempt those types of attacks.

RTP MixSound is a more devious tool. It mixes an audio stream into an existing RTP stream. If you go back to the scenario at the beginning of the chapter where Joe mixed the sounds of an argument into the outgoing call from the CEO, RTP

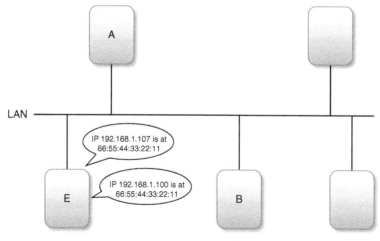

FIGURE 3.12

An Attacker Has Used Ettercap to Get between Two Computers

MixSound could be used to execute attacks like this. If someone were working from home, an attacker could mix in sounds of an amusement park. If someone were working late and called home to their spouse, the attacker could mix in sounds of someone of the opposite sex. Alternatively, the attacker could mix in profanity into the outgoing stream for a customer support line, thus potentially angering the customer who called. The kinds of attacks are really limited only by your imagination.

The entertaining part for the attacker is that the new audio is only mixed into one of the RTP streams. In the examples here, for instance, the attacker could mix it into the streams coming from the caller. The recipient would then hear the mixed audio, but the caller would not. The home worker is suddenly being asked to explain why it sounds like he is at an amusement park. He or she has no clue why they are being asked about this as they don't hear the sounds on their RTP stream. You could imagine the confusion (and marital problems) this could create with the calls to the spouse! Similarly, the attacker could mix sound into only one leg of a multiparty conference call and only into the stream heard by that one recipient. The recipient might then be asking the others on the call about the sound, which they do not hear at all.

RTP MixSound and RTP InsertSound are not the only tools out there that do this, but they are examples of what could be done. It's worth noting that these two tools do not presume that you are able to successfully pull off a MiTM attack. As long as you are on the same network segment, these tools can send RTP packets to target endpoints and have a variety of tricks to try to convince the endpoint to accept the bogus RTP packets as real.

TIP

More media manipulation tools can be found on the Voice over IP Security Alliance (VOIPSA) tools list (www.voipsa.org/Resources/tools.php).

DANGERS OF EAVESDROPPING AND MODIFICATION ATTACKS

While many of the dangers of eavesdropping and modification attacks have been discussed in the previous sections of this chapter, in this section, you will learn more about several of the specific dangers.

Exposure of Confidential Information

Obviously, the most visible and tangible attack is the exposure of confidential information. If someone can gain access to the communication stream inside of a company, they can potentially learn confidential corporate information that could then possibly be used for malicious purposes. This could be information about finances, about new products, and about personnel or any other matter related to the company.

It could also be information from an individual, such as when a person calls into their bank and speaks with someone there. The attacker could use that information for financial gain, public embarrassment (and corresponding reputation loss), or other purposes.

Eavesdropping on UC systems could also be a conduit to other kinds of attacks. Imagine, for instance, that an attacker listens to voice or video calls indicating that the office will be empty for a certain period of time and that something of value is stored in the office. Or imagine that an attacker intercepts someone IM'ing the code to get through the door alarm.

WARNING

Be aware that with voice communications, an attacker might not need to actually gain access to the media stream to obtain confidential information. If a caller is using "dual tone, multifrequency" (DTMF) tones (also known as *touch tones*) to enter information such as a credit card number or voice-mail password, those DTMF tones might travel over the SIP control channel using the method defined in RFC 4733[G] (formerly RFC 2833[H]) and could therefore be obtained via the SIP control channel versus the media channel.

Business Disruption

If a modification attack is successful, it is possible to seriously disrupt the operations of a business. Obviously, there is the blatant case mentioned previously where an attacker changes the use of the word "buy" to "sell" and could potentially create a financial cost to the company. But there could easily be more subtle attacks. Slightly changing the number of units to ship mentioned in an IM message from, say, 150 to 125, could cause a more nuanced disruption of a production process. The possibilities are really only limited by your imagination.

Annoyance

Modification attacks also bring the great opportunity to simply create annoying situations and create internal discord within a company or organization. It could be the mixing of an argument into an outbound media stream as suggested in the scenario back in the introduction to the chapter. It could be mixing in the sound of an amusement park into the background of someone who is working from home. It could be dropping out random words from IM messages or adding in more words. Odds are that these types of attacks may not be perpetrated by an actual external attacker, but rather by someone inside the company intent on annoying or harassing other employees.

[G]http://tools.ietf.org/html/rfc4733
[H]www.disruptivetelephony.com/2007/11/did-you-know-rf.html

Loss of Trust

With attacks that are designed to disrupt or annoy, there is also a corresponding loss of trust in the communication system and potentially a loss of trust in *you* if you are responsible for that system. People may come to discount the system or believe that it is not all that you or other advocates have made it out to be.

THE FUTURE OF EAVESDROPPING AND MODIFICATION ATTACKS

As companies continue to look at UC systems and also at all-IP networks, we will only continue to see growth in eavesdropping and modification attacks. Let's look at some of the particular trends.

Increasing Market Size

The market in general is expanding for communications in all forms over IP networks. Voice, video, IM, social networks, and collaboration technologies are all seeing increased investment. On a larger level, an increasing number of companies are adopting "SIP trunks" as a way to connect from their network out across the Internet to SIP service providers who provide the actual connectivity to the PSTN, a topic you'll learn more about in Chapter 5, "SIP Trunking and PSTN Interconnection." Carriers and service providers already provide much of their internal communication all over IP networks. In fact, in December 2009, the US Federal Communication Commission asked for public comment related to what an "all-IP" public communication network would look like.[1]

As the market increases, so too do the financial incentives for attackers. The larger the market, the more reasons an attacker may look at learning how to eavesdrop on UC systems. It could be for financial gain through market manipulation or blackmail. It could be corporate espionage for a competitor or external advocacy group. It could be journalists digging for content for their articles. Whatever the reason, as the market grows larger the incentives grow for attackers, as do the number of attackers who learn to use the tools out there.

All-IP Enterprise Networks

As part of that increasing market, more and more enterprises are looking at deploying "all-IP" communication networks within their corporations and across their WANs and branch offices. Some of this is driven by cost pressures and looking to reduce PSTN usage, but much of it is driven by the idea of increased collaboration that is possible through UC systems and other collaboration tools.

The security concern is that as UC systems get distributed across larger and larger networks, there become more points at which an attacker can insert the relevant

---

[1]http://hraunfoss.fcc.gov/edocs_public/attachmatch/DA-09-2517A1.pdf

software that can either eavesdrop or modify voice, video, and IM communications. There are more routers, more branch office networks, more potential rogue Wi-Fi hotspots, more servers…just more components to the network in general.

Cloud and Hosted Systems

Along with the distribution of UC system components across an internal network, there is also the movement of pieces of UC functionality out into the hosted "cloud," something we'll discuss in Chapter 7, "The End of Geography." There are tremendous advantages with moving some UC capabilities out into the cloud, but there are corresponding security concerns.

You need to ask questions such as

- What does the connection look like between the on-premise UC systems and the hosted systems?
- Could an attacker insert eavesdropping software in the path between the premise and cloud?
- What does the security of the cloud/hosted provider look like?
- How well do they secure their systems?
- Could an attacker compromise one of their network edge systems or internal servers?
- What about the staff of the cloud provider?
- Can you trust them to not be listening in to your conversation?

All of these are concerns about cloud/hosted providers that need to be taken into account when considering such a solution.

Federation between UC Systems

As companies move to all-IP networks, there is increasing interest in exploring how you can "federate" your UC system with another company's UC system. This may be driven by cost or simply by a desire for better collaboration. As was discussed briefly in Chapter 1, "The Unified Communications Ecosystem" and will be discussed in much greater detail in Chapter 7, "The End of Geography," federation between UC systems brings great challenges for the security professional.

With regard to eavesdropping and modification attacks, the major concern is that the surface area where an attack can occur gets much larger. You now have to worry about the security of the federated systems and understand what potential there is for an attacker to compromise systems in the connected networks and get in a position where he or she could eavesdrop on or modify media streams.

Continued Endpoint Distribution

As you saw in Chapter 2, "Insecure Endpoints," UC endpoints are increasingly scattered across the public Internet and mobile networks. From an eavesdropping perspective, you have to worry about the endpoints and the networks they will connect on. For the endpoints, you have to do the endpoint evaluation mentioned in Chapter 2. This will ensure that the endpoints are in fact secure from someone who might be able to compromise an endpoint and insert software that could listen to a conversation.

You also have to worry about the remote networks upon which those endpoints are connecting. Is it possible for an attacker to capture the traffic on the local network and then decode the RTP streams or IM chat streams to listen in to the conversations? Can an attacker compromise network devices like routers?

The challenge, of course, is that you will have very little control over where people are using their UC endpoints remotely. They will want to use them from their homes, from their local Wi-Fi café, while traveling in trains, sitting in a sports stadium... and anywhere else that they can be. You will have to figure how you can secure the connection to the UC endpoint regardless of where the endpoint may be.

> **NOTE**
>
> Keep in mind, too, that all those UC endpoints that are IP phones also include a local microphone that is managed by the installed software. In October 2009, the winners of the Cisco AXP Dev Contest included a proposal[j] for an "integrated surveillance system" that turned on the microphones on IP phones during nonwork hours to monitor for abnormal audio signals. Obviously, such a system would be helpful to attackers. Similarly, being able to turn on the microphone on an IP phone in a conference room could be quite useful to an attacker. For this reason, you need to ensure that the software installed on IP phones cannot be compromised. Back in the section "Strategy #4: Develop Patch Plans for All Endpoints" in Chapter 2, "Insecure Endpoints," you learned that some IP phones download their software from a central server each time they boot while others have the software installed directly in the IP phone. You need to understand how your IP phones load their software and whether they can be modified by an attacker.

HOW TO DEFEND AGAINST EAVESDROPPING AND MODIFICATION ATTACKS

Defending against eavesdropping and modification attacks really comes down to one primary defense: *encryption*.

The basic concept of encryption is that you take some unencrypted data, commonly referred to as the *plaintext*, and pass it through an *encryption algorithm* to wind up with encrypted data, commonly referred to as the *ciphertext*. The data could be truly text, as it is with many IM messages, or it could be audio or video streams sent between two UC endpoints.

To encrypt data, you need to have an *encryption key* that is known by both parties involved with the communication process. At the simplest level, this may be a "secret key" shared by both parties. At a more complex level, the encryption key may involve "certificates" and "public/private key pairs." There may also be multiple encryption keys involved in a communication session. It is quite common in security design to

---

[j]http://article.gmane.org/gmane.comp.voip.security.voipsa/2852

have a *master key* that is known by both parties and is used to create *session keys* that are used for part or all of a communication session between two endpoints.

Regardless of what key mechanism is used, a fundamental challenge with using encryption is *key exchange*, that is, how do you securely get the encryption key from one party to the other. You will see this is particularly an issue with the Secure Real-time Transport Protocol (SRTP).

A second challenge is whether the encryption will occur "hop-by-hop" or "end-to-end." As shown in Figure 3.13, in hop-by-hop encryption, such as that done with TLS or secure sockets layer (SSL) encryption, the transport is secured between a UC endpoint and a server, then from the server to a second server, and then between that second server and the receiving UC endpoint. However, the media stream is not secured on the servers. The secure transport terminates when the stream hits the server and then the secure transport is re-created when the stream leaves the server. For the brief time the media stream is on the server, though, it is unencrypted. With hop-by-hop encryption, you have to trust the security of your servers. If an attacker can compromise a server and install his or her software, it can see the media streams without encryption. Similarly, if the system administrators of a server were untrustworthy, they could potentially eavesdrop on media streams traveling through the server.

In contrast, with end-to-end encryption, as is shown in Figure 3.14, the media stream is completely encrypted from the software on the sending UC endpoint all the way across the network to the software on the receiving UC endpoint. No one with access to any servers in the path can gain access to the media stream.

Now, you might immediately jump to the conclusion that end-to-end encryption is better, and from a pure security point of view that may be very true. However, in the reality of corporate environments today, particularly with regard to compliance legislation, you may be required to record all calls or archive all IM messages. This may or may not be possible with end-to-end encryption and so you may need to use hop-by-hop encryption in order to comply with other business requirements. Similarly, some multiparty conferencing solutions may not work with end-to-end encryption. Hop-by-hop encryption may also be simpler and easier to set up.

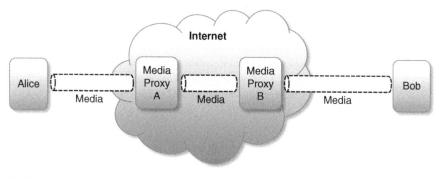

FIGURE 3.13

Hop-by-Hop Encryption

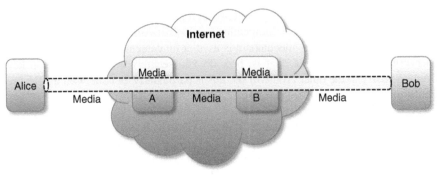

FIGURE 3.14

End-to-End Encryption

Strategy #1: Encryption of Voice and Video

Just as basically most every UC system out there is using RTP (RFC 3550[K]) for sending voice and video across an IP network unencrypted, pretty much every UC system is using SRTP, defined in RFC3711,[L] for sending encrypted voice and video across an IP network. (There are a few systems out there using IP Security [IPSec], which is a topic addressed later in this section.) Note that SRTP is used not just by UC systems based on the SIP protocol but also by UC systems using other standards-based call control protocols (for example, Media Gateway Control Protocol) or proprietary call control protocols. While UC systems may choose different call control protocols, almost all are using RTP and SRTP for sending media across the network.

Part of the reason for this is that SRTP is a strong encryption mechanism that is also lightweight in terms of additional network overhead. SRTP uses the advanced encryption standard[M] as an encryption algorithm and also supports the use of hash-based message authentication code (HMAC), defined in RFC2104,[N] for ensuring the integrity and the authenticity of a SRTP packet. Specifically, SRTP supports "HMAC-SHA1," the version of HMAC that uses the secure hash authentication algorithm (SHA-1).

The beauty of SRTP is that it only encrypts the payload of an RTP packet, that is, the audio or video data included in the RTP packet. This makes it a very fast protocol that adds minimal overhead to a network packet. Given that audio and video both send many very small packets over the network, SRTP does not significantly add to the size of each packet.

[K]http://tools.ietf.org/html/rfc3550
[L]http://tools.ietf.org/html/rfc3711
[M]http://csrc.nist.gov/publications/fips/fips197/fips-197.pdf
[N]http://tools.ietf.org/html/rfc2104

The downside to this approach, of course, is that by only encrypting the packet *payload*, packet *headers* are still exposed and in some cases, such as in an untrusted network, could provide additional information to attackers.

The Challenge of SRTP Key Exchange

The greatest challenge to using SRTP in a UC environment is to address the issue of *SRTP key exchange*. For two UC endpoints to be able to stream audio or video to each other securely, they need to pass the encryption keys from one end to the other.

Unfortunately, there is not a universally agreed-upon way to perform this SRTP key exchange yet. The result is that you might have a UC system from, say, Cisco,[O] and UC endpoints in the form of hard IP phones from Cisco, Avaya,[P] Mitel,[Q] and Polycom.[R] The Cisco IP phones may all be able to communicate via SRTP as they have a common way to exchange the SRTP encryption keys. However, the phones from the other vendors may not be able to exchange SRTP keys, and therefore are not able to have secure communication sessions.

There are solutions out there, though. Let's look at a couple of them.

Security Descriptions

While several proposals for SRTP key exchange were floated around in Internet Engineering Task Force (IETF) discussions, the first to see any significant amount of usage was the "Session Description Protocol (SDP) Security Descriptions for Media Streams," defined in RFC 4568,[S] and alternatively referred to as *SDP security descriptions*, *sdescriptions*, or simply *sdes*.

Sdescriptions added a new "crypto" attribute to the SDP[T] used in SIP to establish a communication session between two endpoints. As shown in RFC 4568, sdescription usage looks like this:

```
a=crypto:1 AES_CM_128_HMAC_SHA1_80
inline:PS1uQCVeeCFCanVmcjkpPywjNWhcYDOmXXtxaVBR|2^20|1:32
```

The crypto attribute includes information about the encryption and the authentication algorithms and then some keying material that can be used to generate the appropriate keys for communication.

Sdescriptions is very easy to use, as the endpoints simply add another line to the SDP information being sent in the SIP packets during session establishment. However, it has the very fundamental flaw that essentially the encryption key is sent in the clear. Sdescriptions can only be used securely with an encrypted SIP connection. As you will learn in Chapter 4, "Control Channel Attacks: Fuzzing, DoS, SPIT, and Toll Fraud," today most encrypted SIP connections occur with the use of TLS. The challenge is that TLS only encrypts communications hop-by-hop. This means

---

[O] www.cisco.com/
[P] www.avaya.com/
[Q] www.mitel.com/
[R] www.polycom.com/
[S] http://tools.ietf.org/html/rfc4568
[T] http://tools.ietf.org/html/rfc4566

that the SIP packets – and the corresponding SDP with the SRTP encryption key – are exposed in any SIP proxies or other servers between the caller and the recipient. If an attacker can compromise one of those proxies or servers, he or she can gain access to the SRTP encryption key and can then decrypt all of the encrypted media sessions.

Potential Solutions

A great amount of effort was spent within the IETF over the past few years to arrive at a better solution than sdescriptions that solved both the hop-by-hop key exposure problem and also a number of call scenarios where encryption usage was problematic. To fully understand all the issues involved, your best plan would be to read RFC 5479,[U] "Requirements and Analysis of Media Security Management Protocols," which explains the problems and then also reviews the current and proposed solutions to address the issues.

In the end, it looks like there will probably be two potential solutions out there to provide a higher level of SRTP key exchange than what is currently available via sdescriptions:

- **DTLS-SRTP** After a long evaluation process that at one time was considering around 13 different protocols, the IETF has identified that the protocol to be used in the future for SRTP key exchange should be the "Datagram Transport Layer Security (DTLS) Extension to Establish Keys for SRTP" otherwise known as *DTLS-SRTP* and defined in the Internet Drafts *draft-ietf-sip-dtls-srtp-framework*[V] and *draft-ietf-avt-dtls-srtp.*[W] (Note that both of these drafts have been submitted to the RFC Editor and may be out as RFCs by the time you read this book.) DTLS-SRTP essentially starts out by exchanging some basic fingerprint information in the SDP and then using DTLS (RFC 4347[X] – think of DTLS as TLS over UDP instead of TCP) to perform the key exchange in the actual RTP media channel.
- **ZRTP** During this IETF evaluation process, Phil Zimmermann of Pretty Good Privacy (PGP) fame submitted his "ZRTP" Protocol defined in *draft-zimmermann-avt-zrtp*[Y] for consideration. ZRTP is a bit different in that it exchanges the SRTP keys entirely in the media path. There are no SIP or SDP messages involved. As you might expect from someone with Phil Zimmermann's cryptographic background, ZRTP has a number of interesting crypto aspects with regard to perfect forward secrecy, MiTM protection and more.

At the time of this book, neither DTLS-SRTP nor ZRTP are widely available yet, although ZRTP is available in Phil Zimmermann's "Zfone" project as well as a number of other implementations,[Z] including one for the Asterisk open-source PBX.

[U]http://tools.ietf.org/html/rfc5479

[V]http://tools.ietf.org/html/draft-ietf-sip-dtls-srtp-framework

[W]http://tools.ietf.org/html/draft-ietf-avt-dtls-srtp

[X]http://tools.ietf.org/html/rfc4347

[Y]http://tools.ietf.org/html/draft-zimmermann-avt-zrtp

[Z]A list of ZRTP implementations can be found at www.voip-info.org/wiki/view/ZRTP

Please note that both of these protocols would provide end-to-end security where you would not need to worry about the security of the intermediary proxies and servers. However, as noted in the introductory text to this section, "How to Defend against Eavesdropping and Modification Attacks," end-to-end encryption may not be compatible with other enterprise requirements such as call recording or conferencing. You'll need to understand what requirements you have and whether vendors with end-to-end encryption can provide appropriate solutions.

What to Do Today?

To protect your UC systems from eavesdropping and modification attacks of the voice and video streams today, you really have three main options with regard to SRTP.

1. Use sdescriptions with TLS-encrypted SIP and ensure you can trust intermediary servers/proxies – and test all endpoints. If your UC system is being deployed entirely on your own network where you can trust the people who have access to SIP proxies or other media servers and where you can trust that those systems receive a high degree of security scrutiny, then you certainly can consider using sdescriptions for SRTP key exchange. Note that you'll need to protect the SIP control channel with something like TLS encryption. You also will have to test the endpoints from various vendors to ensure that they will in fact provide the TLS-encrypted SIP and sdescriptions support you need.

2. Purchase all endpoints from a single vendor. For a variety of reasons this is probably not an overly favorable option, as there is a good probability that you can wind up being "locked-in" to proprietary equipment, services, and so on. However, assuming the vendor supports SRTP across all the endpoints, you should at least be all set with SRTP key exchange. Note, of course, that if they are using sdescriptions, the same caveat applies as in the previous paragraph about needing to protect the SIP channel and also ensuring you are okay with the security of SIP proxies and other servers.

3. Ask your vendors about timeframes for DTLS-SRTP and/or ZRTP support. As mentioned earlier, there is very little commercial support yet for either DTLS-SRTP or ZRTP. Now, neither has been formally adopted as a standard, so it is understandable for vendors to wait until RFCs are issued. Having said that, DTLS-SRTP has been identified by the IETF as "the way forward" and those drafts are currently in the queue to become official RFCs. Once that happens, you should expect to see some vendors moving to supply endpoints that support the specification. It is not clear right now what the future holds for ZRTP, but it is seeing interest within some parts of the developer community and may evolve in interesting ways.

The challenge for either DTLS-SRTP or ZRTP is to actually get into more UC endpoints. Until that time, we are basically stuck with sdescriptions as the only cross-vendor way of doing SRTP key exchange.

IPsec

You may have noticed that in this entire section, there has been no mention yet of the IPsec protocol commonly used for VPNs. There are, in fact, a few vendors out there who have offered IPsec for IP phone endpoints. IPsec may also be the VPN mechanism used to connect a remote worker back into the corporate office for access via a softphone or UC endpoint.

The challenge with IPsec is that it involves a fair degree of overhead for processing each packet on the network. Where SRTP only encrypts the payload of a packet, IPsec encrypts the entire packet and adds some extra encryption headers as well. What once was a small packet with a small slice of audio may balloon into a much larger packet by the time IPsec is done with it. The larger packet must then traverse the network and be decrypted on the other side.

Historically, this has been a significant enough amount of overhead to cause vendors to look at alternatives like SRTP, especially when looking at securing a large number of endpoints. Given that both computing power and network bandwidth have grown exponentially over the years, IPsec may perform better and have a role to play in securing UC systems. It certainly may be the VPN technology you use to connect your remote workers in to use their UC collaboration clients and/ or softphones. You just may want to spend some time evaluating the performance of softphones over an IPsec connection versus over a TLS-encrypted SIP/SRTP connection.

The good news about IPsec is that in its usual mode of operation, it does encrypt the entire packet stream from the remote endpoint to your network. The bad news is that (a) there may be a performance hit and (b) it is still only hop-by-hop because the IPsec connections will typically terminate on a VPN concentrator on the edge of your network.

> **NOTE**
>
> In most IPSec deployments today, IPsec is used in "tunnel mode" where the entire packet is encrypted. However, you should be aware that the IPsec specification does define a "transport mode" where, similar to SRTP, only the payload is encrypted.

Strategy #2: Encryption of IM

Beyond voice and video, the other major media channel you typically have in UC systems is the IM text channel. The good news is that encrypting IM is well understood at this point and there are many different solutions out there, both proprietary and open standards-based. In this section, you'll look at three of those solutions:

1. TLS/SSL
2. PGP/Gnu Privacy Guard (GnuPG)
3. Off-The-Record (OTR)

The reality is that almost all UC solutions will probably be using TLS/SSL to encrypt IM, but this section also covers PGP and OTR because they do provide options for end-to-end encryption and because you will see mention of them in public information about securing IM.

> **WARNING**
>
> When looking at encryption of IM systems, be sure to understand how IM messages are stored on your local machine. It is quite possible that logs of IM chat sessions may be stored locally as unencrypted text files. This means that while they may be secured across the network, someone may be able to compromise the local machine and view all the chat logs there.

Concerns about Encrypting IM

Before you go off encrypting all your IM traffic, it is worth considering two important issues. First, in the United States and many other countries, there are now significant amounts of compliance legislation such as Sarbanes–Oxley that require you to archive all IM messages. Now, you may still be able to do this while also providing encrypted transport of IM. For instance, if you use TLS/SSL with your IM clients, it is a hop-by-hop encryption method and so the IM messages are unencrypted on the IM servers. You can simply have software there on the IM servers route a copy of all IM messages to a system for archiving. If, on the other hand, you use an end-to-end encryption method, you may need to figure out some other method of complying with archive requirements.

Second, being a text-based medium like e-mail, IM represents another vector for potential viruses, phishing scams, malware, and so on. For instance, a URL could circulate via IM that goes to a malicious Web site that aims to compromise your users' Web browsers. You or your IT department may want to have some mechanism to scan IM message traffic to protect your user base. Such scanning systems may or may not be compatible with the encryption you make available. You need to ask the questions as you consider options.

TLS/SSL

If SSL works for Web browsers to secure home banking, for instance, why not use it to encrypt IM messages? In truth, that's what most IM systems do.

TLS, defined in RFC 5246,[AA] is based on the SSL 3.0 specification originally created by Netscape although TLS did evolve substantially away from SSL 3.0. For communicating with people outside the security space, you may find you need to speak of it like this section is titled, "TLS/SSL." The reality is that many people to whom you need to speak about securing IM may not be familiar with the term *TLS* (even though it's been around for almost a decade) but will know the term *SSL* from their Web browser usage. It may even be the case that in their UC or IM client there is a check box somewhere that says "Use SSL" when in fact it is actually using TLS.

Many if not most of the enterprise UC solutions as well as the public IM networks do support TLS. It is by far the predominant way to protect the traffic over IM and is used by both Jabber/XMPP and SIP/SIMPLE systems. In many cases, UC solutions or IM networks enable it by default. In other cases, you may need to go into the

---

[AA]http://tools.ietf.org/html/rfc5246

preferences/settings for your UC client and find the appropriate check box. Do recall, though, from the beginning of this section, "How to Defend against Eavesdropping and Modification Attacks," that TLS/SSL is a hop-by-hop encryption method and so the IM messages are unencrypted on the IM servers. This may be perfectly fine if you are comfortable with the security of those servers.

PGP/GnuPG

Another option for encrypting IM is to use a public/private key pair in the OpenPGP format[BB] from either commercial PGP providers or the free software Gnu Privacy Guard[CC] (referred to as either *GnuPG* or *GPG*). You provide your public key to the person with whom you want to communicate. You obtain their public key. You configure your IM client to use their key and, ta da, you are IM'ing securely.

The challenge with PGP/GPG is that there is a bit of setup/configuration work that must be done and the process is not entirely intuitive to a nontechnical user. There are, though, a fair number of IM clients, particularly in the Jabber/XMPP world, that do support PGP/GPG encryption and, once set up, do allow you to have completely secure end-to-end encrypted IM sessions.

Another issue with a PGP/GPG system is the central importance of your private key. Should your computer get stolen, for instance, and an attacker is able to figure out whatever pass phrase you have used to protect your private key, he or she is then able to decrypt and read any of your IM messages, including all of your past messages.

OTR

Primarily as a reaction to that last point about PGP, another system called *OTR*[DD] messaging has emerged in recent years. OTR works in a somewhat similar fashion to PGP in that you do have key pairs but it has two fundamental differences:

1. **Perfect forward secrecy** If someone compromises your OTR key later, it cannot be used to decrypt your past messages.
2. **Deniability** The messages do not have digital signatures, and so after a conversation is over, there is no way that someone else can tie a message directly to you. So again, if someone compromises your OTR key, they cannot cryptographically prove that you sent earlier messages.

The whole idea is to create a situation where a casual conversation can be "off the record" and truly as confidential and private as possible. OTR is not widely available in commercial clients but is included in common multiprotocol IM clients such as Pidgin[EE] (formerly Gaim) and Adium[FF] and is also mentioned in security literature around IM encryption.

[BB]OpenPGP is defined in RFC 4880: http://tools.ietf.org/html/rfc4880
[CC]www.gnupg.org/
[DD]More about OTR at:www.cypherpunks.ca/otr/
[EE]www.pidgin.im/
[FF]http://adium.im/

SUMMARY

In the world of UC, voice, video, and text are simply bits inside of packets being sent across the network. If an attacker can get to the right point in your network, he or she can eavesdrop on that communication, either actively watching/listening to the sessions in real-time or passively collecting all the communication sessions for later viewing. Potentially worse, of course, the attacker can modify those bits and change the communication you are having, probably without you even knowing it.

What is perhaps most tragic about defending against eavesdropping and modification attacks is that the vast majority of UC system vendors out there do have encryption for voice and video available in their software and most endpoints – but it is not enabled by default! Raising your protection level may be as simple as configuring a couple of options in your administrative interface. You do, though, need to be sure you can enable encryption and also meet any compliance or other IT security requirements you may have in place.

NOTE

Sadly, one of the barriers you may run into is that people within your organization may have come to rely on unencrypted media or signaling in order to troubleshoot problems with the UC system. You may need to find tools or systems that let them perform the troubleshooting they want with encryption in place or develop appropriate processes where encryption can be dropped long enough to troubleshoot an issue and then be reenabled. All too often encryption may be dropped for troubleshooting and then never turned back on.

In the next chapter, we'll look at channels for controlling our UC systems and how those channels can be attacked. Perhaps not surprisingly, you'll find that one of the strategies for defense is quite similar to the strategy here....

Control Channel Attacks: Fuzzing, DoS, SPIT, and Toll Fraud

4

INFORMATION IN THIS CHAPTER

- Anatomy of Control Channel Attacks
- Dangers of Control Channel Attacks
- Future of Control Channel Attacks
- How to Defend against Control Channel Attacks

In June 2006, the US Federal Bureau of Investigation (FBI) arrested Edwin Pena, a 23-year-old Miami resident, and accused him of masterminding a Voice over Internet Protocol (VoIP) fraud scheme that stole over 10 million minutes of calling worth about $1.4 million from a number of VoIP service providers. The FBI complaint[A] details how Pena allegedly represented himself as a legitimate provider of wholesale telecommunications services and solicited business from a range of companies. Pena then routed the calls from those customers across the networks of various VoIP service providers where he had illegally obtained free access. He was making money providing this service and routing his traffic for free, which allowed him to purchase fancy cars, real estate, and even a speedboat. In August 2006, Pena fled the United States and remained a fugitive until February 2009 when he was arrested in Mexico. He was extradited to the United States in October 2009[B] and pled guilty to the fraud charges in February 2010.[C]

To pull off his scheme, Pena paid Robert Moore, a developer in Spokane, Washington, to develop software that, among other things, would scan networks and find vulnerable systems that Pena could use to route his illegitimate traffic. The FBI complaint alleges that Pena and Moore used brute force attacks to determine the call-routing prefixes used by VoIP service providers to route legitimate calls. Pena then used the vulnerable systems discovered to route his phone calls to those VoIP service providers. This scheme hid the origins of the calls from the VoIP service providers, confusing their billing systems so that the service providers could not bill anyone for what appeared to be legitimate traffic. The complaint notes that in one

---

[A]www.justice.gov/usao/nj/press/files/pdffiles/moorecomplaint.pdf
[B]http://newark.fbi.gov/dojpressrel/2009/nk101509.htm
[C]http://voipsa.org/blog/2010/02/19/voip-fraudster-and-fugitive-edwin-pena-pleads-guilty/

case Pena routed around 500,000 calls through one provider over a 3-week period while disguising where that traffic actually came from.

Robert Moore, who was also arrested in June 2006, was convicted in July 2007 and sent to prison for his role in the scheme. Before he reported to prison, Moore gave an interview[D] where he outlined how he had pulled off some of the attacks. Sadly, many of the intermediary systems were compromised purely through the use of default or weak passwords. For instance, Moore indicated that some of the systems had an administrative username of admin and a password of admin. Other known vulnerabilities were exploited that should have been patched if system administrators had been paying attention to their devices connected to the public Internet.

In the end, the Pena and Moore VoIP fraud case represents the largest public disclosure to date of a scheme that exploits the *control channel* of a VoIP system. While the Pena and Moore scheme turned out to exploit the older H.323 signaling protocol, the lessons are definitely applicable to the Session Initiation Protocol (SIP) and other control channel protocols used widely today throughout Unified Communications (UC).

ANATOMY OF CONTROL CHANNEL ATTACKS

Before you begin looking at specific attacks against control channels, let's review how the call flow occurs within SIP-based UC systems. As shown in Figure 4.1, the control messages flow via SIP through one or more SIP proxies to reach the receiving endpoint. The media stream flows directly between the two endpoints along a separate path.

In an enterprise UC system, there might only be a single SIP proxy, that is, the IP private branch exchange (IP-PBX) or call server. SIP-related call or IM messages might be limited to a single network or within a certain set of networks. Alternatively, as shown in Figure 4.2, the UC network might be much more complex.

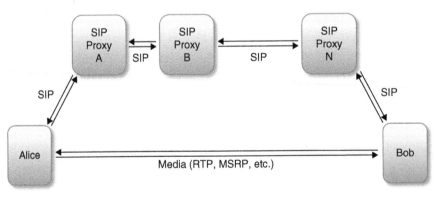

FIGURE 4.1

Control Channel and Media Streams Follow Different Paths

[D]www.thevoicereport.com/TelecomJunkiesArchive-VoIPHacker.html

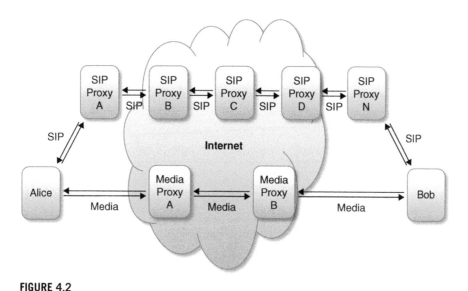

FIGURE 4.2

A UC Network Might Involve Numerous Proxy Servers

The complexity of your UC network, and in particular whether there is communication across the public Internet, will directly impact what dangers are most relevant to you and what defenses you need to put in place. The more complex the UC architecture, the more points there are for an attacker to inject software and the more points at which you need to consider defenses.

Eavesdropping Attacks

In Chapter 3, "Eavesdropping and Modification," you learned about how the *media channel* could be intercepted and observed. The same attacks and the same tools can be used to observe the control channels. If you recall Figures 3.6 and 3.7 in Chapter 3, Wireshark has some easy options to let you identify VoIP calls and graph out the flow of a SIP call. Figure 4.3 shows that Wireshark also let you dig deeper into the actual contents of the SIP packets to view their contents.

Similar to the eavesdropping attacks against media channels, the attacker only needs to get to the same network segment where the control channel traffic is occurring. The attacker can then capture all the traffic on the network segment and analyze the traffic at some later time. By analyzing the control channel traffic, the attacker can potentially learn the following information:

- Who is calling whom?
- What are common external numbers that are being called or external IM contacts?
- Presence information about who is or is not available, and any other available "rich presence" information (such as status messages about where someone is right now)

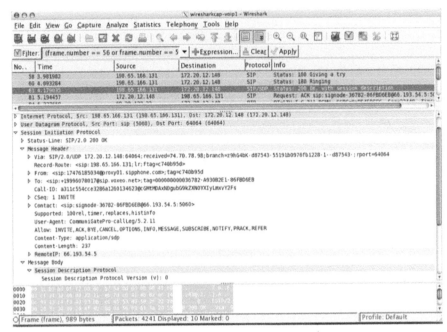

FIGURE 4.3

Wireshark Can Show You the Contents of a SIP Packet

- What systems are used by SIP service providers to route calls out to the public switched telephone network (PSTN)?
- What gateways are used to connect to federated UC systems, to public IM networks, or to any other collaboration systems?
- Usernames and passwords to external systems
- Encryption keys for the encrypted Secure Real-time Transfer Protocol (SRTP) media channel (if the attacker compromises a hop in the routing path where the keying material is briefly unencrypted)
- Patterns of communication sessions – volume, usage, busiest endpoints, and so on

This information may allow an attacker to gather important information about the company in and of itself, or it may give the attacker more information that he or she can use to undertake further attacks against your UC system.

NOTE

Do note that there are many other network analysis tools that also allow an attacker to capture and read packets. Wireshark is mentioned as an example purely because it is freely available across all the major operating systems of Windows, Mac OS X and Linux/UNIX. See the VOIPSA VoIP Security Tools list at www.voipsa.org/Resources/tools.php for more specialized scanning tools.

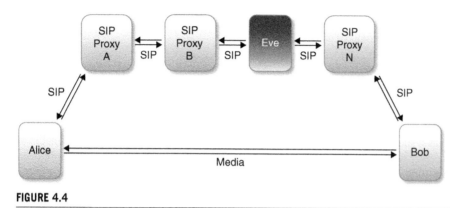

FIGURE 4.4

An Attacker, Eve, Inserts Herself in the Control Channel between Alice and Bob

Modification Attacks

Back in the "Modification Attacks" section of Chapter 3, "Eavesdropping and Modification," you learned about how an attacker could get in the middle of a media stream and make modifications to the media being sent from one endpoint to another. Using the same techniques and tools, an attacker could get in the middle of a control channel, as shown in Figure 4.4, and be able to both intercept and modify control messages.

The attacker can potentially observe and modify network traffic if he or she can

- get in the *network path* between the two endpoints
- get between two of the *servers* or *proxies* involved with sending the traffic between the endpoints
- get on the same *network segment* as one of the endpoints
- compromise the local system of either endpoint.

What you learned about these attack vectors in Chapter 3, "Eavesdropping and Modification," applies equally to control channels as it does to media channels. Consider the types of modifications an attacker could make to the control channel if he or she were to get in the middle of it:

- Redirect calls to another extension or number where the attacker could answer it.
- Modify presence information so that a person appeared to be available or busy when in fact they were in the opposite state.
- Change the identity information of the sender so that the call or IM appeared to be coming in from someone else. (A topic to be discussed in more detail in Chapter 6, "Identity, Spoofing, and Vishing.")
- Remove information about encryption support from the headers to attempt to cause the media stream to be unencrypted (and therefore that much easier to intercept or observe).

- Change billing information included in SIP headers so that calls are billed to another account or are unable to be billed.
- Add another extension under the attacker's control to a conference call.

The amount of chaos or business disruption an attacker could cause is truly only limited by the attacker's imagination.

An attacker in the middle of a control channel can of course also cause no end of denial-of-service (DoS) attacks. The attacker could simply drop certain control messages, such as endpoint registration messages, resulting in endpoints being unable to interact with the system. In a more targeted attack, the software could simply drop any outbound sessions from Alice to Bob with the result that Bob would never know Alice was trying to contact him. This could be particularly effective if the attacker were to block both voice or video and IM communication between Alice and Bob, but allow it to work for Alice to everyone else in the company.

Once the attacker is in the middle of a control channel, there is very little he or she cannot do to use and abuse your UC system.

Denial-of-Service Attacks

There are, though, a range of other DoS attacks that do not require a man-in-the-middle attack to be effective. Let's look at several of these attacks.

Flooding

Network flooding attacks have long been a standard part of an attacker's toolbox for denying service. The basic concept is

1. either send a massive amount of traffic at a particular server or service with the aim of exhausting all its resources trying to respond to bogus traffic so that it cannot process legitimate requests for service
2. or send a massive amount of traffic onto a specific network segment with the goal of creating so much network congestion that legitimate traffic cannot reach the target server or service. This type of attack isn't specific to UC as the traffic sent onto the network could really be of any type.

Regarding the first type of flooding attack, there are a good number of tools out there that will, for instance, send thousands of simultaneous SIP INVITE messages to your UC systems to see how it stands up to the bombardment. Examples include SIPp,[E] sipsak,[F] and SipBomber.[G] These tools, and many other similar tools, attempt to exceed the number of simultaneous sessions a server can handle, which can result either in the server not being able to accept further sessions or in some cases the server rebooting or otherwise ceasing operation.

[E]http://sipp.sourceforge.net/
[F]http://sipsak.org/
[G]www.metalinkltd.com/downloads.php

Distributed DoS/Botnet Attacks

Obviously, if an attacker is launching a flooding type of attack, the attacker may want to hide the source of the attack so that they cannot be simply shut down by blocking one or just a couple of addresses. This is essentially what Pena and Moore were attempting to do in the fraud scheme outlined at the very beginning of the chapter, although they were using their intermediary systems to hide the source of their traffic to evade billing.

When this type of attack method is used for a DoS attack, in today's terminology, we refer to this as a "distributed DoS" (DDoS). In a DDoS, a large number of systems are used to send traffic to a particular network address to disguise the origins of the attack and deny system administrators an easy route to blocking the traffic.

An attacker could do what Pena and Moore did and go around establishing a series of intermediary systems from which to launch attacks. Today, though, odds are that an attacker would instead look to either create or hire a "botnet" to perform the attack. In a botnet, there are hundreds, thousands, or millions of computers out there that have been compromised and have a "bot" installed on their system waiting for commands. Typically, these are personal computers where the bot has been installed as a result of opening a virus-laden e-mail, inadvertently installing spyware, or visiting some type of malicious Web site. Today an attacker would typically contract with a botnet provider to perform the designated DDoS attack, which would then be launched against the victim's servers by the software installed on these many compromised systems.

Now the botnets available today are generally designed to target Web or mail servers. At the time of this book, there have been no reports of production botnets targeting UC systems. However, back in May 2007, reports circulated[H] about proof-of-concept code that is still available today,[I] which would allow the creation of a SIP-focused botnet. As UC systems and other SIP-based systems continue to be deployed – as they move closer to allowing full interconnection between systems across the public Internet – there will come a time when the potential target market is big enough to be financially viable for some attacker to create a SIP-based botnet. Until that time, though, expect to see botnets continue to be used more for more standard network attacks, like those against Web and e-mail servers.

Misuse of Legitimate SIP Signaling

Rather than flooding a server with SIP packets, it may be possible to cause a DoS simply by sending legitimate SIP packets. A classic case is the "SIP BYE" attack where an attacker writes a script that simply sends a SIP BYE message to the default SIP port 5060 across a range of Internet Protocol (IP) addresses, effectively telling all SIP devices to hang up whatever call they have in progress. Any endpoint receiving the BYE message would just terminate whatever call it was making. In the early days of SIP, this attack would often work with literally that simple of a script. Over

---

[H]http://voipsa.org/blog/2007/05/07/ready-or-not-here-come-the-irc-controlled-sipvoip-attack-bots/
[I]www.loria.fr/~nassar/readme.html

time, vendors added protections against this brute force attack by, for instance, only accepting BYE messages from endpoints with whom a session was in progress. Still, there are scripts available out there on the Internet that will attempt this kind of BYE attack against SIP endpoints.

EPIC FAIL

In April 2008, Cisco reported[J] that two DoS vulnerabilities existed in Cisco Unified Communications Manager where the processing of specific legitimate SIP messages would cause the call server software to restart, thus terminating any calls in progress. Other examples exist out there from a variety of vendors. The point is that vendors' SIP implementations may respond to what appears to be legitimate SIP traffic in ways that cause the system to be unresponsive or to terminate existing communication.

Registration Erasure or Modification

Another more subtle DoS attack involves erasing or modifying the registration of a SIP endpoint to the UC system. When a SIP endpoint first starts up, it sends a SIP REGISTER message to a system component referred to as a "Registrar" with the information about the endpoint like its extension ID, IP address, domain name, etc. This Registrar component is the directory that is used to route SIP traffic. For example, in Figure 4.5, when Alice wants to call Bob, her local SIP proxy queries the registrar to find Bob's address and then routes the traffic to Bob's endpoint.

The endpoint registering with a SIP Registrar does so for a defined period of time, which could be as long as a several hours or as little as 20 or 30 s. At the end of that time period, the endpoint will be removed from the Registrar unless a subsequent REGISTER message has been received restarting the time period. An endpoint's registration can also be explicitly removed if a REGISTER message is sent in with an expiration time of "0."

The attack is then fairly straightforward. The attacker sends in false REGISTER messages that attempt to do one of the following:

1. Remove the registration entirely.
2. Register the endpoint's extension ID pointing to a bogus destination (if the intent is simply a DoS but the attacker wants the endpoint to still appear as registered).
3. Register an alternative destination (if the intent is interception, fraud, or DoS through redirection).

Now, as shown in Figure 4.6, if this last attack is done, when Alice attempts to call Bob, she in fact winds up talking to Eve.

To pull this off, the attacker has to somehow keep Bob's endpoint from legitimately registering, but this could be accomplished through several methods. First, the attacker could launch a separate DoS attack against Bob's endpoint causing it to fail or at least not be available. Second, the attacker could simply send many frequent

---

[J]www.cisco.com/en/US/products/products_security_advisory09186a0080a0156a.shtml

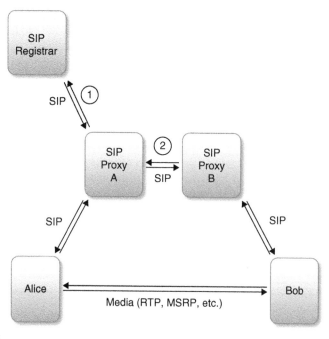

FIGURE 4.5

A SIP Registrar Is Used to Look Up a Destination Address

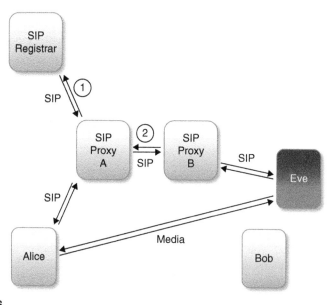

FIGURE 4.6

The Attacker, Eve, Has Modified Bob's Endpoint Registration

REGISTER messages. If Bob's endpoint was, for instance, set to register every hour, the attacker could be sending registrations every 30 s to ensure that Bob's extension was always redirected to the bogus or alternative address.

An interesting aspect about this attack from Bob's perspective is that he might not necessarily notice (depending upon his system) that his endpoint is no longer registered. The symptom to him is purely that he is not receiving inbound calls. His endpoint might continue to work perfectly fine for outgoing calls, but no one can reach him with an inbound session.

One obvious solution to protect against these attacks is to require some form of authentication when SIP REGISTER messages are received, and in practice, most UC systems do in fact do this. However, there can be nuances missed in how registrations are handled that can lead to further exploitation. As an example, in 2007, Sipera Systems reported[K] that the consumer service Vonage only checked the credentials on the initial REGISTER message sent to Vonage's registrar server. Subsequent messages appearing to be from the same IP address were not checked, allowing an attacker to replay registrations and wind up receiving calls intended for the Vonage user.

> **NOTE**
>
> An attacker could also use the SIP REGISTER command to register an additional endpoint attached to a specific extension or address. In this way, a call to Bob would also ring the attackers' endpoint and the attacker could in fact pick up before Bob and wind up speaking with the caller.

Elevation of Authority or Password Cracking

Another very common attack against a control channel is purely to scan a UC system, to identify all the addresses on the system, and to break the passwords associated with those addresses. There are any number of commonly available tools that will help with this. If an attacker is able to obtain compromised logins, he or she could then attempt to register endpoints with that log-in information and gain access to the system and its resources.

Fuzzing

The term *fuzzing* or *protocol fuzzing* refers to essentially modifying or manipulating a protocol beyond its intended use or valid format to cause some unintended effect on the target endpoint. If you recall back to the "Protocol Fuzzing" section of Chapter 2, "Insecure Endpoints," you saw a brief mention of Siemens IP phones that rebooted if they received specially crafted SIP packets and a Zoiper softphone that crashed if a specific SIP header was empty.

[K]www.sipera.com/index.php?action=resources,threat_advisory&tid=358&

These are the types of outcomes that fuzzing software attempts to identify. Test suites are available that try out various permutations of SIP (and other protocols) headers and messages to see whether a particular product or service will respond in an unpredicted way. Essentially, they are looking to see whether vendors' products are adequately handling malformed SIP messages. The vendor may have made an assumption that a specific SIP header would always be sent and always be sent in a specific format. What happens if that header isn't there? Or is there but has the wrong format? Will the system just ignore that and continue? Will the system crash? Or will it do something else?

For the SIP protocol, one of the reference test suites for this kind of testing is the PROTOS test suite created by the University of Oulu, Finland, back in the early 2000s. The test suite is freely available,[L] and you can use it to test how your SIP-based systems respond. The PROTOS test suite has been eclipsed over time by newer tests, most notably by those from the commercial firm Codenomicon,[M] but it still can provide a useful baseline to understanding how susceptible your systems are.

Spam for Internet Telephony

A final control channel attack that bears mentioning primarily because of the hype it has received in the popular press is the attack of Spam for Internet Telephony (SPIT). The idea is that an attacker would connect to your system and iterate through the possible recipient addresses (for example, 111@sip.example.com, 112@sip.example.com, 113...), and whenever a valid address is found, the attacker would initiate one or more calls and send through automated messages.

It truly makes for great headlines in the media... where else in the security field can you write headlines like "SPIT Happens" or "When SPIT Hits the Fan"? The concern is also very real – what if someone were able to send in a large amount of unsolicited traffic into your UC system? Filling up users inboxes, filling up the disk drives of voice-mail servers, and generally creating a very frustrating and annoying situation for your users. All of us have at some point been drowning under e-mail spam, so the very concept of having that type of traffic entering a UC system causes great concern.

The reality, though, is that today the circumstances that would allow for SPIT generally do not exist. For a SPIT attack to be carried out, your UC system would need to accept SIP connections from random, untrusted people out on the Internet or other wide area networks. While there may be some few companies that do allow these kind of random connections, the vast majority of systems out there do not. Generally, most companies may use SIP for connectivity out to a SIP service provider and then on to the PSTN, but they do not allow other connections via SIP. The PSTN serves as a de facto firewall preventing these types of direct SIP connections.

[L] www.ee.oulu.fi/research/ouspg/PROTOS_Test-Suite_c07-sip
[M] www.codenomicon.com/

This will change over time, and you will learn more about this in the next chapter, Chapter 5, "SIP Trunking and PSTN Interconnection," and in the final Chapter 7, "The End of Geography." We will reach a point where you will be able to receive a connection over the IP communications network from any random endpoint out there, just as you can receive a phone call today over the PSTN from any random phone out there. That point is not today… but when we get there, we will need to have addressed issues around SPIT creation, or we will be drowning in SPIT then. For the moment, though, it remains more of a hypothetical attack for the vast majority of users out there.

DANGERS OF CONTROL CHANNEL ATTACKS

Let's now take a look at some of the specific dangers of control channel attacks, including toll fraud, denial of service, exposure of confidential information, patterns in aggregation, annoyance, and loss of trust.

Toll Fraud

Obviously, as outlined in the Pena and Moore fraud scheme introduced at the very beginning of the chapter, *toll fraud* is a serious potential danger of control channel attacks. In the Pena and Moore scheme, they were able to convince service providers to accept illegitimate voice traffic as real traffic. This incurred very real costs for the victimized service providers as they were routing calls over other service providers and out to the PSTN but were in turn not being able to bill for those calls.

At the enterprise level, the potential is definitely there for the same type of abuse. At a local level, if an attacker is able to register an unauthorized endpoint with your UC system, he or she can then make calls out through your connections to the PSTN. Separately, if you connect to the PSTN through an SIP connection from your on-premise UC systems to a SIP service provider out on the Internet, an attacker can attempt to compromise your log-in credentials at the SIP service provider and route calls through that service provider using your billing information. In either case, you will wind up being charged for those illegitimate calls. (You will learn more about attacks toward SIP service providers in the next chapter, Chapter 5, "SIP Trunking and PSTN Interconnection.")

Denial of Service

While perhaps not as directly financially damaging as toll fraud, DoS attacks definitely represent one of the major dangers of control channel attacks. Let's look at several examples.

DoS against Endpoints

An attacker could target a range of endpoints with something like a SIP BYE attack and cause all those endpoints to hang up their calls. Alternatively, other scripts exist out there that will cause endpoints to reboot. In either case, an attacker could write a script that periodically executes these attacks against endpoints, rendering the endpoints to be largely unusable. A more subtle attack would be removing the registration for a particular endpoint so that it would appear to be in operation but would in fact not be receiving any calls.

DoS against the UC Server

Using some of the attacks in the "Anatomy of Control Channel Attacks" section, an attacker could shut down the server (or servers) that form the core of the UC system. With the IP-PBX or call server down, obviously calls cannot go through.

DoS against the SIP Connection to the PSTN

If your UC system connects to the PSTN through a SIP connection out to a SIP service provider, an attacker could target that connection with an attack aimed at denying use of that link. You will learn more about this in the next chapter, Chapter 5, "SIP Trunking and PSTN Interconnection," but for the moment consider what would happen if an attacker were to flood the externally exposed SIP connection on your UC system with a huge amount of SIP traffic. Your UC system may not be able to keep up with all the responses and will be unable to send or receive legitimate traffic. Similarly, an attacker could target the connection point at your SIP service provider and attempt to shut down the connection there. Either way, the net impact would be that you would be unable to send or receive any significant volume of calls to and from the PSTN.

If the types of DoS attacks outlined in the previous sections were launched at a particularly crucial point for the victimized business, such as the prime time when the company is taking calls, the cost to the business could be quite huge. Consider a flower store that does most of their business around Valentine's Day and what the impact would be if their phone lines were shut down for even a few hours. Or consider a tight political election where one campaign arranges for a phone bank of volunteers to make calls urging people to get out and vote. What would the impact be if a political opponent or some other third-party group were to take the campaign's phone system offline for a period of time? The particularly heinous part of an attack like this is that the attacker could insert the software into the network many months in advance (or have it ready externally) and then trigger it at the identified time.

There are also more subtle DoS attacks an attacker could undertake, such as erasing an endpoint registration so that calls never get through to that particular endpoint. Another example could be modifying a user's presence so that he or she appears busy even though they are in fact available. These cases might only affect a single individual, but if that individual were waiting for an important call or IM, say, to close a major sales deal, the impact could be quite significant.

Exposure of Confidential Information

If an attacker can see the control channel, he or she can gain information about the configuration of your network and thereby learn where else to attack. Depending upon what exactly is sent in the control channel, the attacker might be able to use the information in the control channel to gain access to other pieces of information. For instance, as discussed earlier in Chapter 3, "Eavesdropping and Modification," if a UC system is using SRTP for encrypting voice or video and is using sdescriptions to pass the SRTP keys in SIP headers, an attacker with access to the SIP control channel could also use those SRTP keys to decrypt the media channel and be able to listen or view what is being said there. As another example, any number of applications is also using SIP INFO messages to pass information between servers and clients. These messages might contain information considered confidential.

Similarly, presence information from the IM component of your UC system might give away information related to where a specific person is or is not. Some UC systems include the ability for a user to include a "mood message" or "status message" that might include additional information beyond the simple presence state. For instance, a manager might set their status to "Away at training conference in San Francisco for the week." Knowing whether someone is available or is away could aid an attacker in a "social engineering" attack where he or she contacts other people in the organization and attempts to gain access to information by pretending to be someone else in the company.

Patterns in Aggregation

A more subtle danger is that an attacker can discern patterns in the aggregation of all the messages in the control channel. For instance, an attacker might notice an extremely large number of calls from one internal extension to an external number. A bit of research might find that it is the company's legal team calling the legal counsel at a smaller, financially troubled competitor. Even without access to the media stream, this might lead the attacker to conclude that an acquisition is in the works, which could be useful information to someone else out in the larger market. Being able to see patterns in who is interacting with whom can provide much useful intelligence about communication within a company and with partners.

Annoyance

Obviously, there is a great potential for annoying people within a company. The prankster who gains access to the control channel could, for example, cause someone's phone to ring every hour or so... just one or two rings and then when the person picks up, no one is there. An attacker could repeatedly cause an individual's phone to disconnect or reboot, or could reroute someone's extension to another phone. While these kinds of attacks may not directly impact the company's operations, they can annoy employees and raise the level of frustration within a company.

Loss of Trust

Control channel attacks can definitely lead to a loss of trust in the UC system. If the system comes to be seen as unreliable or untrustworthy, people may speak negatively of the system inside the company and make it difficult for you to obtain further funding requests or system expansion if you are responsible for the system. Obviously, that loss of trust could carry over to you and your team as well.

FUTURE OF CONTROL CHANNEL ATTACKS

Control channel attacks will continue to grow as UC systems continue to expand and interconnect. Back in Chapter 3, "Eavesdropping and Modification" in the section "The Future of Eavesdropping and Modification Attacks," you learned about the trends of

- All-IP enterprise networks
- Cloud and hosted systems
- Federation between UC systems
- Continued endpoint distribution

All of those trends apply equally to control channel attacks. They all expand the surface area for potential attacks and expand the "zone of trust" you need to worry about when interacting with other external networks and systems.

Federation between UC systems, in particular, is of concern regarding the control channel because in federation you are explicitly sharing control information and allowing remote systems, and conceivably remote endpoints to interact with your UC system. Presence information is also typically being shared. As more companies deploy UC systems, the interest in federation will only increase.

There are also three other trends that are more applicable to control channels: integration with social services, PSTN bypass, and the growth of Extensible Messaging and Presence Protocol (XMPP).

Integration with Social Networks and Services

You would have to live under a rock to not be aware of the rise of "social networking" services like Facebook[N] or Twitter.[O] While targeted at consumers, such services are also being heavily used by businesses. Some services, like LinkedIn,[P] are aimed primarily at the business world. All of these services also make application program interface (API) available so that other applications and services can interact with the social network. The challenge you have is that your user base may want to have interconnection between your UC system and the social networks. For instance, your users may want to be able to send IM messages to Facebook users. For another example, at least one UC vendor is looking at how to integrate Twitter into the UC system so that a user's status on the UC system could be updated by the user's last tweet.

From a security point of view, there are multiple challenges here. For a start, the most common social networks are operated by private corporations who control the APIs and other interactions. Twitter, Facebook, and LinkedIn are all owned by private companies who control all aspects of the service. There are no open standards here. What this means is that you are at the mercy of the company who may decide to change the API or service at any time. Similarly, you are trusting that the company

---

[N] www.facebook.com/
[O] www.twitter.com/
[P] www.linkedin.com

has thought through the security of their systems and do themselves operate a secure environment.

For instance, if you were to connect your IM system to Facebook chat and expose presence information from your internal UC network to select Facebook users, can you be sure that only those select users will see that internal presence information? Can you trust that Facebook won't start sending you bogus control channel messages? How much can you trust the security of the social networks? Maybe you can... maybe you can't... it is just more research you will need to do to determine what kind of exposure you may or may not have.

Another security concern with social networks is that of availability. Mostly, all of the popular social networks are centralized services operated by a single company and concentrated in that company's data centers. You are again at their mercy. This is in contrast to most of the regular Internet services like Web or e-mail servers that are highly distributed and decentralized. If you interconnect and the service goes down, is there any impact on your UC system? What about when the system returns to service? Will there be a flood of messages coming at your system?

TIP

For more information about security issues with social networks, please consider taking a look at *Seven Deadliest Social Network Attacks* (ISBN: 978-1-59749-545-5, Syngress).

The reality is that integration with social networks and services is only going to continue to increase in the months and years ahead. You do need to understand how these services will interact with your control channels and how you can protect your systems while still allowing the interconnections to occur.

PSTN Bypass

As companies move to all-IP networks and also use SIP connections out to SIP service providers to get to the PSTN, those companies are increasingly able to bypass the PSTN entirely and communicate directly from one company to another over the IP network. Companies are even inching toward the day when they might be able to accept SIP connections from random endpoints anywhere out on the public Internet in a similar way to how they can accept a phone call from any random phone out on the PSTN.

You will learn more about this in the next chapter, Chapter 5, "SIP Trunking and PSTN Interconnection," but for the moment consider that particularly accepting random SIP connections requires that you have a publicly exposed SIP port. With this, you need to have a higher degree of security hardening on that public connection. You can no longer rely solely on access control lists or other means of limiting connections. The potential sources of attacks are now near-infinite. It's a complicated situation. But we as an industry are slowly moving toward that point, so you need to understand what the security ramifications will be as we edge closer.

Growth of XMPP

One curious trend to watch regarding control channel security is the continued growth of usage of the XMPP in public IM networks, UC systems, and emerging collaboration systems. XMPP originated with the Jabber IM Protocol, server, and clients back in 1998–2000[Q] and over time evolved to where it is now used by literally tens of thousands servers across the public Internet,[R] including major services like Google Talk and LiveJournal Talk. XMPP was standardized through the XMPP Standards Foundation[S] and the Internet Engineering Task Force (IETF)[T] and is continuing to garner increased usage.

In September 2008, Cisco acquired Jabber, Inc.,[U] the private company championing the overall XMPP effort and provider of the largest enterprise XMPP server. Cisco indicated that they would be incorporating XMPP into their collaboration products and services. In October 2009, Microsoft announced[V] that an XMPP Gateway would be available at no additional cost to users of Microsoft Office Communications Server (OCS) 2007 R2, allowing OCS users to share presence and IM with other XMPP systems. Similarly, IBM has supported XMPP interconnection to Lotus Sametime since 2006[W] and has continued to expand that support in more recent software releases. In the social network space, Facebook announced[X] in May 2008 that they were building a XMPP interface to Facebook Chat, and in November 2009 it was reported[Y] that this connection was close to being launched. Over the summer of 2009, Google also rolled out Google Wave,[Z] a new collaboration platform that is ultimately based on XMPP and includes a federation protocol[AA] that will, when fully launched, allow for a massively distributed and decentralized collaboration infrastructure. Finally, the XMPP community has also developed Jingle[BB] as a way to use XMPP to control voice or video sessions, and implementations are starting to be available.

The point of all this for a security professional is that XMPP is continuing to evolve as another control channel for real-time communication and collaboration. Given the momentum, you may see even more services announcing XMPP support and you may need to pay more attention to how XMPP works and how to secure connections using XMPP.

[Q]http://xmpp.org/about/

[R]http://xmpp.org/services/

[S]http://xmpp.org/xsf/

[T]http://xmpp.org/rfcs/

[U]http://newsroom.cisco.com/dlls/2008/corp_091908.html

[V]www.microsoft.com/Presspass/Features/2009/oct09/10-01UCInterop.mspx

[W]www.eweek.com/c/a/Messaging-and-Collaboration/Lotus-Sametime-75-Interoperates-with-AIM-Google-Talk/

[X]http://developers.facebook.com/news.php?blog=1&story=110

[Y]www.process-one.net/en/blogs/article/facebook_chat_supports_xmpp_with_ejabberd

[Z]http://wave.google.com/

[AA]www.waveprotocol.org

[BB]http://xmpp.org/extensions/xep-0166.html

HOW TO DEFEND AGAINST CONTROL CHANNEL ATTACKS

Similar to defending against eavesdropping and modification attacks, one of the best defenses against control channel attacks is encryption. As you will see in this section, there are other defenses as well, but using some level of encryption is a basic foundation of your defense.

Strategy #1: Encrypting the Control Channel

Control channel encryption is typically performed by either Transport Layer Security (TLS) or IP security (IPsec), and in this section, you will learn about the differences between the two approaches.

One important fact is that control channel encryption is *hop-by-hop* encryption because at each hop in the network path, the servers need to act on the control information to understand what to do next. There is no *end-to-end* encryption option as you learned about for media channels in Chapter 3, "Eavesdropping and Modification." The security challenge is that as shown in Figure 4.7, in hop-by-hop encryption, the *transport* is secured between a UC endpoint and a server, from the server to a second server, and then between that second server and the receiving UC endpoint. However, the control channel is not secured on the servers. The secure transport terminates when the channel hits the server and then the secure transport is recreated when the channel leaves the server. For the brief time the control channel is on the server, though, it is *unencrypted*. With hop-by-hop encryption, you have to trust the security of your servers. If an attacker can compromise a server and install his or her software, it can see the control channel without encryption. Similarly, if the system administrators of a server were untrustworthy, they could potentially view the control channel traveling through the server.

Let's now look at two different ways to encrypt the control channel.

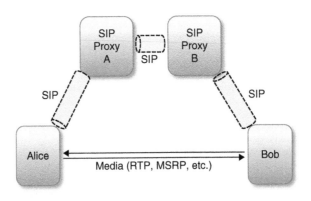

FIGURE 4.7

Hop-by-Hop Encryption

WARNING

Before you enable encryption on your network, you need to check that all devices and applications on your network can support encrypted control channels. Call recording systems, for example, my rely on unencrypted SIP to gather information about the calls you are recording. If such applications or devices cannot support encryption, you will need to determine how they can continue to perform their function if you enable encryption. Keep in mind that if you disable encryption on their network segment, you are then providing an opening where an attacker could gain access to the control channel.

TLS Encryption

With TLS, defined in RFC 5246,[CC] the UC client initiates a TLS connection to the UC server and a "handshake" process ensues that involves the server sending its digital certificate to the client, the client validating that certificate, and then both sides establishing the keying material to be used during the communication session.

NOTE

In a typical TLS deployment, authentication is *unilateral*, in that the client authenticates the server's identity by way of a digital X.509 certificate, but the server does not authenticate the client by way of a certificate. However, the TLS protocol also does support the concept of *mutual (or bilateral) authentication*, where both ends of the connection authenticate to each other using certificates. In UC systems, mutual authentication has not been common as it involves embedding a X.509 certificate in every endpoint, including all hardphones and softphones. However, in recent years, a number of UC vendors have started to embed certificates in their endpoints, so mutual TLS authentication is actually becoming possible in some UC systems.

An important point to consider with TLS usage in UC systems is that TLS only encrypts the control channel. As shown in Figure 4.8, the media channel is encrypted separately from the control channel.

Now, back in Chapter 3, "Eavesdropping and Modification," you learned that media channel encryption via SRTP often sends the encryption key material through the control channel using the sdescriptions method. With sdescriptions, the SRTP key is passed as a Session Description Protocol attribute in the SIP packet. However, the encryption of each channel still happens separately.

Internet Protocol Security

In contrast, with IPsec, a tunnel is typically set up between the endpoint and the UC server, and all traffic between the two hosts is sent across the IPsec tunnel. Both the control channel and the media channel traverse the IPsec tunnel.

[CC]http://tools.ietf.org/html/rfc5246

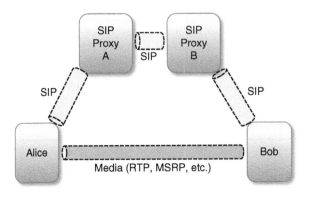

FIGURE 4.8

With TLS, the Control and Media Channels Are Encrypted Separately

While this may have some benefit for greater simplicity in implementations, you learned in Chapter 3, "Eavesdropping and Modification," that a challenge with IPsec is that it can add significant overhead to the very small packets that make up the typical RTP media stream. If you choose to go this route, you may want to do some testing to be sure that the performance of the UC clients over the IPsec virtual private network (VPN) meets your requirements.

> **NOTE**
>
> You should note that TLS can also be used to create a tunnel from a remote system back to a corporate network. So-called Secure Sockets Layer (SSL) VPNs have become increasingly popular given that they typically can traverse a firewall or network address translator (NAT) gateway easier than IPsec and have some other advantages regarding, for instance, more granular access control. You may find that you are using an SSL VPN from laptops back into the corporate network to use softphones or other UC clients. In this case, again you may want to do some performance testing.

Strategy #2: Limit and Secure Interconnection Points

Another layer of defense is to identify all the interconnection points within your UC system and from your UC system to external systems and to limit what devices can connect to those interconnection points. For instance, if you have a SIP proxy server on the edge of your corporate office network that only communicates with your central call server and with SIP proxies at each branch office, you can restrict the IP addresses allowed to communicate to that SIP proxy to the IP addresses of the other branch office SIP proxies and the central call server. Similarly, if your externally exposed SIP proxy (or session border controller [SBC]) only communicates with your SIP service provider for PSTN access, you can restrict the IP addresses that can communicate with it to only those of your SIP service provider.

Similarly, on your internal network, you may be able to impose limits depending upon how your UC system architecture is configured. Some UC systems are configured in a "hub-and-spoke" or "star" configuration where all endpoints communicate only with the central IP-PBX or call server. In such a configuration, the endpoints would never receive any SIP communications directly from other endpoints – all SIP communications would be relayed through the central call server. With a system like this, you could then configure the endpoints to only accept SIP messages coming from the central server's IP address (or addresses in a clustered environment). Yes, an attacker could still potentially spoof the IP address of the central call server, but it is just one more layer of work you are making an attacker to do, and may also eliminate or at least greatly reduce the risk from people downloading and playing with various VoIP security tools from their own systems on the internal network.

In a mesh configuration where endpoints can send SIP messages directly to other endpoints, you can't lock down the IP addresses to quite the same extent, but you could, for instance, only assign endpoints a certain range of IP addresses and limit connections to come from that range. Again, it's not foolproof by any means, but it just provides another layer in your defense in depth posture.

Strategy #3: Use Strong Authentication

It should go without saying that you need to use the strongest possible methods of authentication wherever possible. If you go back to the Pena and Moore fraud scheme outlined at the very beginning of chapter, Robert Moore indicated that they were able to compromise not only intermediary systems but also accounts on VoIP service providers simply because the accounts used weak passwords. Pena and Moore ran a series of scripts that used "brute force" methods to guess usernames and passwords, and it worked.

If you have externally exposed SIP connections in particular, you need to ensure that you are using the strongest possible ways of authenticating incoming connections, using mutual TLS authentication, for instance, or at the very least using very strong passwords.

NOTE

Be aware that some systems may be configured to allow a session to "fall back" to a less-secure encryption or authentication methods. If you know that all your systems support a certain level of authentication, falling back should be disabled because the falling back occurs only if unauthorized systems were trying to connect.

Strategy #4: Deploy SBCs or SIP-Aware Firewalls

For those external SIP connections, you should also strongly consider deploying either a SIP-aware firewall or a SBC on the edge of your network in front of your UC system. Such devices are hardened and designed specifically to be used on the edge of a network. An SBC, as its name implies, is designed to be at the border of your network and securely handle the incoming and outgoing connections to and from other SIP devices. Some networks will include both an SBC and an SIP-aware firewall in front of the SBC. You have many options here in different price ranges. The key is to look for software or a device that is designed to be used on the edge of a network and is hardened against attacks coming in from the public networks. Odds are that most UC systems by themselves have not been tested to this level of hardening.

Strategy #5: Auditing or Monitoring

As yet another layer in your defenses, you should consider some system to monitor the SIP-related traffic on your network. It's not clear exactly how Pena and Moore were discovered, but the FBI complaint indicates that at least one victimized provider was able to identify a large amount of bogus traffic that traversed its network. Now, the FBI complaint doesn't indicate whether this traffic was discovered in a forensic investigation after some trigger to indicate something was wrong or during the time the calls were going on.

The point is, though, that the provider did have auditing in place so that they could identify this traffic. Certainly with the level of network monitoring tools available today, though, you could develop some scripts or monitoring tools that could watch for SIP traffic within certain levels and trigger alerts when certain thresholds are exceeded or when there are strong deviations from certain baseline patterns. Again, this isn't entirely foolproof as an attacker could throttle the rate of incoming calls to attempt to evade such monitoring, but it does create yet another layer of work for an attacker and may catch those who simply start sending large volumes of traffic through your network.

SUMMARY

In this chapter, you've seen the kinds of attacks that can be carried out against control channels, the dangers inherent in those attacks, and some of the strategies you can use to protect against these kinds of attacks. Similar to eavesdropping and modification defenses, one of the tragedies here is that many UC systems do include support for TLS-encrypted SIP, for instance, but the encryption is disabled by default. Providing your system with a higher level of security may be as simple as enabling a few options in your administrative interface.

Having said that, though, encryption may not protect you from the realm of DoS attacks out there, so you do need to take a look at precisely what systems you are allowing to send SIP packets to your UC system components. Particularly for external SIP connection such as those to the public Internet, you need to seriously understand what kind of security hardening you have in place to protect those connections.

On that subject of external connections to SIP systems and the PSTN, you are now going to do a deeper dive into that subject in the next chapter.

SIP Trunking and PSTN Interconnection

INFORMATION IN THIS CHAPTER

- Anatomy of Attacks on SIP Trunks and PSTN Interconnection
- Dangers of Attacks on SIP Trunks and PSTN Interconnection
- The Future of Attacks on SIP Trunks and PSTN Interconnection
- How to Defend against Attacks on SIP Trunks and PSTN Interconnection

Consider this hypothetical scenario: Kroy Flowers is a major provider of floral arrangements and gifts for a small city in the United States. As a small business looking to save on costs and provide the best possible service, Kroy Flowers recently installed a new IP-PBX and as part of that decided to get their phone service using a Session Initiation Protocol (SIP) trunk. This "SIP trunk" connects their IP-PBX across their Internet connection to an Internet telephony service provider (ITSP) and from there on out to the public switched telephone network (PSTN). Calls to Kroy Flowers go across the PSTN to their ITSP and then from there across the IP network to Kroy Flowers' IP-PBX, where they ring an extension. Outbound calls follow the opposite path across the IP network to the ITSP and then out to the PSTN.

A SIP trunk works great for Kroy Flowers because, being a very seasonal business, they don't have to worry about maintaining excess capacity in their office. Their ITSP lets them make and receive as many calls as their IP bandwidth can handle. A SIP trunk has also reduced their costs and given them the ability to set up some local numbers in nearby states as well. It's all been working very well for them.

Unfortunately, ZYX Flowers recently opened up in town and is competing quite heavily for business. It's early February and both companies are gearing up for their traditional rush of orders around Valentine's Day.

As Kroy Flowers enters the final few days before the big day, all of a sudden their phone system starts to become unreliable. Calls get dropped midway through. When people do get connected, they complain that it's taken them a number of tries to get through. The folks at Kroy Flowers wonder how many other people are getting turned away. Then on what is usually their busiest day, February 13th, the phones stop ringing. They try to call their own number but can't get connected. They can't seem to make outbound calls either. Frantically, they call their telecommunications vendor and their ITSP trying to find out what is going on. Their ITSP sees that they are unable to connect but is unable to provide much guidance beyond that. Kroy Flower's staff calls their Internet service provider (ISP), and some investigation shows that a large number of connections are being opened from all across the Internet to the systems on Kroy Flowers' premise. They try a number of different techniques but struggle to reduce the packet flow to Kroy Flowers. Mystically, around the middle of the day on February 14th, the problems stop. Calls make it through again and everything seems back to normal. Except, of course, that they had an abysmal Valentine's Day sale and lost an enormous amount of business.

Meanwhile, across town, the folks at ZYX Flowers had a hugely successful time. When all is said and done and they are counting their profit, the ZYX Flowers owners agree that paying what seemed at the time like a large fee to that botnet operator they'd found on an obscure Web site turned out to be an excellent move on their part.

Fiction? In this case, yes…but it's not far off from what is possible today.

When we talk about unified communications (UC) systems, we are talking about more than just telephony. However, a UC system isn't terribly useful if you can't communicate with people in the larger communications infrastructure, and so UC systems need to connect to the PSTN. Increasingly, those connections are coming by way of SIP trunks – and many if not most of those are insecure. In this chapter, we will focus on the telephony side of UC and look at both the advantages and the challenges of "SIP trunking."

ANATOMY OF ATTACKS ON SIP TRUNKS AND PSTN INTERCONNECTION

Let's take a step back and talk about what a "trunk" is and how that relates to a "SIP trunk" so that you can understand why people use SIP trunks and what the security implications then are.

Understanding SIP Trunking

In the traditional telephony of the PSTN, a company would arrange to have a "trunk" line brought into their facility from their local carrier or service provider. This trunk would be in the form of a physical cable that would be connected to some type of gateway device on the company's premises, which in turn would be connected to the company's PBX and phone system. The trunk might be a regular analog line, a time-division multiplexing (TDM) connection, or an Integrated Services Digital Network (ISDN) connection. Separately, as shown in Figure 5.1, a company would have a connection to the Internet.

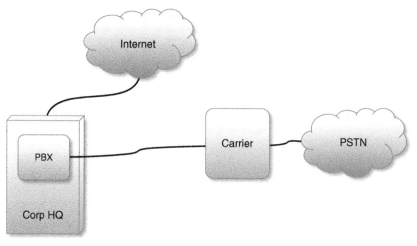

FIGURE 5.1

In Traditional Telephony, a Company Has a Dedicated Connection to the PSTN

These TDM trunks might be in the form of a "T1" line, a "fractional T1" or ISDN in either the basic rate interface or primary rate interface form. There are numerous challenges with TDM trunks, which are as follows:

- Installing a trunk initially involves a physical installation, which can take quite some time to be scheduled and completed.
- Special hardware devices are required to terminate the TDM connection, either as separate physical devices or as special cards in a PBX.
- There are hard capacity limitations that you simply cannot exceed.
- Adding extra capacity may involve additional physical installation and be both time-consuming and expensive. Additional hardware devices may also be required.
- Generally, your only source for a TDM trunk is your local telecommunications carrier. You may have a few options but typically the actual physical connection is still from your local provider. This lack of choice is reflected in the usually expensive cost of TDM trunks.

Overall, there is a lack of flexibility in terms of usage, capacity, equipment, and providers.

Enter the concept of creating "trunks" using Voice over Internet Protocols (VoIPs) like SIP. With a SIP trunk, the connection occurs over your existing Internet connection. As shown in Figure 5.2, the on-premise IP-PBX connects out over the Internet to an ITSP who provides the actual connection to the PSTN.

It is important to be clear that there is no physical connection for this "trunk." Certainly, there is a physical layer connection for the underlying Internet link. That connection could be via a fixed line, a cable modem, a wireless link, or even a dial-up connection. But that connection is not specific to your "trunk" and is shared by all other data uses. In fact, for this reason, there has been some resistance to even using

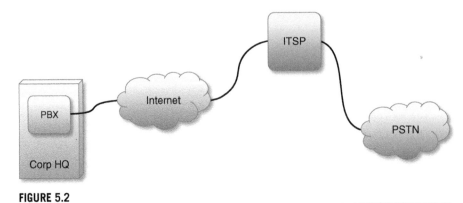

FIGURE 5.2

With a SIP Trunk, the Connection to the PSTN Occurs Over an Existing Internet Connection

the term *trunk* to refer to such a connection over an IP network. However, a "SIP trunk" functions in many similar ways to a "TDM trunk," and so it is useful to speak of it in that way.

> **NOTE**
>
> Do note that such a "trunk" does not have to use the SIP protocol. It is also quite possible to create a connection over IP using the older H.323 protocol, the newer Inter-Asterisk eXchange (IAX) protocol, or even proprietary VoIP protocols from vendors. This chapter focuses on SIP trunks because that is what the vast majority of UC systems use today. If your system uses a different protocol, the principles of this chapter will still generally apply.
>
> A SIP trunk may also not travel over your primary Internet connection. Some companies may have a separate Internet connection for the SIP traffic or even a direct private link between the premise and the ITSP.
>
> It is also worth mentioning that within the industry, there has been some confusion over the exact definition of a "SIP trunk." As Jonathan Rosenberg noted in a now-expired Internet Draft document in 2008,[A] the term has been used to apply to the following:
>
> - A connection from an on-premise IP-PBX to a service provider for PSTN connectivity.
> - A connection between two IP-PBXs.
> - A virtual port on an IP-PBX to which other systems can connect.
>
> This book uses the term *SIP trunk* to refer to a connection from an on-premise system out to the PSTN.

It's also important to realize that without the physical connection, there is no inherent limitation of a cable. Trunks in the TDM world are *circuit-switched*. A regular T1 line has 24 channels and can, therefore, support 24 simultaneous calls. There is a limitation in the way signals are sent across the cable that precludes a 25th call from being added. With SIP trunks, there is no limitation of the connection media itself. The primary limitations are really due to software and policy constraints. Yes,

---

[A]http://tools.ietf.org/html/draft-rosenberg-sipping-siptrunk

there may be very real network constraints such as that your Internet link will only support 50 simultaneous voice sessions, but there is nothing that may prevent you from sending 51 simultaneous calls (except your users may then experience degraded audio quality). Most ITSPs seem to charge for SIP trunks in a similar fashion to TDM trunks, that is, on a per-simultaneous-call basis. You pay a monthly fee for the number of simultaneous connections you will be allowed to have.

However, an ITSP could charge on a bandwidth utilization basis or on simply a per-minute basis. Also, note that the IP-PBX vendor may charge a "per-port" charge for a SIP trunk, but again, this is a software limitation rather than a physical limitation.

NOTE

With an industry that is still developing as the SIP trunking space is, the term *ITSP* is not always used. You may also hear people refer to ITSPs as "SIP service providers," "VoIP (or Voice) service providers," "VoIP providers," or simply "service providers" or "carriers."

Let's discuss in more detail the advantages and reasons why people are shifting to using SIP trunks.

Ease and Speed of Installation

Without a physical connection, the installation of a SIP trunk can be as easy as signing up with an ITSP through a Web site, providing a form of payment, getting the log-in credentials, and configuring your system. Now, odds are it may not be that simple. You may need to test to ensure you have adequate bandwidth and that your on-premises IP-PBX is compatible with the ITSP's service. You may also have to determine if your firewall or other devices on the network edge are compatible, but overall, that is the simple experience ITSPs are aiming for. No need to "roll trucks" and get a technician on site. No need to schedule an appointment weeks or months out. No need to purchase extra, expensive hardware.

WARNING

Be aware that "SIP is NOT always SIP," in that the SIP specifications are loose enough in some areas that the SIP messages sent by one vendor may not be 100% acceptable by another vendor's product. You will probably want to do some interoperability testing to ensure that your IP-PBX can interoperate with the ITSP without any problems. The SIP Forum[B] has an initiative underway called *SIPconnect*[C] which is designed to help with this. Vendors and ITSPs go through a certification program, and the idea is that a "SIPconnect-compliant" IP-PBX should be able to interoperate with a "SIPconnect-compliant" ITSP with a minimum of testing. The SIPconnect program is still relatively new but bears watching in the time ahead. The SIP Forum also sponsors a series of "SIPit" test events to assist vendors in testing how interoperable their SIP-related products are. If you are a vendor of SIP-based equipment, you may want to visit www.sipit.net to investigate attending a SIPit event.

[B] www.sipforum.org/
[C] www.sipforum.org/content/view/273/227/

Ease of Expansion and Flexibility with Capacity

Along with the ease of installation, expansion of your capacity is typically trivial. In most cases, you simply contact your ITSP, indicate you want additional capacity, and arrange to pay for it. They make a software change on their end. You might need to make a change on your end and it's done. (Depending upon your IP-PBX vendor, you may need to purchase additional "trunk ports" on your IP-PBX.) No waiting for installation. No technician visits. Plus, if you want to decrease your capacity, it is similarly just a phone call away.

Additionally, because again the limitations are in software, your ITSP may allow you to burst above your agreed-upon capacity for seasonal or overflow traffic. Depending upon your contract terms, and indeed even if you have a contract, you may have the flexibility to rapidly change your capacity based on the needs of your business.

Business Continuity/Disaster Recovery

An interesting aspect of SIP trunking is that nothing prevents you from obtaining SIP trunks from multiple ITSPs. In fact, you can use this fact to create a great business continuity/disaster recovery (DR) plan. Consider Figure 5.3, where your company has multiple SIP trunks going out through different ITSPs to the PSTN. If there is a problem at any of the ITSPs for outbound calls, you can simply route the calls through one of the other ITSPs.

Inbound calls can be a bit more difficult because direct-inward-dial (DID) numbers are typically established at the ITSP. If an ITSP has a failure, the DIDs associated with that ITSP may not work. However, the DIDs associated with other ITSPs will continue to work so you could still receive calls via some number. There are also services out there that would allow you to redirect a central phone number to a different ITSP.

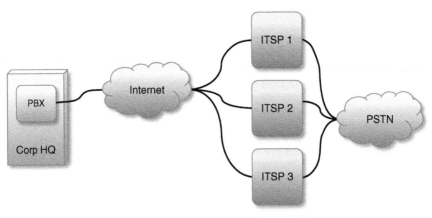

FIGURE 5.3

You Can Use Multiple ITSPs for Business Continuity Purposes

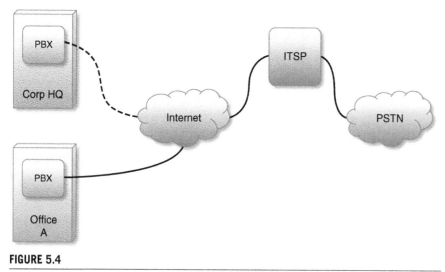

FIGURE 5.4

ITSPs Can Redirect Traffic in the Event of a Local Failure

SIP trunks can also assist in the case where your company or one of its locations becomes unreachable. As shown in Figure 5.4, because the call routing configuration is simply happening in their software, an ITSP (or multiple ITSPs) can simply redirect their DIDs to the SIP connection at another location.

With a bit of forethought, you can set your systems up so that a failover can happen quickly with minimal calls lost.

Expanded Geographical Coverage

Because you can establish relationships with multiple ITSPs, you can make interesting decisions around geography. For instance, say you are a small business in Boston and you find that you get a lot of traffic to your Web site and customers from people in France. You'd like to make it even easier for those French customers to interact with you. You could find out from your current ITSP if they can get a French phone number for you or, if they can't, you can simply sign up with a French ITSP. Now you can publicize that French number and have your customers call you that way. Even though they call you at a French number on the PSTN, their calls will go over the IP network back to your IP-PBX in Boston and ring your extensions there. As shown in Figure 5.5, you could establish SIP trunks with multiple ITSPs in various parts of the world to very quickly give your company a global appearance.

There is a reverse benefit to this arrangement as well. Just as you can *receive* calls from customers in France via your French ITSP, you can also *make* calls in France via that same connection. Suddenly, what was previously an international long-distance call becomes a local or at least national phone call. You pick up the phone in Boston, dial the number and the call goes across the IP network to the French ITSP where it then exits onto the PSTN there in France.

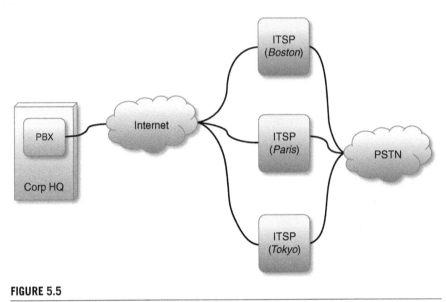

FIGURE 5.5

Using Multiple ITSPs to Have a Global Telephony Presence

Innovation and Communication beyond Just Voice

As you've seen throughout this book, "UC" is about not just voice, but also video, IM, presence, and other collaboration technologies. SIP trunks allow you to communicate by more than just the voice of the PSTN, although obviously not with endpoints on the PSTN. In Chapter 7, "The End of Geography," you'll take a look at federation between UC systems and how it allows richer communication between systems. SIP trunks are steps along this path. For instance, if you have a SIP trunk to an ITSP and a partner company has a SIP trunk to the same ITSP, the ITSP can start to do things like routing calls from your company to the partner company directly over IP, bypassing the PSTN completely. The stage is now set for you and the partner company to start using more that just the low-quality voice of the PSTN. You could start using wideband codecs, for instance, for so-called *high-definition voice* or start doing direct video connections to each other.

A SIP trunk can also enable you to keep up with innovation that is happening in the larger telecommunications space. For instance, Voxbone,[D] a VoIP service provider headquartered in Europe, launched the iNum initiative[E] where you obtain a "global phone number" that is not tied to any specific country. At the current time, the iNum service works mostly with SIP-based networks. Voxbone is also planning to add support for SMS and other modalities to iNum numbers. These kinds of innovations are available over the "all-IP" networks and not over the traditional PSTN.

[D]www.voxbone.com
[E]www.inum.net

Competition and Cost

Because there is no physical connection and all the traffic goes entirely over the IP network, there are a great number of competitors in the SIP trunking space. For you as a consumer of SIP trunks, the good news is that you have many choices to choose from with different kinds of service offerings, service level agreements (SLAs) and, of course, different cost structures. One of the main sales pitches for SIP trunks is that they will greatly slash your PSTN telecommunication costs. The result is that you can find some seriously low prices for your traffic to the PSTN.

There are also three other cost-saving sides of SIP trunks. First, there is a savings in that you are no longer paying for two physical connections into your company, one for data and one for voice. Your data connection is the only link in now. Yes, you are paying for voice traffic on top of that data connection now, but you also don't have the maintenance and equipment for that second physical connection anymore. Second, there is the previously mentioned fact that you can establish SIP trunking relationships with ITSPs in different parts of the world in order to reduce or eliminate long-distance or international phone calls. Third, you can establish SIP trunks with multiple ITSPs and then perform "least cost routing" using software from companies like Transnexus[F] to route a call through whichever ITSP is cheapest for the target destination.

All this competition may be great for consumers of SIP trunks, but it's not so great for you as a security professional. When you have a market that's kind of like a chaotic "Wild West" marketplace where anyone can jump in, how many of the newer ITSP entrants are necessarily paying attention to security? And as per-minute prices continue to get commoditized toward zero, how many ITSPs can afford to focus on security?

That is the topic of the rest of this chapter. Now that you understand why people are using SIP trunks, let's look at the attacks against them.

Attacks against SIP Trunking

If you take a look back at Figure 5.2, a SIP trunk as defined in this book is a connection between an on-premise system such as an IP-PBX and an ITSP located typically somewhere out on the public Internet or at least across a private IP network. Then, the possible attacks are going to be the ones you learned about in Chapter 3, "Eavesdropping and Modification" and Chapter 4, "Control Channel Attacks: Fuzzing, DoS, SPIT, and Toll Fraud."

An attacker is going to target:

- the point at which your premise system exposes a SIP connection to the Internet (trunk termination point);
- the path your trunk traffic takes across the Internet;
- the connection point (trunk termination point) at your ITSP.

Let's look at some of the specific attacks possible against these points.

[F]www.transnexus.com/

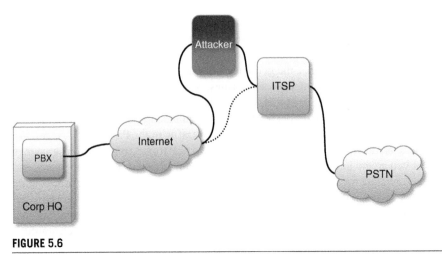

FIGURE 5.6

An Attacker Needs to Get in the Network Path of a SIP trunk

Eavesdropping and Modification on SIP Trunks

As you saw in Chapter 3, "Eavesdropping and Modification," the main attack is for an attacker to get in a position where he or she can observe and potentially modify the traffic. The attacker needs to do one of the following:

- Get in the *network path* between the two trunk termination points;
- Get between two of the *servers* or *proxies* involved with sending the traffic between the trunk termination points;
- Get on the same *network segment* as one of the trunk termination points;
- Compromise the local system of either trunk termination point.

As shown in Figure 5.6, if the attacker can get into one of these situations, perhaps by exploiting unpatched security vulnerabilities in a system along the path, default/weak passwords, or via malware such as viruses, then he or she can use common tools like Wireshark or any of the many other network sniffing tools that are out there in order to capture and later view SIP communications.

To modify the traffic going across the SIP trunk, the attacker would need to get truly in the middle of the network path and then, as in Chapter 3, "Eavesdropping and Modification," use commonly available tools to monitor the traffic and change the contents.

TIP

A useful Web site to find network scanning tools is the "Top 100 Network Security Tools" site at http://sectools.org/

Denial of Service against SIP Trunks

As noted in the scenario in the introduction to this chapter, denial-of-service (DoS) attacks are a serious potential issue with SIP trunks. The attacks you learned about in Chapter 4, "Control Channel Attacks: Fuzzing, DoS, SPIT, and Toll Fraud," are all relevant here. If the attacker can truly get into the middle of the network path, he or she could drop packets, modify packets, and so on, to deny service to either end of the connection. The attacker can also flood one component in the SIP trunk with bogus requests or send malformed SIP packets to see if he or she can compromise a system.

The attacker can also just unleash massive Distributed DoS (DDoS) attacks against your connection, your ITSP, or any point along the path. Being on the public Internet, attackers have access to extremely large-scale botnets with tens of thousands (or more) of individual bots spread out all across the Internet. Such systems can paralyze and shut down your network for quite some period of time.

An attacker could also go after pieces of the underlying network infrastructure. For instance, if you use a host name to connect to your ITSP, the attacker could attempt to poison the Domain name system (DNS) servers involved in resolving the host name so that they would deliver the traffic to a different site. Alternatively, an attacker could seek to disrupt or deny DNS service entirely, preventing the connection.

Theft of Service/Toll Fraud

In this attack, the attacker tries to figure out how to inject illegitimate traffic into the path of your SIP trunk. The easiest way is usually for the attacker to try to connect to your ITSP with your credentials. The attacker may try to brute-force guess any kind of credentials, or the attacker may have sniffed the traffic, seen the hashes used in SIP digest authentication and will try a "replay" attack using the hashes.

Alternatively, the attacker may target your on-premise IP-PBX and try to see if it can be convinced that there is another endpoint out there that can send "legitimate" traffic. In this way, the attacker's traffic would flow through your IP-PBX and then up the SIP trunk and out to the PSTN.

DANGERS OF ATTACKS ON SIP TRUNKS AND PSTN INTERCONNECTION

Attacks against SIP trunks have most all of the dangers you read about in Chapter 3, "Eavesdropping and Modification" and Chapter 4, "Control Channel Attacks: Fuzzing, DoS, SPIT, and Toll Fraud." The major issue is that those dangers are heightened significantly because the traffic from your premises to the ITSP may be traveling across the public Internet. That is really the key point.

In the chapters mentioned above, you learned about the concerns of attacks on your own network. Now, add in traffic across any number of networks that are outside of your control. The surface area for any attack expands dramatically and the number of potential attackers is now exponentially greater. Let's now take a look at some of the specific dangers of attacks against SIP trunks and the corresponding interconnection to the PSTN.

Toll Fraud

Obviously, as outlined in the Pena/Moore fraud scheme at the beginning of Chapter 4, "Control Channel Attacks: Fuzzing, DoS, SPIT, and Toll Fraud," *toll fraud* is a serious potential danger and can incur very real financial costs to your organization. If an attacker is somehow able to compromise the authentication credentials you use with your ITSP, he or she can then send out traffic to the PSTN at your expense.

> **EPIC FAIL**
>
> In January 2009, Western Australian police indicated[G] that a small business in Perth, Australia, had their VoIP network attacked and thieves made over 11,000 calls costing over $12,000.

DoS

As the scenario with the competing floral businesses at the beginning of this chapter outlined, a DoS attack launched at a particularly crucial point for the victimized business, such as the prime time when the company is taking calls, could cause a huge disruption to the business. Beyond the example of the florist business, consider a tight political election where one campaign arranges for a phone bank of volunteers to make calls urging people to get out and vote. What would the impact be if a political opponent or some other third-party group were to take the campaigns' phone system offline for a period of time? Back in May 2007, Web sites of the government of Estonia were taken offline for significant periods of time in what later turned out to be politically motivated massive DDoS attacks.[H] While those attacks were targeted at Web sites, what would the effect have been if they had been targeted at the UC channels? Pick your scenario...the reality is that with voice, video, IM, and so on being simply data packets over the IP network, the opportunity is there to severely disrupt those channels with DoS and DDoS attacks.

Note that an attacker could launch a DoS attack like this by inserting the software into the network many months in advance (or have it ready externally) and then trigger it at the identified time.

Corporate Espionage/Exposure of Confidential Information

As discussed previously in both Chapter 3, "Eavesdropping and Modification," and Chapter 4, "Control Channel Attacks: Fuzzing, DoS, SPIT, and Toll Fraud," there is a great amount of confidential information that can be gathered both from the media channel and from the control channel that could be of interest to other parties.

[G]www.zdnet.com.au/news/communications/soa/VoIP-hackers-strike-Perth-business/0,130061791,339294515,00.htm
[H]www.scmagazineus.com/russia-confirms-involvement-with-estonia-ddos-attacks/article/128737/

Obviously, eavesdropping and listening to or viewing corporate conversations is a very tangible way that information can be gathered.

Information can also be gleaned from patterns in the control channel about who is calling whom, how often, and so on. Additionally, information about the components used in the UC system may be found in control messages and can help attackers learn about further devices they can attack.

The discovery and analysis of this information could be simply done by an attacker exploring systems but more often than not there may be a strong financial incentive. The attacker may be able to gain information about a public company that could be used to make a profit in financial trading. The attacker may be getting paid to find this information by a competitor or a third-party group. Perhaps the attacker is aiming to blackmail someone or perhaps he or she is looking for information that will help them make further and deeper attacks.

Now you may consider these types of attacks to be more in the realm of Hollywood movies than reality, but consider that many SIP trunks are going out across the public Internet without any encryption. As more and more communication moves toward IP communications, the opportunity for this type of espionage is increasing exponentially.

Modification

Along with the more passive attack of eavesdropping, an attacker could of course try to get in a position to modify the contents of communication that are flowing across the SIP trunk. As you learned in Chapter 3, "Eavesdropping and Modification," an attacker needs to get directly in the middle of the communication path, but, once that is done, can make changes to whatever flows through the path. Consider, again, the idea of a company interacting with their customers who have called in from the PSTN. What if the attacker were to, for instance, inject profanity or insults into the audio stream heard by the customers?

Spam for Internet Telephony

In Chapter 4, "Control Channel Attacks: Fuzzing, DoS, SPIT and Toll Fraud," you learned that spam for Internet telephony (SPIT) remains a more distant threat to UC systems. However, SIP trunks are one area where the threat can potentially be very real. The threat is to both your UC system and also to the ITSP and PSTN.

With regard to the threat to your on-premise system, the issue is that if you have an open SIP port on the public Internet to which anyone can connect, you are potentially opening yourself up to receive spam from anyone who discovers your open port. A spammer can simply connect to your SIP port and start sending messages. If the attacker scanned across a range of possible extensions, he or she could very rapidly start sending messages to all your employees. The attacker could wind up filling up your voice-mail servers with messages and causing a DoS of the voice-mail system because other legitimate callers would not be able to leave messages.

The attacker could of course annoy your employees with the bogus calls. A simple way to prevent this can be to restrict who can connect to your external SIP port to specific hosts or IP addresses. Without this restriction, the open port that terminates your end of the SIP trunk can make you open to these types of attacks. Granted, these types of attacks are not yet highly visible, but as the market for SIP trunks continues to grow, financially motivated attackers may migrate over into the SIP space to look to increase their operations.

THE FUTURE OF ATTACKS ON SIP TRUNKS AND PSTN INTERCONNECTION

For all the reasons outlined in the "Understanding SIP Trunks" section in the beginning of this chapter, you can expect to see the growth of SIP trunks continue.

Reasons for Growth

Some of the major reasons for increased growth in SIP trunks include costs savings for PSTN bypass, the move to all-IP networks, and DR/business continuity planning (BCP).

Cost Savings for PSTN Bypass

With price pressure and commoditization happening across pretty much all market segments, companies continue to be pressed to lower costs. One of the major attractions of SIP trunks is that they can dramatically lower telecommunication costs. Expect to see this continue to be one of the major drivers for SIP trunking expansion.

The Move to All-IP Networks

Companies of all sizes are looking at how moving to an "all-IP network" can make them more efficient and competitive. Many are looking at or have deployed UC systems. Large enterprises and service providers are building out their "next-generation networks." Driven by the increasing availability of ubiquitous high-speed network bandwidth and the decreasing cost of network components, companies are looking to understand how they can use the Internet and other data networks to connect with their customers faster and more efficiently. Even governments are getting into the act; the US Federal Communications Commission has recently indicated it is looking for guidance on its role in helping in the transition from the legacy PSTN to a new "all-IP" network.[I] Governments in other countries are already building out IP networks.

There's a race on to reinvent and rewire our communications infrastructure. For an enterprise or company to play in that game, they need the IP connectivity of a SIP trunk.

[I]http://hraunfoss.fcc.gov/edocs_public/attachmatch/DA-09-2517A1.pdf

DR/BCP

As mentioned in the "Understanding SIP Trunking" section, SIP trunks can be extremely helpful in DR or BCP. SIP trunks can assist in BCP both for what happens if a telecommunications service provider becomes unavailable and for what happens if one of your offices becomes unavailable. They offer an immense amount of flexibility in creating systems that will ensure that communication can continue in the event of some kind of major failure or catastrophe.

For all of these reasons, the outlook seems extremely favorable for the continued growth of SIP trunking.

Increased Market Size

The downside of this growth from a security point of view is that as the market grows so too do the financial incentives for attackers to consider getting into the space. As more attackers look at SIP trunks and PSTN interconnection, the sophistication of the available tools and attack methodologies will continue to grow. Over time, those tools will become easy enough that unsophisticated "script kiddies" will be able to perform more attacks than are already possible today. With the success of the market will come an increasing number of attackers, and undoubtedly, an increasing number of successful attacks.

More ITSP Entrants with Few Cares about Security

As has been mentioned several times throughout this chapter, the market for SIP trunking providers is exploding rather dramatically. Anyone with a decent Internet connection can conceivably set themselves up as an ITSP. They can do something as simple as install the open-source Asterisk PBX on a server, buy some connectivity from an upstream ITSP, and start selling "SIP trunks" locally or through their Web site. The barriers to entry are almost nonexistent.

The downside, of course, is that many of these newer entrants may not even be aware of the security concerns. Or if they are aware, they may not care in their focus on making a profit.

The challenge for you and your company is to sort out which ITSPs have a clue with regard to security and which do not. In the next section, "How to Defend against Attacks on SIP Trunking and PSTN Interconnection" you'll learn some questions to ask potential ITSPs.

Expansion of the PSTN Trust Boundary

A more subtle trend going on today is the expansion of the security "trust boundary" that exists in the world of the PSTN. With the traditional PSTN, it has historically been a relatively small "club" of carriers who have interconnected and exchanged traffic as depicted in Figure 5.7. To be a member of that exclusive club, you needed to have expensive equipment, your own network, and so on. It was pretty much limited to the

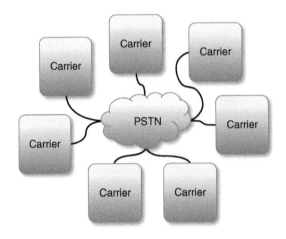

FIGURE 5.7

The PSTN Previously Had a Smaller Number of Interconnected Carriers

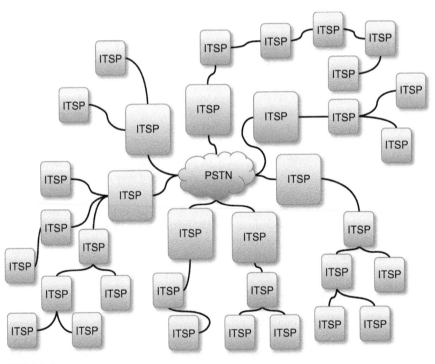

FIGURE 5.8

IP Communications Expands the Security Trust Boundary of the PSTN

extremely large traditional carriers from the private sector in some countries or the government-run telecommunication agencies in other countries. The club members knew each other and more importantly could basically trust each other (within certain limits) to send only appropriate and legitimate traffic through the interconnection.

With IP networks, all of that changes. As noted in the previous section, basically anyone can enter the market as an "ITSP." Many of the top-level ITSPs will sell connectivity to companies so that those companies can become ITSPs themselves. Those second-level ITSPs will sell to a third-level ITSPs, who in turn will sell to a fourth level of ITSPs…and so on. Somewhere down at the bottom of the chain will be IP-PBXs and other on-premises systems that connect to an ITSP and thereby into the larger network. The impact shown in Figure 5.8 is that the "exclusive club" no longer exists. There are many more players in the network formerly known as the PSTN, and there is no way that top-level ITSPs can even remotely know who all is connecting in to them through the many potential layers of ITSPs.

Should one of these lower level ITSPs let illegitimate traffic come in through a connection or should a local IP-PBX be compromised, the traffic is going to bubble up through the next levels and eventually out to other top-level ITSPs as if it were legitimate traffic. It is going to get a wee bit messy in the years ahead.

HOW TO DEFEND AGAINST ATTACKS ON SIP TRUNKS AND PSTN INTERCONNECTION

Given that a SIP trunk is really a combination of both a media channel and a control channel, the defenses are going to involve those you learned about in Chapter 3, "Eavesdropping and Modification," and Chapter 4, "Control Channel Attacks: Fuzzing, DoS, SPIT, and Toll Fraud." A primary foundation for your defenses is that of encryption. First, though, let's consider questions you should be asking your ITSP.

Strategy #1: Understand Your ITSP

Given the market volatility and the ease at which ITSPs can enter the market, you need to perform a level of due diligence before signing on. Your list will obviously vary based on your situation, but here are some questions to consider.

1. Basic questions to assess their viability (some of which they may not answer):
   a. How long have you been in operation?
   b. How many commercial customers do you have?
   c. How many people do you employ full-time?
   d. What was your overall revenue last year? This year?
2. Are you directly connected to the PSTN?
3. If not, whom do you purchase your SIP connectivity from? Whom do they in turn purchase their connectivity from? (You want to try to understand if they are a top-level ITSP or if not, how far down the chain they are.)

     a. What does your network architecture look like?

     b. Do you have redundant components in your network. Where are the Single Points of Failure (SPOFs)?

     c. Where are your data centers located? (or is it all virtualized out in the cloud?)

4. What kind of SLAs do you have available?

     a. In the case of an incident where, for instance, calls are not going through, how can you be contacted? Phone? e-mail? IM? Live Web chat?

     b. What kind of response times can be expected?

     c. How large is your support organization?

     d. What is the internal escalation process if the initial person can't answer my questions?

5. What was your uptime over the past 12 months?

     a. Do you have third-party validation of that?

6. What are your business continuity plans?

     a. What happens if one of your data centers suffers a failure?

     b. Have you tested your business continuity plans? If so, how did the test go?

7. What are the security procedures at your facility?

     a. How is physical access to your servers and equipment protected?

     b. How many people have administrative access to your equipment?

     c. What kind of security policies do you have in place related to server access?

     d. What level of security training or experience does your staff have? What security certifications do any of them hold?

     e. Do you periodically test the security of your systems? With an external firm? What were the last results?

     f. What are your patch management plans?

8. What kind of SIP interoperability testing do you have in place?

     a. Are you "SIPconnect" compliant?

9. What kind of transport security options do you support? TLS-encrypted SIP and SRTP? IPsec or TLS/SSL virtual private networks (VPNs)? Specific devices?

10. What kind of authentication methods do you support?

11. For business continuity/DR purposes, how easy is it to redirect calls to another location?

12. What kind of self-service console or other admin interface is there?

Your list can of course go on at quite some length. Your goal is overall to determine how available the ITSP will be for you and how confidential they will keep your information.

TIP

As technology changes and as feedback is received, an updated version of this list of questions will be available at the book's Web site at www.7ducattacks.com

Strategy #2: Establish a Secure Transport Layer

After you understand more about your ITSP, your first step should be to establish some form of a secure transport layer between your on-premise trunk termination point such as your IP-PBX (or similar system) and your ITSP, as shown in Figure 5.9. As was discussed in the section "How to Defend against Control Channel Attacks" in Chapter 4, "Control Channel Attacks: Fuzzing, DoS, SPIT, and Toll Fraud," one important fact to remember is that your control channel encryption is *hop-by-hop* encryption because at each hop, the SIP proxy server will need to decide what to do with the call next. Odds are that your media channel is also hop-by-hop purely because the end-to-end media encryption techniques of DTLS and ZRTP are not yet widely available.

There are two primary methods of securing the transport layer between your IP-PBX and your ITSP: TLS/SRTP and VPNs.

TLS-encrypted SIP and SRTP

One method of securing the transport is to use the combination of TLS-encrypted SIP and secure RTP discussed earlier in Chapter 3, "Eavesdropping and Modification," and in Chapter 4, "Control Channel Attacks: Fuzzing, DoS, SPIT, and Toll Fraud." In this scenario:

1. A TLS-encrypted SIP control channel session is established between the on-premises IP-PBX and the ITSP;
2. A Secure RTP session is established for the media channel; and
3. Sdescriptions is used to pass the SRTP encryption key from one end to the other over the TLS-encrypted SIP channel.

As discussed in Chapter 3, "Eavesdropping and Modification," and Chapter 4, "Control Channel Attacks: Fuzzing, DoS, SPIT, and Toll Fraud," this results in two separate connections for each call: one connection for the call control channel and a separate connection for the media channel.

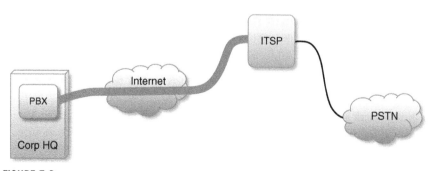

FIGURE 5.9

Securing the Transport Layer from Your IP-PBX to Your ITSP Is a Critical Defense Mechanism

VPNs

A second approach is to establish a VPN between your IP-PBX and your ITSP. This VPN may be using IPsec, TLS/SSL, or another VPN protocol. The key difference from the first TLS-encrypted SIP and SRTP approach is that an encrypted tunnel is established through which all traffic flows. The tunnel is created from the premise to the ITSP and remains connected indefinitely.

At the premise location, the VPN might be established from the actual IP-PBX itself, but it is more likely to be established from some system or device on the edge of the premise network. This could be an existing device that establishes a software VPN connection out to the ITSP. It could be a session border controller or perhaps a SIP-aware firewall. The point is that some device on the premises network is connecting out to a similar device or VPN termination point within the ITSPs network.

Making the Choice

Whether you choose to go the TLS-encrypted SIP/SRTP or VPN route is really a matter of preference, performance, and really what your ITSP will support.

The advantage of the TLS-encrypted SIP/SRTP route is that connections are only made for each individual call so there is no permanent connection established between your premise and the ITSP. This is also a disadvantage in that each call requires the setup of the individual connections and the overhead associated with that. You also may need to have "SIP aware" firewalls and other network edge devices that can handle the dynamic allocation of ports required for the various SRTP connections.

On the other hand, nailing up a VPN between your premise and the ITSP has the advantage of simplicity. Once the connection is up, you simply are sending regular, unencrypted SIP and RTP across the connection. If you use an IPsec VPN, the disadvantage is that as mentioned in the "IPsec" section of Chapter 3, "Eavesdropping and Modification," IPsec does involve a bit more overhead in the way it encrypts the packets. This may or may not be a problem for you depending upon the available bandwidth between you and your ITSP.

Ultimately, it will come down to what your chosen ITSP supports. The key point is really that they support some form of transport layer encryption.

Strategy #3: Ensure Strong Authentication Is in Place

If you go back to the beginning of Chapter 4, "Control Channel Attacks: Fuzzing, DoS, SPIT, and Toll Fraud" and the Pena/Moore VoIP fraud case, Pena and Moore were able to route their illegitimate traffic over legitimate accounts at service providers because the authentication between the account owner and the service provider was weak and could be guessed by brute force techniques. To avoid having your account hijacked like this, you need to ensure that some form of strong authentication is in place. The good news is that the SIP (defined originally in RFC 3261[J]) does not simply send usernames and passwords in clear text. SIP instead uses the digest authentication defined for HTTP in RFC 2617[K] which involves essentially sending a one-way hash of the password. While better than passing passwords in the clear text, digest authentication is potentially vulnerable to replay attacks or man-in-the-middle attacks.

A better plan is to look into solutions that involve mutual authentication using certificates in some form. For instance, setting up TLS between your premise and the ITSP with mutual authentication would be much stronger.

Along with that, consider also restricting the IP addresses that can authenticate to your ITSP and premise equipment. If you and your provider have only a limited number of systems that will be sending SIP messages, you can put access control lists or firewall policy in place within your network, as can your ITSP, so that SIP messages are only accepted from the agreed-upon IP addresses. Sure, an attacker can spoof an IP address and try to use your account credentials, but he or she would not be able to sustain a conversation from that spoofed IP address. Then, the attacker could send bogus SIP INVITEs, for instance, to attempt to trigger the ITSP to initiate new calls, but when the ITSP tried to connect back to the spoofed IP address to connect the call, the communication would fail.

TIP

If you restrict communication with your ITSP to be from specific IP addresses, do not forget to include IP addresses of any backup servers you may have. It would be difficult to recover if you had a failure at your primary site and brought up the secondary only to find out that it was locked out of communication with your ITSP.

Strategy #4: Consider the Same Service Provider as Your Data/Internet Provider

Another strategy to consider for securing your SIP trunk is to explore using your ISP as your ITSP for SIP communications if they offer such services. The advantage, as shown in Figure 5.10, is that if your ISP is directly connected to the PSTN and not another upstream ITSP, your SIP traffic never actually touches the full public Internet. It would stay entirely within your ISPs network and then go on out to the PSTN from there.

This reduces your zone of exposure to just your network and that of your ISP. Most ISPs, too, are extremely paranoid about the security of their own network and will take extra pains to ensure that their network is not damaged by traffic from customers.

[J]http://tools.ietf.org/html/rfc3261
[K]http://tools.ietf.org/html/rfc2617

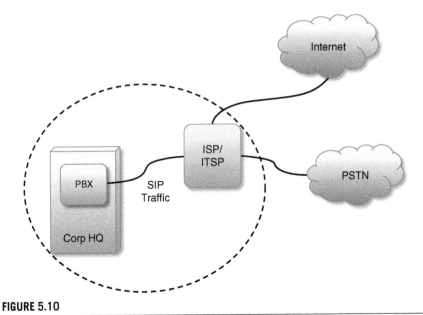

FIGURE 5.10

Using Your ISP as Your ITSP Keeps Your SIP Traffic off the Public Internet

The downside of using your ISP as your ITSP, of course, may be… cost. You may be able to find significantly cheaper ITSPs available to you out on the public Internet. It's the classic trade-off between cost and security. In any event, this may be an option for you to consider.

Strategy #5: Establish a Business Continuity/DR Plan

Earlier in this chapter, in the section "Business Continuity/DR," you read about how SIP trunks can be used to ensure your business can continue to receive or make calls in the event of a failure at either your location or your ITSP. As part of setting up SIP trunks, you need to look at having a business continuity plan for both your ITSP's failure and that of one of your locations.

ITSP Resiliency

What happens if your ITSP has a network failure or some kind of catastrophic incident at one of their data centers? Hopefully, by asking the questions back in Strategy #1 you ruled out ITSPs that had too many SPOFs, but even an ITSP with the most redundant and reliable network can still have occasional problems and outages.

To make your network resilient in the face of these types of outages, the simplest approach is just to set up accounts with multiple ITSPs, as seen in Figure 5.11. You

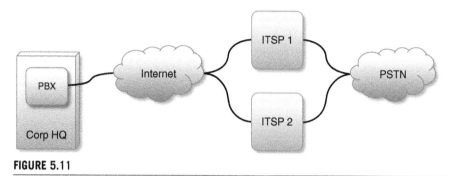

FIGURE 5.11

Multiple ITSPs Can Allow Your Business to Continue in the Face of ITSP Outages

can send and receive most of your traffic through ITSP #1, but in the event of a failure there, you can shift to sending traffic out through ITSP #2.

You could of course extend this and have a third and fourth ITSPs as even further backups, but you may run into commercial issues in trying to do this. Many ITSPs may quote you a rate based on certain expected traffic levels. If you are giving all your traffic to ITSP #1, odds are that ITSP #2 (and #3 and #4) will charge you a higher per-minute rate since you are hardly using their service. They may also have certain minimums. Those may just be minor details in the grand scheme of having a plan to keep your communications going, but they are certainly topics to think about. Rather than route all your traffic through one ITSP and use a second as a backup, you may want to look at balancing traffic between them.

Catastrophic Failures at Your Locations

What if you have a failure at one of your locations? An extended power outage… a hurricane… earthquake… fire… pick your disaster, but it could happen. What can you do? As shown earlier in Figure 5.4, one solution is to ensure that from your ITSP you can easily redirect your incoming calls to another location. If your main location fails, then, you need to be able to call your ITSP or access some Web interface (securely, one would hope!) and change the destination address for all your inbound calls to go to another SIP address. Obviously, there are security protocols you need to set up around who can initiate such a transfer, and so on, but the beauty of SIP and IP communications is that this can be a trivial way to handle what would have been catastrophic outages with traditional TDM telephony.

SUMMARY

SIP trunks offer tremendous benefits to companies in terms of flexibility, innovation, and cost savings, but they do so with the very real security issues around availability and confidentiality. As you consider how to link your UC system to the legacy

PSTN, you need to seriously think through how you will protect that communication channel you have up to an ITSP. As we collectively build the next "all-IP" communications infrastructure, SIP trunks can help your company ensure they are a player in that space..., but you need to make sure this can be safely done.

Next in Chapter 6, "Identity, Spoofing, and Vishing," you'll learn about the incredible challenges relating to "identity" in the world of UC....

Identity, Spoofing, and Vishing

INFORMATION IN THIS CHAPTER

- Anatomy of Attacks on Identity
- Dangers of Attacks on Identity
- The Future of Attacks on Identity
- How to Defend against Attacks on Identity

In March 2009, residents of Sanford, Maine, started getting phone calls that appeared to be from the Sanford Institution for Savings (SIS), a local bank, informing them that their accounts had been frozen, and they needed to provide complete account information in order to keep their accounts open.[A] The calls were not from SIS, of course, but were from attackers seeking to trick people into providing their financial account details.

In May 2009, *APC Magazine* in Australia reported[B] a similar scam where people were receiving an e-mail that appeared to be from Commonwealth Bank asking them to call a specific number. When they called that number, they heard an automated Interactive Voice Response (IVR) system that prompted them for their account details and then indicated that it was activating their card. *APC Magazine* reported that the number being called was registered with a local VoIP provider from whom anyone can easily register numbers.

A year earlier, Brian Krebs reported in his *Washington Post* "Security Fix" blog[C] on a massive scam where text messages were sent to mobile phone users, indicating that their bank account had been suspended due to suspicious activity. To reactivate their account, the message recipients were instructed to call a phone number where they were then prompted to enter their account information. Krebs reported that in one such scam, over a 5 week period, millions of text messages were sent,

---

[A]http://blog.banksis.net/?p=211&cpage=1
[B]http://apcmag.com/commonwealth-bank-targeted-in-massive-phishing-scam.htm
[C]http://blog.washingtonpost.com/securityfix/2008/03/the_anatomy_of_a_vishing_scam_1.html

approximately 4,400 people actually called the number, and 125 people entered their full credit or debit card number, expiration date, and personal identification number (PIN).

At the SpeechTEK 2008 conference in New York, renowned hacker Kevin Mitnick demonstrated[D] in his keynote address how he could publicize a phone number for a bank that, when called, *appeared* to be from the bank and in fact *did* access the bank's real IVR system. However, the phone number was actually for his attack system that was sitting in the middle, relaying the bank's audio to the caller and relaying (and logging) the caller's keypresses to the bank's system. After someone called this number and interacted with the bank's system, he then had all the information necessary to call back to the bank and identify himself as the caller. While this was only a demonstration, Mitnick was pointing out that attackers could very easily create this type of system and then send out e-mail or text messages trying to convince people to call the *attacker's* "customer service number" instead of the real customer service number for the bank.

In that same keynote address, Mitnick also relayed another example where he spoofed the caller identification (caller ID, or sometimes calling line ID [CLID]) on his phone to call a company and then convinced an employee to give him the information he needed to carry out a separate attack on the company's system.

The common thread through all of these attacks is how the attacker tries to convince the target of the attack that the interaction is legitimate by showing an identity that appears to be real. For instance, in an enterprise setting, the target sees on his or her phone what looks like a real phone number from somewhere inside their company. They accept the call believing they are in fact talking to a coworker. The attacker could prey on fear a bit by presenting a caller ID of CORP SECURITY or something similar to cause the target to be anxious or uncertain. In addition, if the target calls out to an automated IVR service as a result of receiving an email, for instance, the attacker could make the attack system sound identical to the real system or even interact with the real system such as the Mitnick example mentioned above, thus further convincing the target that they are communicating with the real system.

Attacks on identity are not new in the communications infrastructure. Scammers have been trying to defraud people over the public switched telephone network (PSTN) for ages, and techniques like "orange boxing"[E] have been in existence since the early days of "Caller ID" mass availability on the PSTN. The difference is that now with unified communications (UC) and VoIP, it is far easier for an attacker to modify and change identity information.

[D]www.speechtechmag.com/Articles/Editorial/FYI/Former-Hacker-Tackles-IVR-and-Voice-Biometric-Security-50358.aspx
[E]www.artofhacking.com/files/OB-FAQ.HTM

NOTE

Interestingly, it is currently *legal* within the United States to spoof caller ID when calling someone. It is obviously *not* legal to execute a crime such as impersonating a person to defraud someone else, but the act of spoofing caller ID is allowed. To address this issue, members of the US Congress have been trying since 2006 to pass the "Truth in Caller ID Act," but so far they have been unsuccessful.[F]

ANATOMY OF ATTACKS ON IDENTITY

Let's look now at how attacks on identity can be carried out. Within UC systems, the greatest challenge is that the Session Initiation Protocol (SIP) is a *text-based* protocol that can be easily modified.

Think of e-mail for a moment. Do you honestly trust the "From" addresses on e-mail messages you see in your inbox? Are all those 50 messages in your inbox this week *really* from PayPal? Is that offer really from the last remaining son of the now-dead finance minister of some African country? Did your bank really send you the message saying that your account was compromised and you need to visit a certain Web site to fix your account?

Thanks to the overwhelming volume of spam in e-mail, as well as the great amount of publicity about identity theft and "phishing" scams; most people today seem to understand that e-mail addresses cannot be trusted completely. Just because it says it is from Elvis or some prominent politician doesn't mean that it actually came from them.

However, people generally place a much higher degree of trust in the caller ID that they see coming in on their phone. They believe that if the phone says it is someone calling, then it must be certainly the same person. As an exercise, ask 10 people outside the security profession a question like "When you get a call that shows it is from someone, do you trust that it is in fact from that person?" Odds are that probably almost all of them will say yes, and they do. (The caveat of asking people "outside the security profession" is because most security professionals have an ingrained sense of paranoia that prevents them from trusting *any* information they see.)

What people do not understand *yet* is that the caller ID they have come to trust can be modified today just as easily as an e-mail "From" address can be changed. Particularly in the world of VoIP and UC, the identity is just a text string that can be easily modified or replaced. People *shouldn't* trust caller ID – but for now, they do.

From an attack perspective, note that for an attacker to attempt to trick someone by appearing to be an internal user, the attacker does not need to have an internal extension. Most UC systems will simply pass along the caller ID they receive from the sending endpoint. The attacker can therefore set up his or her *external* attack system or endpoints and give them *internal* caller ID information. The target receiving the call will see what appears to be an internal caller ID, even though the call may be originating outside the network.

[F]http://voipsa.org/blog/category/identity/

> **NOTE**
>
> Note that caller ID is a different service from automatic number identification (ANI) or the dialed number identification service (DNIS). ANI and DNIS are lower level protocols within the PSTN for sending telephone numbers primarily related to billing (ANI) or call routing (DNIS). While an attacker could attempt to spoof ANI or DNIS, doing so is a more complex process and is outside the scope of this book. For the vast majority of telephony attacks, spoofing caller ID will be sufficient and far easier.

Note that this applies, in particular, to voice or video calls as they can connect through the PSTN or the SIP infrastructure. Modifying Instant Messaging (IM) may be a bit more challenging because of the general lack of federation between IM systems. This is changing, though, and attackers may be able to set up their own attack systems for IM in the future.

Caller ID Spoofing on the PSTN

Before we get into modification of identity in UC systems, you should be familiar with how easily caller ID can be modified on today's PSTN. If you haven't tried this, simply turn to your favorite search engine and search for "caller ID spoofing." Beyond a couple of explanatory sites, most of the links will be to services where you can easily make calls to other people with a spoofed caller ID (for a fee, of course). One spoofing service even has a Facebook application and mobile applications for iPhone, Blackberry, and Android devices, making it easy for you to make calls with spoofed caller ID from wherever you are.

All of these services make it extremely easy today for *anyone* to spoof caller ID through a simple Web site or application. VoIP and UC systems, though, provide a few other mechanisms.

Identity Modification at the Originating Endpoint

Perhaps the simplest way to modify an identity in a UC system is to change the display name or other identity information within the endpoint itself. Almost every "hard" endpoint such as an IP phone will have a Web administrative interface. Every "soft" endpoint like a softphone will have a menu named something like "preferences," "options," or "settings," where you can configure the endpoint. As an example, Figure 6.1 shows where you could set the user ID string in a Grandstream IP phone.

As another example, Figure 6.2 shows on the left side the *Preferences* menu option in SJphone,[G] a free SIP softphone available for Windows, Mac, or Linux. The name has been set to "Pres. Barack Obama." On the right side of Figure 6.2, you can see an inbound call from this SJphone to a Gizmo5[H] softphone where the modified name is displayed.

[G]www.sjlabs.com/products.html

[H]www.google.com/gizmo5/ – Gizmo5 was a standalone SIP phone that was purchased by Google in late 2009.

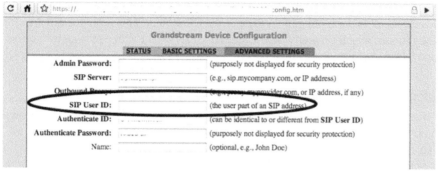

FIGURE 6.1

You Can Configure the User ID in an IP Phone Admin Interface

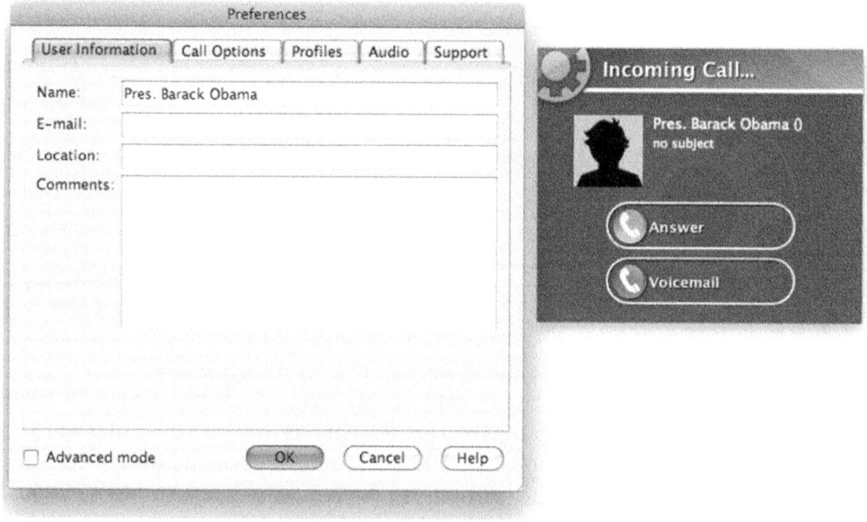

FIGURE 6.2

Identity Spoofing Using Softphones

This call could obviously have been made to a hard phone or to any other UC endpoint, and the endpoint would have displayed in the format and style most appropriate for that endpoint. Similar identity modifications can be made in other hard or soft clients.

There is one major caveat regarding modifying identity at the endpoint level: the UC system to which the endpoint is connected must *allow* identity modification. In many UC systems, endpoint identity is locked down in the central system. The identity is assigned to the endpoint when it starts up and may not be changed by the end user. The endpoint may even appear to allow the user to change the identity, but the UC system will not accept messages from that endpoint or will change the identity back as the message goes through the UC system. This is particularly true for IM systems, which generally have a centralized server through which all traffic goes and where identity can be enforced.

Identity Modification at Source System

Of course, there is nothing that prevents an attacker from setting up his or her own VoIP or UC system complete with whatever endpoints the attacker wants to use. An attacker could download a free, open-source platform like Asterisk,[I] set it up on a very basic computer system, connect it to the Internet, and start making calls as someone else. Within Asterisk, SIP endpoint configuration takes place within the "sip.conf" configuration file. As shown in the code below, the caller ID can be easily set to whatever the administrator wants it to be.

```
[basic sip phone]
type=friend
username=sip1
callerid="John Doe" <1749>
host=dynamic
nat=yes
canreinvite=no
disallow=all
allow=ulaw
allow=alaw
```

As mentioned in the Section "Expansion of the PSTN Trust Boundary" in Chapter 5, "SIP Trunking and PSTN Interconnection," the PSTN relies on implicit trust between service providers that they will not send illegitimate traffic to the rest of the network. An attacker can exploit this trust by connecting an IP-PBX under his or her control up to an Internet Telephony Service Provider (ITSP) and from there out to the rest of the PSTN. Because there is no global identity system to verify the origin of the traffic from the connected system, the ITSP has to accept and pass on the traffic as legitimate. Instructions are also commonly available[J] to help create applications for spoofing.

Note that instead of an attacker setting up a separate attack system, the attacker could also attempt to exploit some vulnerability in an IP-PBX or other UC systems to compromise the system and make modifications to identity information there. For example, if an attacker had already compromised an extension and learned a valid username and password, the attacker might want to try to modify the displayed caller ID to present a different name associated with the extension.

[I]www.asterisk.org/
[J]For example, www.voip-info.org/wiki/view/Spoofing+Extension

Identity Modification in Transit

Finally, the attacker can modify the identity information while the SIP packet is in transit. As you learned in Chapter 4, "Control Channel Attacks: Fuzzing, DoS, SPIT, and Toll Fraud," if an attacker can insert themselves into the SIP control channel, the attacker can modify SIP headers and other information between the sender and recipient.

For example, consider Figure 6.3 where an attacker has inserted himself between Alice and Bob. Imagine that the attacker wanted to create some confusion between Alice and Bob and disrupt their communication. As Alice calls Bob, the attacker could rewrite the SIP headers so that Bob sees a caller ID that he is unlikely to want to pick up, perhaps "Collections Department" or "Telemarketing Research." Similarly, the attacker could change the identity information going back to Alice to be something completely different in an attempt to trick Alice into thinking that she was dialing the wrong number. If the attacker is successful, Alice may hang up before Bob even answers.

To execute this kind of attack, the attacker has to look at potentially modifying two of the headers sent in a typical SIP INVITE message. First, the "From" header is defined in the original RFC 3261[K] and is present in all SIP messages. By default, this is the header used by endpoints for caller ID."

A second header, called *P-Asserted-Identity* and often referred in writings on SIP as simply "PAI," was established by RFC 3325,[L] and it enables SIP servers within a *trusted domain* to assert what the identity of an end user is. When the SIP proxy server receives an outgoing INVITE from an authorized user, the server can add the PAI header with information from the server's data store. As shown in the example of excerpted SIP headers below, the P-Asserted-Identity can be different from the

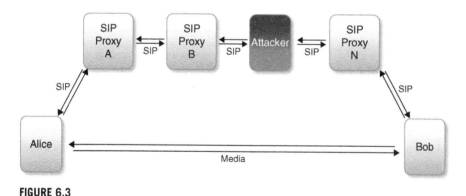

FIGURE 6.3

An Attacker in the Middle of the Control Channel Can Modify Identity Information

[K] http://tools.ietf.org/html/rfc3261
[L] http://tools.ietf.org/html/rfc3325

"From" address. There can, as shown, be two P-Asserted-Identity headers added: one for an SIP URI and the other for a TEL URI, although most often only the PAI header with an SIP URI may be included.

```
INVITE sip:bob@example.com SIP/2.0
To: <sip:bob@example.com>
From: "Alice" <sip:alice@example.net>;tag=1234567
Call-ID: 342681985700452324
CSeq: 1 INVITE
P-Asserted-Identity: "Alice Wonder" <sip:alice@example.net>
P-Asserted-Identity: tel:+16035551212
Privacy: id
```

The result of this is that SIP endpoints within the trusted domain can ignore the "From" header address and use the P-Asserted-Identity as the caller ID. Given this, the user can change the identity inside their endpoint to whatever they want because that value will be ignored when caller ID is displayed on the receiving endpoint.

WARNING

Remember that P-Asserted-Identity is designed to be used only within the domain of a trusted set of servers and endpoints. The problem with using it outside the trusted domain is that downstream servers have to trust the upstream servers to accurately and securely pass the PAI header. Say that Server A asserts the identity of a user with the PAI header and sends that to Server B. Server B then sends it to Server C, who sends it on to Server D, who sends it on to Server E, and so on. Somewhere down the line, Server H receives the PAI header and has to trust that it has in fact been passed all the way down the chain intact and with no modification. PAI provides no mechanism to identify *which server* added the PAI header, nor is there any protection against modification. It is truly designed to be used among servers that fully trust each other.

The attacker in the middle of the SIP control channel can modify either or both the "From" header and the "P-Asserted-Identity" header to change the identity of the sender or recipient, or both.

Vishing

Spoofing the identity of a person or a company may be part of a larger identity-based attack known as "*voice phishing* or *vishing*," where an attacker is using the telephony system to attempt to trick a caller into disclosing "personally identifiable information" (PII) that the attacker could typically use for financial gain. This PII could be account numbers, PINs, passwords, US Social Security numbers (or its equivalent in other countries), or other information.

Phishing is the overall name for this broad category of attacks, with the best-known attack being bogus e-mail messages that are sent which warn you of dire consequences unless you visit a Web site to correct the issue. The standard technique for a phisher is to create an e-mail that closely matches a real e-mail from a bank indicating that the recipient is going to, for instance, have their credit card suspended unless they take action *right now*. The phisher registers a domain or a subdomain that is as close as possible to the bank's real domain. Finally, the phisher creates a Web site that closely resembles the bank's real Web site. The phisher then sends out the e-mail to massive numbers of recipients, hoping that some of the recipients will actually have accounts at the target bank and that some percentage of those recipients will go to the bogus link and fill out the form requesting the PII data.

TIP

You can learn more about phishing in general at the Web site of the Anti-Phishing Working Group: http://apwg.org/

Phishing has been a plague for the past several years, and both law enforcement agencies and product vendors have been taking steps to combat the problem. For instance, e-mail programs may now warn when an e-mail is suspected of being a phishing scam. Web browsers may similarly flag a site when you visit it based on blacklists and other technologies.

Given this situation, some phishers have now branched out to include voice in their attack plans, making use of the fact that people have a larger degree of trust in the traditional PSTN and in the caller ID. A very basic form of "voice phishing" or "vishing" may involve sending out that same e-mail warning of dire consequences, but instead of asking people to visit a Web site, they are asked to call a phone number. That number then goes to an IVR system that presents menus that closely resemble those of the bank and include requests for the caller to enter their credit card account number and other information. In fact, the savvy attacker will use the bank's own prompts in the attack system. The attacker can call into the bank's IVR system and record all of the prompts used during the phone call. These recordings can then be uploaded to the attacker's system and played back to the victims.

The goal is ultimately to convince the caller that the attacker's system is the "real" bank and that they should enter their PII data in response to various prompts. The attacker can then use that information to empty the victim's bank accounts, open up new credit cards, obtain documents fraudulently, and so on. The attacker may also simply sell this personal information to someone else who may in turn use it.

As shown in Figure 6.4, more sophisticated schemes are possible where the attack system has the option to transfer to a "live agent," who in fact is an attacker who does his or her best to convince the caller that the call is legitimate. The attacker could even conceivably transfer the caller to the *real* bank's call center if the person had additional questions (at which point the attacker already has all the information he or she requires).

Beyond simply expanding the traditional phishing e-mail scam, phishers can also use voice and other communications media in interesting ways, again trying to

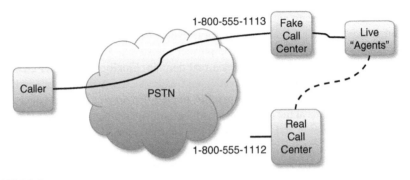

FIGURE 6.4

Sophisticated Vishing Attacks May Involve Live Agents

get the target to call back in and interact with the attacker's system. For instance, the attacker can

- make outbound calls to people, informing them of the dire issue and asking them to call the attacker's number;
- make outbound calls to people seeking to interact with them directly in the course of the call;
- send SMS messages, urging the targets to call in to the number.

If people stop trusting e-mail messages, the attackers will try SMS and voice. At the point in time when these methods stop working, you could see the attackers moving to whatever messaging medium people trust next, perhaps IM or social networking.

The connection to UC and VoIP in all of this is simply that UC and VoIP have made all this phenomenally easier for an attack to be executed. A visher could certainly pull off an attack like this with traditional PSTN tools and systems, but with the traditional PSTN there is a higher cost of equipment, lines, lengthy delays in getting all the connections in place, and so on. Instead, with VoIP and UC, an attacker can simply install free software onto a commodity computer (or even a virtual machine), upload the recorded prompts, build a small IVR application, and get a SIP trunk connection from an ITSP, and they are in business. Once the attacker has built the initial attack system, there is virtually no time involved in setting up additional systems. Should the authorities start to catch the attacker's trail, it's extremely simple to shut down the operation and start it up again on a different IP address using a different ITSP, and so on.

You need to be aware of how these attacks work and educate the users about what to look for. You also need to be aware that while the vishing attacks discussed publicly have generally been related to banks and financial institutions, the possibility is definitely there for an attack on a corporate system. Imagine an attacker setting up a system to mimic a large company's self-service portal to help with, say, password resets. The attacker could send selective e-mail addresses found through online searches, for instance, indicating to those people that their VPN account was expiring, and they were needed to call "support" to reactivate their account. The number they call could then ask them for their old password and then their new password. Or instead of requesting people to call, the attacker could launch outbound calls targeting numbers or extensions associated with a branch of your company.

All these are again using modifications to telephony identity to trick people into believing that they are communicating with someone legitimate, with the end result being the potential disclosure of information to an attacker.

DANGERS OF ATTACKS ON IDENTITY

Let's now look at some of the major dangers of attacks on identity: fraud, identity theft, social engineering, reputation damage, annoyance, erosion of trust, and the deception of automated systems.

Fraud

The most obvious danger of attacks on identity is the entire class of attacks labeled broadly as "fraud," where an attacker attempts to deceive you typically for some type of theft. If an attacker can convince you that he or she is in fact calling from your bank and that you should give him/her the information known only to your bank, he or she can then potentially use that information to pretend to be you and, for instance, empty your bank account. There are many different ways in which an attacker can deceive you.

Now, the identity displayed in a communications session alone will not necessarily convince someone that a caller is legitimate, but it helps in painting the overall picture that the victim sees.

Identity Theft

One particular form of fraud that has received much attention in recent years is that of "identity theft," where an attacker uses PII to pretend to be the victim to, for instance, withdraw money from the victim's accounts, establish new credit cards in the victim's name, or charge purchases to the victim's credit cards.

Communication and telephony can play a role in helping the attacker obtain the information he or she needs. For example, the victim may receive an automated call that appears to be from their bank indicating that their account is in trouble and asking them to call a phone number. The caller ID of the automated call seems to be from their bank, and the message sounds legitimate. When they do call the number they are asked to call, they see a caller identification number that looks like the one from their bank (assuming that their UC system displays the ID of the number being called); and they hear IVR prompts and menus that sound identical to what their bank uses (in fact, they might be the bank's actual prompts). In addition, they might speak with an agent who further convinces them that they are speaking with their bank. They then provide their personal information because they truly believe they are speaking with their bank.

The scam involves a whole number of parts, but the caller identity is one that help convince the victim to accept the initial call or to think that they are talking to a legitimate call center.

Social Engineering

Another danger is the use of identity in "social engineering" to convince you to provide information or access to someone attempting a larger crime. For instance, if you work in a large company, you might receive a phone call that appears to be directly from your CEO or from one of the executives reporting directly to the CEO. He or she asks you a series of questions about the product you are working on, what it is used for, what kind of deficiencies it may have, and so on. You provide all this information, thinking you are being asked to do so by a superior at your company. In fact, you have just provided the information to an attacker, who might now provide that information to a competitor or use that information to attempt to attack the product in question.

From your perspective, the call appeared to be legitimate based on the caller ID displayed on your desk phone. If you are not familiar with the executive's voice, how will you necessarily know that it is not the actual person on the phone?

Consider another example: Your company runs a network operations center (NOC) and has very strict security policies about who can gain access to the NOC. No one is allowed in without proper approval from a limited set of approvers. One afternoon, you get a call that *appears* to originate from one of the legitimate approvers indicating that someone will be arriving shortly at the NOC who should be cleared for full access to the facility. The particular NOC operator receiving the call has not spoken with this approver before, but based on the identity displayed on the phone and other information given by the caller, the NOC operator decides that the call is legit and authorizes the visitor's access. Finally, it turns out that both the "approver" and the "visitor" were in fact attackers who wanted to gain access to the NOC.

Again, identity information displayed by the communications infrastructure is not the sole reason why the attacker is able to gain information or access, but that identity information helps to lay the foundation for the attack. The victims are more open to communicating with the attacker because they *believe* they are talking to the person they think they are. Identity information helps with that.

Reputation Damage

You are sitting down for dinner at home when the phone rings. Immediately, you think to yourself "yet another annoying telemarketer" and vow to never do business with companies that call during your dinner hour. When you look at the caller ID, you see the name of a prominent company that you respect. Immediately, they lose a bit of that respect in your mind.

However, what if that company is not even remotely associated with the call? What if it was an unethical company calling for some other topic but using the prominent brand's name to try to trick people into picking up the call? Think of all the e-mail scams you get on a regular basis that appear to be from someone completely different. The same kind of identity forgery is possible within UC and can have negative effects on your reputation.

Similarly, if someone were to call, text, or IM you and were then abusive in language, you would have a negative view toward them. If that person appeared to be from a company you knew, that company would lose some of the positive reputation it may have had. There are a number of ways that an attacker could use UC communication to damage a company's reputation.

Annoyance

It should go without saying that attacks on identity can be used to annoy other people. Say that you keep receiving a call from what appears to be your bank's call center, but when you pick up the call there is no one there. You may call the bank's call center back, where they will have no record of any calls being made to you. As the calls continue, it becomes annoying to the point where you may simply leave your phone off-hook so that you stop receiving calls.

You could receive calls from what seem like other employees, but they are actually connections to other people. An attacker could change caller identities randomly so that you never know exactly who is calling you. The possibilities are rather endless.

Erosion of Trust

All of these various dangers are symptoms of a far larger and more systemic danger – "an erosion of trust." An erosion of trust between your users and the UC system, between the users and any automated services you have, between the users and yourself, and indeed between the users themselves. This loss of trust may impact a team or a company's ability to perform at its highest level and generally may lead to a less than satisfactory work environment.

As a security professional, you *want* people to think critically and to not necessarily trust the information they receive, but the challenge is to engender that level of vigilance while also keeping enough trust in place that people can work well together.

Deceiving Automated Systems

You may have noticed that that the dangers outlined so far in this section relate to *humans* being fooled by modified identity information. However, UC systems themselves may also be deceived by attacks on identity. Consider, for example, a UC system that routes inbound calls to a person based on the identity of the caller. If the person's boss (or spouse) calls him or her, the call would be routed to them at any time, regardless of whether he or she is in a meeting or not. Perhaps, the UC system will not accept calls at all unless he or she is from particular SIP addresses. In both cases, an attacker may be able to get through to the targeted victim, perhaps with only a one-way audio, but still with a call.

IM systems, similarly, may use identity in making decisions. An IM server may only allow messages in from certain known identities or domains. The server may only allow new registrations from specific domains as well. Automated agents may only return information from a database to specific IM-user IDs. Again, an attacker who is successfully able to spoof the legitimate identity of someone else may gain access to information or services he or she should not be able to access.

EPIC FAIL

In August 2006, it was widely reported[M] that a significant number of people, including celebrity Paris Hilton, had used caller ID spoofing to access voice-mail accounts belonging to other people. It turned out that both Cingular Wireless and T-Mobile USA used caller IDs with no additional password as a way to authenticate a caller into their voice-mail systems. Because of this, if you knew someone's mobile phone number, you could go to any of the caller ID spoofing services and then dial into the Cingular or T-Mobile voice-mail system with the target's mobile number set as your caller ID. You would then have full access to the person's voice-mail system and could listen to all messages and perform other actions such as changing the greeting.

THE FUTURE OF ATTACKS ON IDENTITY

As systems become further interconnected, federated, and generally linked together, the potential for identity abuse will only continue to increase. Let's look at several aspects of the continued interconnection process and attempts to address the issue.

Interconnection and Federation

Back in Chapter 5, "SIP Trunking and PSTN Interconnection" in the Section, "Expansion of the PSTN Trust Boundary," you learned that the PSTN as we knew it no longer exists. Today, we live in this interconnected fabric of Internet Telephony Service Providers who are constantly connecting more and more levels of additional ITSPs. The "old boys club" of a few carriers who more or less trusted each other is gone.

As has been a common theme throughout the chapters of this book, we are increasingly moving to a more interconnected communications infrastructure where UC systems federate with each other and, through SIP trunks and ITSPs, connect out to the larger IP communications network being built today. While there are immense

---

[M]One of the many articles was www.infoworld.com/d/security-central/paris-hilton-accused-voice-mail-hacking-457

possibilities for richer communications, identity in particular faces a challenge with the interconnection as the number of UC and VoIP endpoints increases. How do you know whom you are really communicating with when it is so incredibly easy to change the identity information?

RFC 4474 SIP Identity and Whatever Comes Next

One answer proposed by the Internet Engineering Task Force (IETF) back in 2006 is *SIP Identity* and is defined in RFC 4474.[N]

The idea is fairly simple. If Alice (alice@example.net) wants to send an SIP INVITE to Bob (bob@example.com) to begin a communication session, Alice's end-point sends the INVITE to her local proxy server, which computes a cryptographic hash across the "From" header and a number of other headers. The proxy server then signs the hash with a certificate valid for the domain name (for example, example.net), inserts the signed hash into an SIP header, and sends it over to Bob. On Bob's end, his system computes the same hash and compares it with the signed hash sent in the SIP headers (after confirming the signature is intact and good). If it matches, Bob will know that he is in fact communicating with "alice@example.net."

The basic idea is shown in Figure 6.5: hash some headers (1), sign the hash (2), and send it to the recipient (3). You wind up with a cryptographically provable end-to-end identity. The signed hash is inserted into a new SIP header called *Identity*. To help the recipient obtain the certificate to verify the signature (4) on the hash, an "Identity-Info" header is added, which includes the URL for sending proxy's certificate.

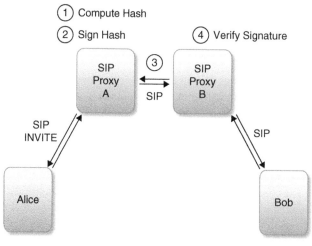

FIGURE 6.5

The SIP Identity Process

[N]http://tools.ietf.org/html/rfc4474

Together, RFC 4474 SIP Identity and the companion "SIP Connected Identity" defined in RFC 4916[O] for the recipient identity provide a solid way of providing end-to-end secure identity assertion (or at least from end-domain to end-domain). From reading the RFCs, you might be inclined to think that the identity problem has been solved.

However, there is one basic fundamental problem: SIP Identity and SIP Connected Identity do not work in most network scenarios common today.

It turns out that in a network environment where SIP endpoints can communicate directly with other SIP endpoints, SIP Identity can work fine; but that is not the reality of most networks today. Instead, the internal network is separated from external networks like the Internet by firewalls, NAT devices and, specific to real-time communications, session border controllers (SBCs). SBCs are "middleboxes" that sit in the SIP control channel path and help in the communication between the internal and external networks via SIP.

The problem is that SBCs modify SIP headers, including some of the SIP headers signed in the RFC 4474 SIP Identity process. The result is that SIP Identity (and SIP Connected Identity) breaks and the other party cannot verify the signature. As Hadriel Kaplan from Acme Packet outlined in his now-expired Internet Draft, "Why URIs Are Changed Crossing Domains,"[P] SBCs have very legitimate reasons for changing SIP headers, including normalization of SIP from one device to another, dealing with IP addresses in SIP headers, network topology hiding, and relationship hiding.

Because of this issue, as well as others like an identified security weakness,[Q] SIP Identity and SIP Connected Identity have seen very little adoption in the marketplace and that is not expected to change. In response, the IETF SIP-related working groups have been digging into the issue in much greater detail in an attempt to find a solution that is secure and also works with current network configurations. To understand the issues better and learn where the IETF work is going, you would be advised to read:

- "End-to-End Identity Important in SIP"[R] by John Elwell of Siemens – This document goes into great detail about why end-to-end identity is important and where the existing mechanisms fail to provide end-to-end identity.
- "Requirements for secure caller identification in SIP"[S] by John Elwell of Siemens and Viktor Pascual of Tekelec – This document lays out requirements for secure caller identification over SIP.
- "Identity Handling at an SIP User Agent"[T] by John Elwell of Siemens – This document examines the various different types of caller identification information an SIP endpoint can receive and how the endpoint can use that information.

[O]http://tools.ietf.org/html/rfc4916
[P]http://tools.ietf.org/html/draft-kaplan-sip-uris-change
[Q]http://tools.ietf.org/html/draft-kaplan-sip-baiting-attack
[R]http://tools.ietf.org/html/draft-elwell-sip-e2e-identity-important
[S]http://tools.ietf.org/html/draft-elwell-dispatch-identity-reqs
[T]http://tools.ietf.org/html/draft-elwell-sip-identity-handling-ua

- "SIP Identity using Media Path"[U] by Dan Wing of Cisco and Hadriel Kaplan of Acme Packet – A proposal for another way to assert SIP identity that should work through SBCs.

These documents, particularly the first two from John Elwell, also contain links to a number of other documents that relate to this overall discussion, within the IETF.

In the end, the important point to remember is that the IETF is working on potential solutions within the open standards world of SIP. Will a solution be found that works for all involved? Will we see that solution commercially available in the next few years? All are good questions.

Social Identity Systems

Meanwhile, in the larger world of the Web, there are several different competing systems that would like to be the source for your "online identity." Today, these systems are used primarily to help you log in to various different Web sites; that is, rather than needing a separate username and password for each site, you can simply log in with your identity from the identity provider. However, the services are competing heavily and various advocates are looking at how these systems can be extended to provide identity for other services beyond that of Web sites. It's quite conceivable that, over time, someone may look at how to extend these systems into providing identity information for UC systems. At the time of this writing, the major systems include

- Twitter – The super successful microblogging site's "Sign in with Twitter"[V] initiative now lets you log in to sites all over the Internet with your Twitter ID.
- Facebook Connect[W] – Claiming over 300 million users now, Facebook Connect lets you easily log in to sites with your Facebook ID.
- Google Friend Connect[X] – Running third behind Twitter and Facebook, Google Friend Connect lets you log in to sites using your Google account.
- OpenID[Y] – The open standard of the bunch, OpenID now claims[Z] over 1 billion OpenID-enabled accounts and over 9 million Web sites accepting OpenIDs.

There are other systems out there, of course. Yahoo, AOL, MySpace, and TypePad, among others, have all competed in this space, but the reality is that Twitter and Facebook are the primary log-in systems you see when you go to any random Web site. You can't rule Google out of course, with their vast reach and Web properties. The "open stack" of protocols, too, that includes OpenID, OAuth,[AA] and a number of other open technologies are also experiencing high growth as companies

---

[U]http://tools.ietf.org/html/draft-wing-sip-identity-media
[V]http://apiwiki.twitter.com/Sign-in-with-Twitter
[W]http://developers.facebook.com/connect.php
[X]www.google.com/friendconnect/
[Y]http://opened.net/
[Z]http://openid.net/2009/12/16/openid-2009-year-in-review/
[AA]http://oauth.net/

and individuals look for options that do not lock them in to the major commercial vendors. You can expect to see the "identity wars" to continue over the next few years as all these systems compete to be your provider of online identity information.

As a security professional, you need to be aware of these different evolving identity schemes and how they may impact your overall Web site security. You also need to keep watching, as it is only a matter of time before some of those systems start being considered for real-time communications and UC systems.

HOW TO DEFEND AGAINST ATTACKS ON IDENTITY

Your strongest defense against identity attacks, as outlined in Strategy #1, is to educate your users about the threats. Sadly, the technical solutions that may help with this issue are probably several years away from being widely available.

Strategy #1: Educate Your Users about Potential Threats and What Not to Trust

The first step is to educate your users about how easy it is to spoof what they think of as caller ID. Demonstrations are probably best here, perhaps at informal departmental or branch meetings within your company or a "Lunch and Learn" lunchtime seminar. This information could be conveyed as videos posted on your intranet or as a webinar or even at a company-wide meeting or annual training session. The exact forum will vary based upon the size of your company, what kind of events you already do, and so on.

For demonstrations, you could consider the following:

1. Setting up an account with one of the various caller ID spoofing services and calling the mobile phones of audience members with a spoofed ID.
2. Modifying one of your UC systems' endpoints to have a different ID and showing how easy it is to make this modification.
3. Setting up a separate test system using something like Asterisk with an application to spoof extensions[BB] that lets you call into the application and enter the number to call and the number you want to appear as the caller ID.
4. Creating an IVR application with prompts uploaded from another IVR system (perhaps your own company's order processing system if you have one) that shows how an attacker could create a system that mimics another system.
5. Sending an e-mail out within the company that looks legitimate and directs people to your bogus IVR application. Report later on how many people were fooled into providing some type of information. (Admittedly, this one may be getting too uncomfortable for many people.)

[BB]For example, this app: www.voip-info.org/wiki/view/Spoofing+Extension

You may also want to educate people about phishing issues in general. The key point is that you want people to develop a healthy understanding of the kind of threats out there and also that they cannot simply trust the caller ID that they see on their phone, whether they are receiving a call or making one.

Strategy #2: Understand and Lock Down Holes that Allow Spoofing

You need to understand where in your UC system identity can be modified and ensure that only the appropriate people can make those changes. Can an end user change the identity in their IP phone endpoint? If so, can you lock that part of the Web management console down while still giving them any access they need? (Do they need to access the Web management console at all?) Can you override their settings from central proxy servers? For softphones, can the users again make changes in the settings for the soft client? Can you restrict or override those settings?

On your UC server, IP-PBX, call server, or whatever you call the central device, who has access to the list of user identities? Who can configure new extensions or additional identity information? Do you trust them to not change or modify the identity information?

As you perform the overall security assessment of your network, you need to look at it from the "identity" point of view. Where can identity be asserted? And who has the power to do so?

Strategy #3: Evaluate Strong Identity Solutions

Where possible, consider evaluating mechanisms that provide a strong assertion of identity. For example, can your system support within your network the usage of RFC 4474 SIP Identity; that is, does the SIP traffic not cross over an SBC? Does the equipment from your vendor even remotely support it?

Alternatively, can your endpoints and UC system support mutual TLS authentication, which will provide the authentication of not only the endpoint to the server but also the server to the endpoint?

On the IM side of UC, can your endpoints again support mutual TLS? Or can they support something like PGP for encryption and asserting identity?

Strategy #4: Monitor and Participate in Ongoing Identity Discussions

As noted in the earlier sections on "RFC 4474 SIP Identity and Whatever Comes Next" and "Social Identity Systems," there is a great amount of evolution happening right now in what online identity systems will look like. The next few years will be a crucial time as both more and more systems become interconnected and also as the evolving identity systems start to mature.

If you are dealing with UC systems based on SIP, you might consider joining one of the IETF mailing lists such as that of the DISPATCH working group[CC] to stay up

---

[CC]www.ietf.org/mailman/listinfo/dispatch

on what new discussions and actions occur around SIP identity issues. If the IETF mailing lists are too high volume for you (and they can be), you may want to consider setting up a Google Alert or some other way to track online discussions related to SIP identity.

Regarding the other emerging online identity systems like Facebook Connect, Twitter, and OpenID, you may want to try them out on test or private Web sites to understand how they work. For monitoring, your best bet may be to follow some of the blogs from the different vendors or again set up news alerts or periodic searches. It is going to be a crazy time for a while. It's best to keep watching, so you know what is coming.

SUMMARY

As we have moved from the traditional PSTN to the new IP communications networks, the challenge is that we are now in a space where "identity" can be spoofed even more easily than it was possible before. Yet, at the same time, we have a user population that is accustomed to trusting the caller identification information and is therefore currently more susceptible to abuses of the identity process. Your challenge is to help people understand where the security issues are while also paying attention to what solutions are evolving and how they may assist you in helping your users know better exactly who they are communicating with through their UC system.

An added challenge, of course, is that UC systems let you distribute and decentralize components all across the IP networks, but that is the subject of Chapter 7, "The End of Geography."

The End of Geography

You call the corporate office of a company in Montreal, Quebec, in January, enter an extension, and connect to your account representative. While you are waiting for him to pull up some information, you try to make small talk and ask about how cold it is right at that moment in Montreal. He laughs and says he has no clue because he actually works out of a home office in Austin, Texas.

Later in the day, you stop in to your local coffee shop for a coffee and a snack. As you sit at your table, the woman next to you starts talking to her computer, "Hi, this is Sylvia, how can I help you?" By her actions and what she says it dawns on you that she is having a video conversation with someone at the headquarters of her employer, mapping out plans for an upcoming event.

As you head toward the door, you see a friend of yours getting ready to leave and so you stop to say hello. While he's putting on his jacket, his mobile phone buzzes and he stops to look at it. "Oh, let me just answer this IM question," he says, sitting back down and typing madly with his thumbs.

Welcome to the ultra-distributed and always-on world of unified communications (UC), where your physical location no longer matters. Calls from the public switched telephone network (PSTN) enter your organization's Internet Protocol (IP) "cloud" and travel over IP to endpoints wherever they may be located. Video, instant messaging (IM), and other collaboration tools are all over IP networks to begin with and they, too, traverse whatever networks are necessary to get to your endpoint. The people communicating can, of course, be in the same building, but they could just as equally be anywhere in the country – or, for that matter, anywhere in the world.

Geography doesn't matter.

The "IP network" recognizes no geographic borders. Wherever you can get an IP address and sufficient network bandwidth, you can put an endpoint on your UC system. Your users can be using dedicated endpoints like IP phones, laptop computers, desktop computers, Web-based programs on a shared computer, or applications running on the incredibly powerful mobile "phones" of today.

Beyond your users, your UC systems can be distributed all over the larger IP network. There is no reason why you need to have all your UC systems concentrated in one location. Gone are the days when the "PBX" was a box or two screwed onto a plywood wall in some room. Today's UC systems are typically running on commodity servers and communicating with different internal components via network connections over IP. If the internal communication is all over IP, there is no reason those components cannot be distributed to where they make most sense. The "call server" can be in one data center while the voice-mail server can be in another data center with more storage. The IM server can be co-located with the call server or located in yet another data center. Even better, the UC system can have redundant components located in each data center for disaster recovery or for load balancing.

Your UC system can distribute functionality even further over IP out into hosted services existing "in the cloud." You've already seen this in Chapter 5, "SIP Trunking and PSTN Interconnection," where gateways to the PSTN have been pushed from being expensive hardware located on your premise to being inexpensive services out in the cloud. Now, there are services where you could push all of the telecommunications functionality out into the cloud. The entire PBX would be out in a hosted center. The phones on your desk would connect out through your IP network across the Internet (or a wide area network [WAN]) to the hosted provider. The business case may make sense for you to do this.

You can push applications out into the cloud as well. Say that, for a brief time, you wanted to have a customer satisfaction survey after every call into your call center, but you did not want to run the application on your own network. For this, you could use Session Initiation Protocol (SIP) to have the call transfer from your call center across the IP network to a hosted application platform where the survey application runs. You could also create automated IM agents or "bots" that connect to your IM network and provide information to your users (such as looking up information in a database) that could be on your premises or out in a hosted cloud. You could create "mashups" where through voice or IM you are interacting with an application, either on your premises or in a hosted service that then uses "Web services" to communicate with services in the cloud for additional information. For instance, if you wanted to be able to provide someone with directions to get to your office from wherever they are, you could make a query to Google Maps or Yahoo!Maps to get the information and return it to the person requesting the information. The possibilities are near endless.

The question for you, naturally, is: how in the world do you secure such a distributed system?

ANATOMY OF ATTACKS AGAINST DISTRIBUTED SYSTEMS

Complexity is the enemy of security in that the more complex a system becomes the harder it is to secure. Today's UC systems can have a great number of different components and a high level of complexity. Given the idea of a distributed system where functionality is spread out all across the IP network, let's think again of what the attackers are most likely trying to disrupt with their attacks:

- **Confidentiality** – The attackers want to gain access to information that you and your organization have. Eavesdropping on communications may provide this.
- **Integrity** – The attackers want to modify the communications traffic within or to and from your organization. They may want to modify the actual media sessions as you saw in Chapter 3, "Eavesdropping and Modification," or they may want to modify the control channel as you saw in Chapter 4, "Control Channel Attacks: Fuzzing, DoS, SPIT, and Toll Fraud," to, for instance, route their own traffic across your network at your cost.
- **Availability** – The attackers may simply want to disrupt your communication architecture so that either the entire organization cannot communicate well or the specific individuals may not be able to communicate.

Of these three kinds of attacks, *availability* is perhaps the largest concern simply because it is the easiest kind of attack to pull off. If the attacker can identify the source address of a remote worker's home office, for instance, then taking that person off your communication network can be a matter of simply launching a denial of service (DoS) or distributed DoS (DDoS) attack against their home IP address. If the attacker wants to disrupt the ability of people to leave voice-mail messages at a hosted service, the attacker can again launch a DoS or DDoS attack at the connection points between that service and your data center. As you saw in Chapter 5, "SIP Trunking and PSTN Interconnection," an attacker can target your SIP trunks to try to disconnect your system from the PSTN. A DoS or DDoS attack may not be something an attacker can sustain for a long time, but if executed at a critical time could cause some serious disruption to your business. For example, consider a home-based salesperson trying to win some large contracts in the final days of a month. If they were to be knocked offline for that time period, the sales of the company could be impacted.

Obviously, both confidentiality and integrity are also very important, but as you saw in Chapter 3, "Eavesdropping and Modification," such attacks often require the attacker to get to a precise spot in the network path to be able to undertake such attacks. DoS and DDoS attacks have no such requirements, and availability is, therefore, far easier to disrupt.

Let's break the attacks into several categories and look at each attack individually:

- Attacks against remote workers
- Attacks against branch offices
- Attacks against distributed systems
- Attacks against federation
- Attacks against cloud-based services

Attacks against Remote Workers

First, let's consider the case of the remote "teleworker." You need to think in terms of two different types of remote workers: those with a fixed location and those who are mobile. Note, of course, that many remote workers may fit into both categories. They may have a fixed location home office with UC equipment there, and then they also may go on the road with their laptop or mobile phone and use the UC client on those devices while traveling.

Fixed Location Teleworkers

The first type is the "fixed location" teleworker who has a UC endpoint in, for instance, a home office. The endpoint doesn't typically move around. As shown in Figure 7.1, it is probably deployed behind a home firewall or in some similar type of scenario and connected to the Internet through a cable, digital subscriber line (DSL) or fiber connection.

Given the nature of mixed communication modalities within a UC system, there may, in fact, be multiple UC endpoints at the single location. For example, a user may have an IP phone on her desk for voice calls and a UC client on her home computer for IM, video, and other collaboration services. Alternatively, she may only have the UC software client and have all communication occur through that client. She may also have an additional UC client on her "smart phone" like a Blackberry or iPhone that may or may not be using her local Wi-Fi network for connectivity.

Note that the Internet connection is typically shared by the teleworker between the teleworker's work activities and the personal activities of the teleworker and his or her family. Traffic going in and out from the network will be related to the UC endpoint and the teleworker's corporate computer or laptop, but it will also come from other systems within the location. This is in contrast to, for example, a branch office where all the Internet traffic will be "work" traffic going from the branch office to the corporate office and back.

For an attacker, the fixed location teleworker represents a fairly straightforward attack. If the point is to disrupt availability, a standard DoS or DDoS attack can be

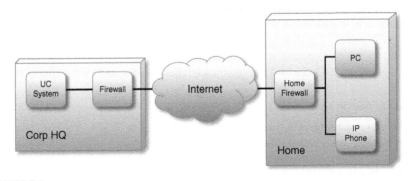

FIGURE 7.1

A Teleworker with a Fixed Location

launched against the IP address of the home network. Similarly, the fixed IP address clues the attacker in to where they have to attempt to get with regard to the network path to be able to eavesdrop or modify packets.

> **NOTE**
>
> Given that home networks are usually receiving dynamic IP addresses from their Internet service provider (ISP), those addresses will typically change when the cable/DSL modem or other connection device is power-cycled. For this reason, the attack might stop after a modem power-cycle and then return again once the attacker has again identified the IP address.

The attacker can also attempt to disrupt or compromise the home gateway device such as a router or firewall that the remote worker is using. Through simple network device fingerprinting techniques, the attacker may be able to find out the make and the model of the home gateway and perhaps the version number of the included software. The attacker can then research vulnerabilities and attempt to compromise the home gateway device directly. Depending upon the vulnerability, the attacker may be able to shut down the home gateway or execute commands. Given that many of these home gateways may be commodity boxes purchased at local electronics stores, home users are probably not thinking about regularly checking for updates to firmware, and so on, and so the boxes may over time become quite vulnerable.

Sadly, as noted in the description of the Pena/Moore VoIP fraud case at the beginning of Chapter 4, "Control Channel Attacks: Fuzzing, DoS, SPIT, and Toll Fraud," the attacker may just be able to login to the gateway device with the default administrative username and password if the home user hasn't changed it. Once into the system, the attacker may be able to modify the system in various subtle ways. For instance, the attacker could change the DNS server addresses being given out to point to DNS servers under the attacker's control, which might give incorrect or malicious addresses for specific sites. If the home gateway runs a standard operating system, the attacker might be able to install monitoring software that would let the attacker execute the attacks you learned about in Chapter 3, "Eavesdropping and Modification." The home gateway represents a network traffic "choke point" that is the ideal place for an attacker to place monitoring software.

Finally, the attacker can always try to compromise one of the computer systems behind the gateway device through viruses, malware, and so on. For example, the attacker could send the home user an e-mail message with a malicious attachment or pointing to a malicious Web site. If the user could be tricked into opening the attachment or visiting the Web site, malware would then be installed on the computer system which would, presumably, make contact with the external attacker from inside the home network. Once this occurs, the attacker now has a conduit into the internal network for whatever kind of attacks he or she wants to make.

Mobile Teleworkers

Truly mobile teleworkers (like "road warriors," who spend most of their time traveling around to various locations) are a different story. On the one hand, they are a bit harder for a focused attacker to attack purely because their IP address will be constantly changing. The attacker has to somehow identify where the remote worker is, perhaps by monitoring traffic to and from a company's SIP gateway. Once the attacker can identify where the remote attacker is, then he or she can begin their standard list of attacks, but the initial identification may be troublesome.

On the other hand, the mobile teleworker may be using their laptop or other device on untrusted networks. For instance, they may pop into a "Wi-Fi café" to quickly check e-mail, IM, or to make a few calls. They may use hotel or conference networks or networks at the location they are visiting. In all of these instances, you do not necessarily have any idea about the security of the network they are using. There may be someone on the café Wi-Fi network, for instance, running network scanning tools just to see what kind of "interesting" traffic may be going across the network. They may not be focused on trying to attack your company, but they may just stumble upon your traffic and inadvertently learn interesting information. If, for instance, you had unencrypted Real-time Transport Protocol media streaming from the UC softphone back to the corporate office, an attacker on the café Wi-Fi could conceivably listen to all those conversations.

Another more subtle point is that the mobile teleworker is using their laptop or mobile device directly on a network where an attacker could be, as shown in Figure 7.2. Unlike the fixed location teleworker, there is no firewall device between the teleworker's computer and the attacker when they both reside on the same network segment. A fixed location teleworker will have some sort of home router, gateway, or firewall in place. As mentioned in the section "Fixed Location Teleworkers," this device has the potential to be compromised if not patched regularly, but at least it is there and has almost always been developed with network security or access control in mind. The mobile teleworker, on the other hand, is using a laptop directly on a potentially hostile network with only whatever protections that the operating system installed on that laptop provides.

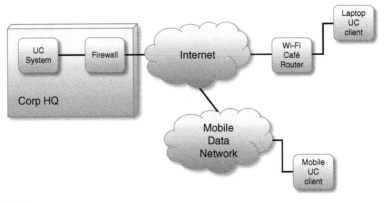

FIGURE 7.2

A Mobile Remote Worker Connects from Wherever They Are

Now, most laptop operating systems do include a firewall to protect the system when on these types of networks, but the question is really one of whether the user has the full protection of the firewall enabled. The user might, for instance, have disabled the firewall while in their home office in order to install or use some specific application. When they then left to travel, they forget to re-enable their firewall and as a result wind up at a Wi-Fi café with a completely open laptop with no firewall turned on.

To attack the mobile teleworker, if the attacker can determine the IP address of the laptop or mobile device he or she can execute a DoS or DDoS against the address. Similarly, the attacker can attempt to find vulnerabilities in the system so that the system can be compromised and monitoring software can be installed or he or she could execute any of the other attacks you learned in Chapter 2, "Insecure Endpoints" or Chapter 3, "Eavesdropping and Modification."

Attacking the Corporate Side

Naturally, rather than attacking individual users, the attacker could instead target the corporate side of the network seen in Figures 7.1 and 7.2. If the attacker can identify, for instance, that all SIP traffic from remote workers goes through a SIP gateway with a specific IP address, the attacker can target that IP address for a DoS or DDoS attack and wind up shutting down communication to all remote workers. Similarly, the attacker can attempt to compromise that gateway system with the goal of installing monitoring software that would give the attacker access to information about all remote communication. Depending upon the purpose of the attack, this may be the best way to achieve the goals the attacker has.

Attacks against Branch Offices

Many UC systems may use the IP network to deploy endpoints into branch offices without installing a great amount of equipment on the premises of the branch office. As shown in Figure 7.3, the branch office may simply have a few IP phones, UC clients on PCs, and perhaps a local PSTN gateway for "survivability" in the case of a failed connection to the corporate office.

The connection between the branch office and the corporate office might be the actual public Internet, particularly in the case of very small branch offices, but it might also be a private WAN created by the company's ISP using a technology like multiprotocol layer switching VPNs across the ISPs network. If the branch office is connected to the corporate office via a private WAN with no visibility to the public Internet, an attacker has a much more challenging task. He or she must somehow gain access to the internal network in order to attack the network of the branch office. It certainly can be done – it is just more difficult.

If the branch office is connecting over the public Internet, the attacks against it are very similar to the attacks against the fixed location teleworker. The attacker can try to execute a DoS or DDoS against the IP address of the branch office. The attacker can try to compromise the gateway device on the network or try to compromise a

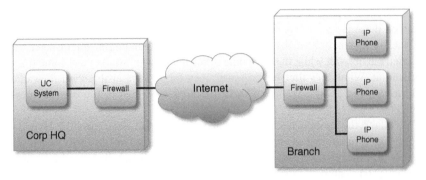

FIGURE 7.3

Branch Offices in UC Systems May Use the Central Services Located Back in the Corporate Office

system on the inside of the branch office. One difference from an individual teleworker location is that with a branch office it may be that *all* traffic will be sent across a VPN into the corporate office. In this case, the attacker will only see one single stream of encrypted traffic going between the branch office and the corporate office versus a number of separate different streams. As the attacker cannot see inside the stream of encrypted traffic, he or she cannot easily deduce patterns from watching the traffic and guess what kind of communication is occurring.

> **NOTE**
>
> Do note that there is research[A] that demonstrates that it is possible to determine if certain kinds of traffic are being encrypted within an IPSec tunnel. You should, therefore, not assume that traffic analysis is not possible on a VPN connection.

Attacks against Distributed Systems

As noted in the introduction to this chapter, organizations can now distribute components of the UC system across the IP network to wherever they make the most sense to be. Figure 7.4 shows a distributed system where IM, presence, and call servers have been distributed across three offices while a self-service Interactive Voice Response (IVR) system is located in one office and voice mail has been centralized in another office. Also, only two of the offices have actual connections out to the PSTN.

It could be that the IVR system makes sense to be in that one location where there are also business systems or databases that feed directly into the IVR's responses. Similarly, the voice-mail system might make sense to be in one data center that has the largest pool of storage servers for all the audio files.

[A]http://citeseerx.ist.psu.edu/viewdoc/download?doi=10.1.1.100.7742&rep=rep1&type=pdf

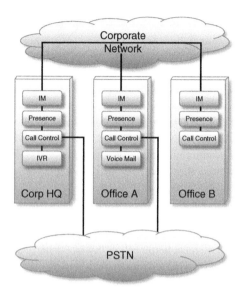

FIGURE 7.4

A UC System with Components Distributed across Three Offices

The business rationale will vary from organization to organization as to why different components may reside in different locations, but the point is that this kind of large-scale distribution is now possible, whereas in the past, it was unthinkable. From a security point of view, there are advantages in this distribution in that you can spread functionality around and create a system that is extremely reliable and able to function in the case of outages or disasters. The disadvantages, though, certainly revolve around the fact that you add complexity to your infrastructure and increase the number of points at which an attacker can attack your system.

This increase in the "surface area" of possible attacks is the biggest difference with attacks on distributed systems. In Chapter 3, "Eavesdropping and Modification," you learned about how an attacker could get software into the network path to listen in to or modify audio, video, or IM sessions. In a massively distributed system, there are just more network paths in which the attacker can potentially insert monitoring software. Now the good news, of course, is that with many more network paths, it is that much harder for an attacker to listen to all conversations. The bad news is that there are many more devices out in the network that need to be hardened, secured, and so on and the chances of an attacker finding one that can be exploited are that much higher.

Now for many organizations, especially larger ones, this distributed system will exist entirely across a private internal WAN between offices. Given this, the attacker needs to first gain access to some part of the internal network and then be able to execute the attacks you have learned about in all the earlier chapters of this book. If the attacker is a disgruntled employee, then obviously he or she may have all the access needed.

Attacks against Cloud-based Services

As organizations have moved increasingly to IP-based communications systems and are able to distribute UC system components around their own internal network, the question naturally comes up: if it makes more sense to do so, why can't I distribute some of those components out to external networks over IP?

Of course, the answer is that you can distribute those components anywhere on the IP network. As a result, you have seen the huge surge of interest in solutions over the past few years that are called *cloud, hosted, managed, software-as-a-service,* or whatever other terms various marketing departments create. Figure 7.5 shows the same network as in Figure 7.4, except with the IVR and voice-mail functions pushed out to the "cloud" of various service providers.

The organization may want to push components out into the cloud for multiple reasons. The hosted provider may be able to provide better scaling of capacity than the organization can provide on their own premises or the hosted offering may be more cost-effective. It may have better reliability or business continuity advantages. It may allow a project to be deployed faster than an on-premise installation would. There are any number of reasons why a company may choose to "use the cloud." They may, in fact, decide to outsource their entire UC system to a hosted offering from any number of vendors including Microsoft with Office Communications Online[B] and IBM with LotusLive.[C]

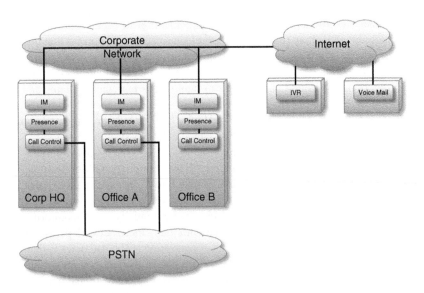

FIGURE 7.5

Components of a UC System Can Be Pushed Out into Hosted Services

---

[B]www.microsoft.com/online/office-communications-online.mspx
[C]www.lotuslive.com/en/a

Alternatively, an organization may use "the cloud" for only a very small service, such as using a Web service for geographic lookups. The security exposure you have related to cloud-based services depends upon how and where you are integrating such services into your communications infrastructure.

With regard to attacks against cloud-based services, the primary difference between cloud services and the distributed systems in the previous chapter is that typically you may be connecting to the cloud service across the public Internet. Now, some of the providers may allow you to bring in a connection directly from your data center, but others may not let you do this. Likewise, some providers may support a VPN from your location to theirs while others may only want communication to occur across the public Internet.

TIP

When evaluating cloud-based services, ask the provider if you can bring a private connection in from your network into the provider's network. If you are able to do so, even at an additional cost, you eliminate the risk of having your corporate traffic traverse the public Internet. If you cannot bring in your own connection, find out about establishing a VPN between your location and the provider.

Obviously, if you have corporate traffic going across the public Internet, you now have many more attack points to worry about and many more network paths that an attacker can attempt to infiltrate. Whether across the public Internet or across a private connection, the key is that if an attacker can get in the right network path, he or she can execute the attacks found in all the previous chapters of this book.

The added dimension is that you have to worry about the security of the service at the cloud provider that is outside of your control. If you establish even a private connection to the cloud provider, what happens if an attacker compromises a system there at the cloud provider? Can the attacker then ride the private connection back into your own network? What defenses do you have in place to protect against this? What about the security and privacy of your data at the service provider? Is it safe there? Could an attacker compromise a server there and read or listen to all your data? (You'll soon learn some questions to ask providers in the upcoming section "How to Defend against Attacks on Distributed Systems.")

Attacks against Federation

As you learned briefly in the "Federation" section in Chapter 1, "The Unified Communications Ecosystem," with organizations moving to using UC systems, there is increased interest in "federating" UC systems between companies. The primary interests are in (1) sharing presence information between companies so that an employee at Company A can know when someone at Company B is available and in which communication modalities the person can be contacted (that is, voice, video, IM, and so on) and (2) being able to communicate from the private internal UC system at Company A directly to the private internal UC system at Company B. This communication between UC systems might take the form of voice, video, IM, or other collaboration technologies.

There are two main forms of federation: intra-domain and inter-domain.

Intra-domain Federation

In intra-domain federation, two or more UC systems exist within the same administrative domain such as a single company or organization. As shown in Figure 7.6, the UC systems connect to each other across the internal corporate network. They could be in separate offices, as shown in Figure 7.6, or they could be in a single building.

The two different UC systems might exist as a form of load sharing where a certain number of users are placed on one system and others are on another system. Alternatively, the different systems may be the result of acquisitions and mergers or as a result of a corporate directive to use multiple vendors or to divide the company across certain organizational lines. Whatever the reason, there are two or more different UC systems connected together and sharing information.

For an attacker to eavesdrop, modify, or disrupt the communication between the two UC systems, he or she obviously needs to get onto the network path between the two UC systems. Unless the attacker is an internal person (such as the proverbial disgruntled system administrator), the first challenge for the attacker is to get through external defenses and get to the internal network where the connection occurs. Once on the network, the attacker can then attempt to perform any of the attacks mentioned in the previous six chapters of this book.

TIP

If you want to learn more about intra-domain federation, for SIP/SIMPLE you can look at the Internet Draft draft-ietf-simple-intradomain-federation[D] and for XMPP you can look at the expired Internet Draft draft-saintandre-xmpp-presence-analysis.[E]

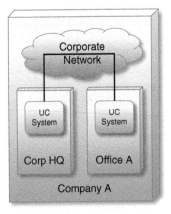

FIGURE 7.6

In Intra-domain Federation, Different UC Systems within the Same Company Communicate

---

[D] http://tools.ietf.org/html/draft-ietf-simple-intradomain-federation
[E] http://tools.ietf.org/html/draft-saintandre-xmpp-presence-analysis-03

Inter-domain Federation

Inter-domain federation extends the federation between two or more UC systems to be between multiple companies or organizations. Figure 7.7 shows the UC system at Company A connected to the UC system at Company B over the public Internet, but the connection could also be over a VPN or a private WAN established by a common service provider.

A connection is established between the two companies, hopefully protected by a secure transport mechanism, that is, a VPN or other forms of encryption. A secure method of authentication between the two domains takes place and then some amount of data from one UC system is allowed to cross over to the other UC system.

Note this potentially large difference between intra-domain and inter-domain federations. With intra-domain federation, because it is all within the same company chances are that the information exchange is basically wide open. All the information in a user's profile or rich status information on the first UC system may be directly shared over to the second UC system. You want to encourage collaboration between people within the same company.

With inter-domain federation, on the other hand, for privacy reasons, you may only want to expose certain attributes across the connection to the other UC system. You may be fine sharing, for instance, the primary telephone number, e-mail address,

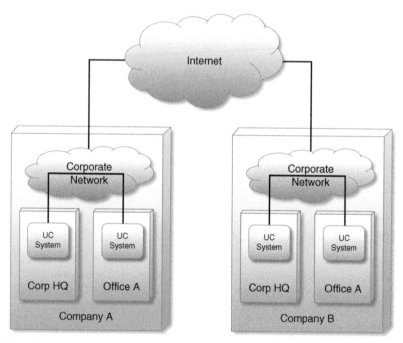

FIGURE 7.7

In Inter-domain Federation, UC Systems within Different Companies Communicate and basic presence status, but you may not want to share additional phone numbers and rich status information (such as mood messages). You will need to look as you set up federation at how you can restrict the information flowing between the two systems. You may also only want to provide presence information from certain people on one system across to the other system.

One of your greatest challenges with inter-domain federation is that the other company presumably has a completely different IT organization with different security policies than your company does. Your zone of trust expands to encompass the users at the other company to the extent you decide to trust them. You certainly can restrict the information to a degree, but in the end, you do need to trust them to not act maliciously.

> **WARNING**
>
> There are nuances here to consider. For instance, what if Company B suddenly started routing call traffic to the PSTN across the federation connection and out the SIP trunk connected to Company A's UC system, running up Company A's bill? How do you restrict that? How would you monitor it? All questions to think about.

Inter-domain routing is obviously a bit easier for an external attacker because in most cases part of the connection is going to be routed across either the public Internet or some other larger network. This simply widens the number of points at which the attacker can attempt to get in or near enough to the network path of your traffic.

As with intra-domain federation, if an attacker can get to the right point in the network, he or she can attempt an attack.

> **TIP**
>
> For more information about inter-domain federation, you may want to look at RFC 5344,[F] "Presence and IM Peering Use Cases."

DANGERS OF ATTACKS AGAINST DISTRIBUTED SYSTEMS

Distributed systems have the inherent issue that they are spread across a large network area and have a correspondingly higher number of points at which the attacker can attempt to gather information or cause disruption. The dangers should be familiar to you at this point in the book and include: availability, eavesdropping, modification, and fraud.

[F] http://tools.ietf.org/html/rfc5344

DoS/Availability

Obviously, as has been highlighted throughout this chapter, DoS and DDoS attacks are among the greatest threats to distributed systems, primarily because by the nature of a distributed system there are that many more points at which the system can be attacked. An attacker can cause serious business damage if he or she can disrupt the connection between components of a company's UC system, between a UC system and a component hosted in the cloud, or between multiple UC systems that are federated.

EPIC FAIL

In August 2007, Skype experienced a major outage where many of the 8 million online users it had at the time were unable to login at all.[G] For the better part of several days, many Skype users were unable to use the service at all. It ultimately turned out not to be a problem caused by an attacker, but rather a problem with Skype's network management routines when the systems were hit by a large number of individual client computers rebooting.[H] With distributed systems of any type, you do need to look at configuration issues to see if they might cause self-inflicted attacks like these.

Eavesdropping

With the eavesdropping attacks mentioned in Chapter 3, "Eavesdropping and Modification," the attacker had to get in the network path between the endpoint and the UC system or between components of the UC system in order to be able to observe the network traffic. With a distributed system, there are more network paths between components and the network paths are likely longer, which makes it easier for the attacker to get into the path or near enough to eavesdrop on the traffic, either in real-time or at a later date.

Also note that in the case of federation, the attacker could potentially learn information about your federation partners. Consider also that you need to think not only about the eavesdropping on the specific messages or media but also the *aggregate patterns* of who is calling whom and so on, if the control channel is not secured.

Modification

Similarly, there are more points where an attacker can execute a man-in-the-middle attack and attempt to modify information flowing between the components of the system. Some of the threats to an individual UC system were discussed back in Chapter 3, "Eavesdropping and Modification," but consider the case of federation where an attacker could modify, say, presence information between two companies so that someone at one of the companies appears to be away when he or she isn't, or

---

[G]www.disruptivetelephony.com/2007/08/skype-disrupted.html
[H]www.disruptivetelephony.com/2007/08/skype-offers-fu.html

appears to be off the phone when they in fact are. These kinds of modifications could impact business communication and also make the users not to trust the system and the presence information.

Fraud

Toll fraud remains a constant threat. As mentioned in the "Warning" in the previous section, what if your federation partner starts to route traffic across the federation bridge and out your SIP trunk? What if you use weak authentication so that an attacker can connect to your UC system as if his or her system was in fact your federation partner's? In both of these cases, the business could be defrauded.

THE FUTURE OF ATTACKS AGAINST DISTRIBUTED SYSTEMS

It is very clear that UC systems will continue to be further distributed across the ever-growing IP network. There is a perfect confluence of three trends:

1. Network bandwidth that is larger and more available;
2. Smarter and more powerful endpoint devices and software;
3. Increasingly powerful hosted "cloud" systems offering all sorts of services.

UC systems will continue to take advantage of all of these trends to provide more collaboration and communication options to users. Let's look a bit more at a few of the trends.

Mobility

The past few years have brought an amazing range of new "smartphone" devices. We have seen the phenomenal success of the Apple iPhone,[I] the openness of Google's Android[J] devices, the solid growth of RIMs Blackberry devices,[K] and the entrance of many other smaller players into the market. You now have incredible power in the mobile device that you generally carry everywhere with you.

These mobile devices are now also carrying UC or VoIP clients on them. Skype is available for multiple devices. Multiple SIP phones can be found. Other collaboration clients are available as well. With some carriers, you can now make VoIP phone calls over the cellular data network. Some devices will also let you stream video over the cellular data network as well. The ability to have your UC client with you always is now very possible.

From a security point of view, there are multiple challenges here. On a base level, there is a physical device out there with login credentials to your UC system that is

---

[I]www.apple.com/iphone/
[J]www.android.com/
[K]www.blackberry.com/

probably set by default to allow the user in so that they don't have to keep entering the credentials. What happens if the user loses the phone in a taxi cab and someone else picks it up? Will that new person be able to make calls? See what is being written on the internal network? On the larger level of distributed systems, your endpoints are now scattered over the mobile data network and the "regular" Internet. More network paths to be concerned about… more potential places for an attacker to probe… all of that must be considered.

Social Networks

UC systems are also interconnecting to social networks and services. Rich presence information is being brought in from Twitter. Chat connections are being made out to Facebook. It's the distributed "cloud," but a consumer-focused cloud where personal and business life is incredibly blurred. It's a cloud run by private companies that are mostly startups. Security is not clear with many of the services – yet, they are being connected to your UC systems in some ways. You need to understand how the connections are occurring and what you can do to minimize risk. There is no sign that interest in social networking is slowing down – if anything the interest is increasing. Expect them to continue to be added in various ways to your UC systems and for information to be distributed out to those systems and networks.

New Collaboration Technologies

The technology underlying UC systems is not standing still. It is continuing to rapidly evolve. There are many new developments in video, new ways to encode the video, many new endpoints, amazing "High Definition (HD)" display systems, and cameras embedded everywhere. Audio, too, is evolving. "Wideband" audio with far better sound quality than the PSTN is now commonly available. Web-based collaboration tools are getting easier and easier to use. All of these technologies are encouraging more and more people to look at IP-based communication tools (and as part of that there is almost the assumption that they can use the tools wherever and whenever they want, further distributing the UC system across the IP network).

New services are launching all the time, too. One of the more recent celebrated launches is Google Wave,[L] allowing people to collaborate in a service that is part e-mail, part wiki, part IM, and part document. Even more, the promise of Wave is that you will be able to run your own Wave server,[M] just as you can run your own e-mail and Web server. Again, as Wave is brought into UC offerings, it will further increase the options for distributing communication and collaboration with the corresponding increase in the attack surface.

An additional challenge is that much of this technology is being used in experimentation and trial without a great amount of research or security review. There are bound to be bugs – and ones that can be exploited.

[L]http://wave.google.com/
[M]www.waveprotocol.org/

Movement into the Cloud

Communication is increasingly moving into the cloud. While hosted offerings have been around for many years, the last few years have brought about the perfect conditions for further movement into cloud (or hosted, managed, or software-as-a-service) offerings. Network bandwidth has become incredibly inexpensive, plentiful, and ubiquitous. For the same price, you now can get better network connectivity in your car driving than you could in a fixed office environment a few years ago. The evolution of microprocessors has brought us extremely powerful mobile devices. With the increased mobility comes the desire to move more functionality out into the cloud.

Additionally, the industry has seen the great success of cloud-based offerings such as those of Amazon Web Services,[N] Google App Engine,[O] Microsoft Windows Azure,[P] and the Rackspace Cloud[Q] to name a few. A business model is now visible and is also being proven out on a daily basis through the use of these cloud platforms by a wide range of companies from startups to large enterprises.

This greater acceptance of the cloud means that more and more services will migrate into the cloud. There are both advantages and disadvantages to this migration. Cloud-based services can provide advantages in the rapid fixing of problems, in keeping up with changes in technology, and in providing options for disaster recovery and business continuity. However, they also mean hosting your applications or services on someone else's network, with all the uncertainties that brings and also the added complexity of connections between your network and the cloud.

The reality, though, is that more and more UC functionality will migrate to the cloud. You need to understand the potential security implications and be ready to ask the hard questions of your network and service providers.

Geography Does Matter

Finally, you should note that even though communication can get to an endpoint technically that doesn't mean necessarily that it should get to that endpoint legally. As much as we talk about how geography "doesn't matter" and about how we can scatter endpoints all over the globe, there is a reality that our legal systems are still very much entrenched in the world of geography. For instance, privacy legislation in some European countries that protects individuals' right to privacy of their data may mean that you cannot store that data on servers (or cloud services) that are located in a country where the laws allow the government total access to data on servers. You will need to understand the legislation of the countries in which you operate with regard to privacy, information protection, accounting reporting, and so on. Compliance with this legislation may seriously impact what your underlying network architecture may in fact look like.

Perhaps someday legislation will catch up with the global aspects of the IP network – but today is very definitely not that day.

[N]http://aws.amazon.com/
[O]http://appengine.google.com
[P]www.microsoft.com/windowsazure/
[Q]www.rackspacecloud.com/

HOW TO DEFEND AGAINST ATTACKS AGAINST DISTRIBUTED SYSTEMS

Let us now look at several strategies to defend against attacks against distributed systems.

Strategy #1: Deploy Secure Firewall Traversal Mechanisms

As you deploy endpoints anywhere you can find an IP address, as you link your on-premises UC system out to hosted systems "in the cloud", and as you federate your system with others – as you do all those things – you need to be sure that you have some way for the traffic to securely traverse your trust boundaries. It may be a session border controller, SIP-aware firewall, or some other device or application. The key is that your SIP or other traffic is securely flowing across the border device to and from UC systems or endpoints out onto the larger IP networks.

It may also help you to understand that many of these devices at the network edge are back-to-back user agents or B2BUAs that terminate a SIP connection on one side of the device and then create a new SIP connection on the other side. This creates a clear separation between the internal and the external connections.

Similarly, there are media proxies that help move the media across network borders securely. The key point is that you need to have a solution that lets you securely pass your traffic through or around your firewall.

Strategy #2: Ensure Understanding of Security at Fixed Locations

In a distributed UC system, you will have endpoints or systems deployed at fixed locations such as home offices or branch offices. You need to ensure that people at those locations have an understanding of what the security expectations are. If, for instance, the company has a VPN between a concentrator at the corporate office and the network device at a branch office, the branch workers need to understand whether or not only some or all traffic on their local network will be routed over the corporate network. So, for example, they shouldn't install an unencrypted Wi-Fi access point that allows just anyone to get onto the Wi-Fi network. Home office workers also need to understand what level of security they need to have in place in their home offices.

Strategy #3: Understand Security Ramifications of Federation

As you consider federation between UC systems, you need to understand the security ramifications of federation and what level of trust and reciprocity will exist with other federated entities, asking questions such as the following:

- Will you have a completely open relationship between the two (or more) federated entities?
- Will you only share some information?
- How can you enforce that?
- What is the security like in the other entity?

- How can privacy be ensured within the other entity?
- How will the transport between the two systems be secured?

You need to look at questions like these to determine which of the various strategies discussed in the previous six chapters will help you in a federated environment.

Strategy #4: Ensure Secure Authentication

Strong authentication is key. Whether you are connecting distributed remote end-points to a UC system, connecting UC systems together over a WAN, or connecting out to a hosted service – in all of those scenarios – there is some level of authentication that needs to occur so that communication can be established. Make sure that the authentication is strong. Where you can, use strong mechanisms like mutual certificates. If you have to use passwords, make sure they are strong. Above all, change default passwords!

Strategy #5: Secure Your Connections to Services in the Cloud

The first steps to being able to understand how you can secure your connections and services in the cloud is to ask potential providers a series of questions similar to the ones below. Your goal is to answer that question: how can I trust the cloud to be there? You are considering moving functionality from your data center out to someone else's. Can you be assured of at least as good, if not better, availability and security than you currently provide in your own data centers?

You can use questions like these below to help develop your list that you will ask the providers you are considering:

1. What kind of availability guarantees/service level agreements (SLAs) does the platform vendor provide?

   The vendor should be able to offer you some type of SLA. You may need to pay more or agree to certain network configuration mechanisms, but you should be able to obtain some kind of contract outlining the level of availability you should expect.

2. What kind of geographic redundancy is built into the underlying network?

   If the provider's service is sitting entirely in one data center in one geographic area, there is always the potential for disruption due to disasters or outages. Hurricanes, earthquakes, ice storms, floods – pick your natural disaster. The point is that you don't want to have your UC system lose some of its functionality because a major storm hit some part of the country. You need to look at hosting providers that do have geographic redundancy or you at least need to understand what exposure you have.

3. What kind of network redundancy is built into the underlying network?

   Does the hosted service rely only on a single Internet provider? Or if it connects to the PSTN, does it only use a single Internet telephony service provider

(ITSP)? Outages do happen and you want to be sure you are not reliant on a single Internet provider or ITSP.

4. What kind of physical redundancy is built into the data centers?

   For example, in the data centers the hosted service uses, are there multiple sources of power and air-conditioning? How reliable is the data center hosting the service?

5. What kind of monitoring does the provider perform?

   If you want your service to be available 24/7, what kind of monitoring does the provider perform? Do they have a network operations center (NOC) where someone is always monitoring the network? If so, is that NOC staffed 24/7? What kind of monitoring will the provider do of your services or applications? It's obviously great if the provider is monitoring their equipment and the overall health of their system, but what about your services or applications specifically? What if one of them stops working? Will the provider notice? How quickly will they respond?

6. What kind of scalability is in the cloud platform?

   One of the big reasons to choose a hosted platform is that you can easily scale and grow your application as your usage increases. How does the vendor provide scalability? What are the limits, if any, to how your usage can grow? Does the vendor have an overall limitation on the capabilities they can provide? How fast can the vendor provide additional capabilities?

7. What operating system or systems is the cloud platform actually running on? What are the patch management plans for the cloud platform?

   Is the platform based on Linux? UNIX? Microsoft Windows? Something else? This helps you have some understanding of the larger risk exposure you have. What are the patch management plans for the servers? How often do they patch systems? Do they test patches before deploying? Will they be testing the patches for your applications or are you expected to do that?

8. What kind of network security is part of the cloud platform?

   What does the provider do with regard to network security of the platform? Do they do periodic scanning or testing? Do they have specific security software in place? Do they have people trained specifically in network security? Does the provider have any certifications such as Payment Card Industry (PCI) compliance?

9. What kind of physical security is part of the cloud platform?

   Similarly, what kind of physical security does the provider have in place? Are the data centers secured against someone walking in pretending to be from the company and gaining physical access to the platform's servers? Is the company's office secured against people randomly walking in and gaining access to systems? For instance, does a company use keycards or similar tokens to restrict office access?

10. Finally, what will the vendor do if there is downtime?

Will the downtime be reflected in your bill? Will the provider give you credit or a refund for the time you lost? While not directly related to security, per se, this shows how willing the company is to stand behind its services.

SUMMARY

One of the most incredibly powerful aspects of UC systems is that you can have a UC endpoint wherever you can obtain an IP address. Even in areas where you might not have sufficient network bandwidth to support voice or video, you may be able to use IM. Where you do have sufficient bandwidth, voice, video, and other technologies can enable rich communication and collaboration between people in ways we could only have imagined in science fiction movies 5 or 10 years ago.

The ability to distribute specific functionality to wherever it makes most sense provides a level of efficiency and resiliency in UC systems that can deliver very real benefits to the business. You can install UC components in offices or data centers where they can most efficiently communicate with other business systems. You can distribute components so that they have extremely high "fault tolerance" and can continue your business in the face of disasters and other service interruptions. You can integrate your on-premises systems with services and applications hosted out in the cloud. All of these pieces can be connected together over the ubiquitous IP network.

You have seen throughout this book, though, that all this power and capability is not without its security challenges. What we call "UC" is actually an entire ecosystem of interconnected and interdependent applications and services. Weak security in one component can compromise the security of the overall system. You saw that some of those components might be endpoints – softphones, hardphones, IM clients, and more. You learned about how media channels could be intercepted or modified and about the incredible dangers of exposing the control channel to attackers. You learned about how SIP trunking is fundamentally changing the way businesses connect to the PSTN and about how the whole notion of "identity" gets changed in an environment where information can be so easily modified.

For all the challenges, though, and there are admittedly many, the truth remains that there are solutions out there and you can secure your UC systems. If you know the right questions to ask and places to look, you can definitely put a plan together to make your UC system secure.

With security done right, you have the potential to make your UC system more powerful, more capable, and more secure than the PSTN could ever be. How many of us had one of those boxes connected to our analog phone where we could press a big red button and "go secure?" Not many – but now we all can have end-to-end encryption that just works and covers not only voice but also video, IM, and other collaboration technologies.

Naturally, with security done wrong, your UC can be a playground for attackers that can cause serious damage to your business and incur very serious costs.

The choice, of course, is yours.

TIP

To learn more about UC security, obtain additional materials and stay up-to-date with information about this book, please visit the Web site for the book at www.7ducattacks.com

---

Index

Page numbers followed by *f* indicates a figure and *t* indicates a table.

If you've enjoyed reading about these attacks you will love *Seven Deadliest USB Attacks*, another book from our Seven Deadliest Attacks Series.

USB-Based Virus/Malicious Code Launch

INFORMATION IN THIS CHAPTER

- Invasive Species among Us
- Anatomy of the Attack
- Evolution of the Attack
- Why All the Fuss?
- Defending against This Attack

We are currently facing a problem of pandemic proportions with viruses and other forms of malicious code being propagated through unexpected avenues. Advanced tactics are making it increasingly difficult to identify the actual source of this mischief. A majority of these threats now appear to be originating from Asia with fluctuating functionality.[A] While the risk of being exposed to malicious code is nothing new, how you can be exposed to it is swiftly transforming.

In this chapter, we will examine the different types of malicious code, concealment practices, and propagation vectors. We will also describe how you can reconstruct an approach leveraging a USB flash drive and favorable methods of mitigation. Once you obtain a solid understanding of the logic behind these programs, you will be in a better position to protect yourself and data from compromise. *Malware* is a general term used to reference all types of malicious code. Throughout this chapter, we will use both of these terms interchangeably.

The culture of business today utilizes many forms of removable media for standard operation. The premise behind these new USB attacks is much like the ancient floppy assault as it relies on removable media devices to be inserted into the host. Nearly all of the recent USB-based malicious code attacks exploit the Windows autorun functionality. Depending on how the host is configured, these USB-based malicious programs can execute automatically without any user interaction.

[A]www.msnbc.msn.com/id/19789995/

INVASIVE SPECIES AMONG US

In the 1990s, dialer-type viruses, which had various payloads and purposes, were prevalent. Disguised as harmless software, some infections would result in dial-up connection redirection to pay-per-minute lines charging users thousands of dollars in fraudulent phone bills. A different attack occurring in the same time frame took aim at data on storage devices. The hack was able to manipulate ActiveX controls that enabled them to compromise computers attaching to their Web site.[B] They used this method to deploy a payload that searched locally attached drives for Quicken database files. Once found, it would modify the bank details, enabling them to wire funds to an account of their choosing.

A report issued by the US Army in November of 2008 indicated their computer infrastructure was under attack by a variant of the SillyFDC worm. Agent.BTZ is the name of this strain, and it used removable media as a primary means to contaminate new hosts. In an attempt to contain the worm, the US strategic command banned the use of all portable media types on its network. This included all USB keys, CDs, digital video discs (DVDs), flash drives, floppies, or any other form of removable media. Other strains of the SillyFDC worm are known to download additional malicious code from the Internet. These infections have been known to cause denial of service on networks using up bandwidth as it spreads and calls for reinforcements. Top Army officers are using this incident to tighten security around the use of personal or otherwise unauthorized devices on the network.[C]

Another interesting incident involving a malware infection of a government computer occurred on board the international space station in September of 2008. Officials from NASA stated that the virus was most likely introduced through an infected flash drive brought onboard by an astronaut for his or her personal use. "This is not the first time we have had a worm or a virus," NASA spokesman Kelly Humphries said. "It's not a frequent occurrence, but this isn't the first time." NASA declined to name the virus, but SpaceRef.com, which broke the story, reported that the worm was W32.Gammima.AG. This worm was first detected in August 2007 and installs software that steals credentials for online games.[1] The virus was able to propagate to other systems on the space shuttle network, which suggests a lack of security infrastructure to mitigate these behaviors.

In the last few years, there has been a considerable increase in these threats being spread via removable devices. Some USB-based devices are actually leaving the manufacturing plant infected. Vendors such as Seagate,[D] TomTom,[E] and Apple[F] top a long list of providers who have distributed infectious components. Again, these are eerily reminiscent of the boot sector virus era, when preconfigured

---

[B]http://news.cnet.com/2100-1023-271469.html
[C]http://articles.latimes.com/2008/nov/28/nation/na-cyberattack28?pg=3
[D]http://news.techworld.com/security/7881/tomtom-pre-infected-with-virus/
[E]www.pcworld.com/article/139576/seagate_ships_virusladen_hard_drives.html
[F]www.apple.com/support/windowsvirus/

floppies were leveraged as a propagation method. During this period, the compromised machines would contaminate additional floppies upon insertion and then spread once introduced into a fresh system. User interaction or a system reset was required for this to take place, but this method still posed a significant threat behind perimeter lines.

An Uncomfortable Presentation

Jessica was a senior sales engineer employed at a major security value-added reseller (VAR) in the Memphis area. Security sales had been skyrocketing recently due to new regulations and increasingly stringent amendments. Her company was having a difficult time keeping up with the demand for proposals, presentations, installations, and other key engagements. They had several openings for positions throughout the organization but were having a difficult time finding qualified personnel.

Matt, an associate sales engineer, had joined the firm a little over a month before and was trying to come up to speed in every direction. He had just graduated college with a BS in computer science and had very little real-world experience. Matt completed an internship at the VAR last spring and did well enough to earn a permanent position post graduation. Once hired, he was immediately assigned to the endpoint security sales team, which was where they were hurting the most. He was a well-rounded young man from a tough background who didn't mind digging in the trenches. This was an opportunity of a lifetime, and he wasn't going to screw it up.

Matt had only been with the firm a week before he fell victim to a twisted initiation prank. This was a new hoax that Bill, another senior sales engineer, had been dying to put into play for some time now. He had used this same trick before on a friend's computer, but this was the first time he had tried to introduce it on a USB pen drive. Included on this pen drive was a sound file with operational parameters defined to execute with gradual occurrence increases. It was also able to raise the speaker volume and disable audio management on the system. He also had a new antivirus (AV) and Host Intrusion Prevention System (HIPS) kill script; he was eager to test it on an unsuspecting victim.

Bill thought it would be best if he included some presentation and training material on the pen drive for misdirection purposes. He gathered up most of the current items he could find and saved them to the drive. Then, Bill strolled over to Matt's desk and tapped him on the shoulder. He told Matt that he should get familiar with the documents contained on the drive as soon as possible because they were recently updated and very relative to some of their new engagements. Matt replied indicating he would get right on top of it after he met with Jessica to work over lunch.

Matt enters the cafeteria and sees Jessica across the room at a table already eating her food and reading something on her laptop. He grabs some chow and sits down across from her, waiting patiently until she acknowledges his presence. A few minutes go by, and she finally initiates a conversation signifying her current state of affairs. Matt listens attentively as she describes her dilemma. After spilling her guts about all the problems Matt can't solve, she finally blurts one out that sparks a reply. She is looking for some updated statistics on data theft related to removable media devices but is unable to locate them on the sales shared drive. Matt chimes in, telling her that he might have just what she's looking for. He pulls out the pen drive that Bill gave him and hands it to her with a smirk of accomplishment.

She puts the pen drive into her laptop, and the autoplay dialogue appears with options. She opens Explorer to view the files and suddenly notices her computer acting sluggish. Just as quickly as the latency appeared, it vanishes, and her laptop performance is as fast as ever. She browses the drive and finds two presentations that might have what she is looking for. Sure enough, the first one she pulls up has data related to the areas that she was missing. She thanks Matt with a grateful grin and asks if he wants to come to a presentation she is giving in one of their conference rooms. Matt can't believe his ears; of course he is going to be there! Just as they are getting up to leave, Jessica hears a light gurgle coming from Matt's direction. She chalks it up to a typical male with an uncontrollable system and a lack of manners. They gather their stuff and head to the meeting room.

They arrive slightly early and begin to set up. A few of the executives have already arrived but are currently being distracted by her management staff. They scramble to get the laptop connected to the projector and place hard copies of the sales material out for everyone to view. Finally, after 10 min, they have everything in place. This is perfect timing, because the first guests are now entering the door. Just as soon as they cross the threshold, she hears that gurgle again, only this time it lasts a bit longer. She turns in disgust and looks toward Matt as if it were him again. He shrugs his shoulders and gives an innocent smile like he isn't to blame. The rest of the crowd finally starts flowing into the conference room, and she asks everyone to take a seat. She plugs the microphone into her computer and then proceeds to turn down the volume level, but she can't find it in her task bar. Hastily, she opens the control panel, and no audio icon shows there either. Then, she tries to use the buttons on the side of the laptop but gets no response when she toggles either direction. Finally, she locates an auxiliary volume control on the microphone, which is able to adjust the volume to a desirable level.

As she begins the introduction, one of the executives interrupts with a question. The inquiry is about a recent merger of theirs, which is completely out of her realm of knowledge. As silence envelops the room, her manager pipes up with a witty answer that pleases the customer. Just as she starts up the presentation, a thunderous, rumbling sound emanates around the room. There is no doubt as to what the sound is, although the question remains of who had done it. She immediately glares at Matt, who is, surprisingly, glaring back at her in the same manner. Her manager has a sincerely frightened look on his face and appears to try to utter something, only to hold himself back. Two of the executives are laughing, while the remaining managers are left with some stiff scowls.

Just as Jessica starts to apologize for the embarrassing incident, another earsplitting grumble cascades around the room. The tone is far too loud for any human to produce, even Matt. She realizes it has to be her PC, because the sounds are coming from the conference speakers. Knowing that no audio controls are available, she decides to shut down her laptop. As she scrambles to shut down everything, another deafening sound protrudes from the speaker system. Four of the customers stand up and begin to exit the conference room. Her manager jumps to his feet to walk with them out the door. Three of the other customers are still sitting in the room, snickering at her dilemma.

Jessica begins to express her regrets and beg for forgiveness when one of them interrupts her. He states that he had seen a similar situation occur with his administrative assistant's computer. His assistant's computer had been doing this for about a week before one of their support staff was able to identify and mitigate the problem. They discovered what was called a *fart virus* that set several audio files into play at random times. Their support staff was able to clean the infection immediately once it was identified. As the executive stood up to leave, he stated that their existing security staff might be adequate when compared to what her VAR could provide.

While this story may seem fictional, it actually occurred to an unsuspecting security professional. Some of the events and names have been changed to protect the innocent, but a majority of the plot is factual. There are a number of real-world cases involving a vast spectrum of entities and types of infections. The example used above could be considered minor when compared with the intent of other infectious material that leverages removable media.

ANATOMY OF THE ATTACK

Malicious code can best be described as any program that is intentionally written to induce an unexpected and undesirable event on operating system, network, application, or any of their dependencies. These are designed to seek and exploit weaknesses in the systems and applications they target and usually run without the express consent of the user. This includes but is not limited to virus, worms, Trojan horses, logic bombs, spyware, and rootkits. The code can also reside on Web pages in the form of Java applets, ActiveX controls, scripting languages, browser plug-ins, or pushed content.

There are several classification methodologies vendors supply or adopt that presently surround malicious code. All of them accentuate similar values but most provide a stale aspect for proper categorization given the current threat landscape. More recent types of malicious code now adhere to multiple categories. For simplicity purposes, we will break these down into a single section, "Malicious Code Methodologies."

Malicious Code Methodologies

Just as a biological virus interferes with the normal functions of the human body, computer viruses impede on customary operations of the infected environment. The digital cousins of the biological versions have been around for over a quarter of a century and are constantly mutating in multiple directions. They have the ability to replicate, inflict damage, modify data, steal sensitive information, and perform many other harmful actions. What is interesting about the current state of affairs is how viruses have transformed to exploit the rapid expansion of the technology sector as it adapts to us. Virus authors have become quite clever in how they are designing their composite creations. Nowadays, malicious programs are designed to call other inter-active components to perform specific tasks. They can be configured to cooperate with almost any part of an application so long as an interface or connector exists to facilitate the communication. By taking this approach, developers no longer have to reinvent the wheel every time they seek to provide enhancements or modifications.

Viruses can best be described as programs that propagate by contaminating other files or programs on a single host. An actual virus is unable to transmit an infection to a new host without human interaction.[G] The payloads delivered by a virus can take on many forms. The next sections will provide a brief overview of the different methods that can be applied.

Worms

A worm is a type of malware that has the ability to propagate itself without user interaction. These do not usually require a host program to exist. Worms take advan-tage of file or other information transports on the system it has infected. One of the most common transports would be e-mail programs. Once a system is infected with a worm, the program will replicate itself by using network services or applications to distribute copies. This particular variety can often wreak havoc on network band-width and system resources.

Trojans

Unlike viruses and worms, Trojans do not reproduce by duplication. These malicious programs attempt to masquerade as a typical application. They work by hiding within the proximity of what seems like normal software running on the target system. Once the machine becomes compromised, a variety of payloads can be deployed, including most viruses and worms.

Many types of the Trojan variants have been known to steal passwords and other personal data stored on the hard drive. They usually send this information to Internet servers or open a backdoor for developer access. Infected users may notice computer performance degradation and strange behaviors that occur without any interaction. Trojans frequently include features that disable or alter the settings on desktop fire-walls, antivirus software, and download reinforcements.

Logic and Time Bombs

A logic bomb is commonly defined as an attribute or a portion of code running within a program that remains inactive until a specific event or time occurs. An excellent example of logic bombs are those used to encourage infected computers to purchase

---

[G]http://irchelp.org/irchelp/security/trojanterms.html

software for artificially induced circumstances. Numerous spyware and AV removal vendors have been known to abuse this type of function for financial gain.[H]

Time bombs are a type of logic bomb that will continuously poll the system date in a dormant state until the authors predetermine rendezvous is reached. At this point, the program will activate and execute its code. These methods are also used commonly by valid software vendors to provide trial periods for evaluation. An example of this would be an application that authorizes only 10 initializations before the program ceases to function.

Rootkits

Rootkits are nothing more than a kit of tools designed to get and maintain root. The term *root* is universally acknowledged as being the highest level of access for UNIX and Linux systems. Dub this into the Windows world and you have a nasty intruder with a bad attitude and administrator access. Primary activities include backdoor admittance, accessing log files, or covertly monitoring any and all activity on the user's computer.

Malicious intent is not the constant rationale behind a rootkit deployment. Sony is probably the most memorable example of a company with legitimate intentions ultimately gone wrong. They attempted to deploy a Digital Rights Management mechanism by way of a rootkit, which was ultimately exploited by malicious code makers. A class-action lawsuit was concluded in 2005 over this issue with additional matters still pending.[I]

Trapdoors

Trapdoors are small amounts of residual code embedded within valid programs originally included by the programmer, which can enable access into the system. They typically have a genuine purpose, such as an alternate path for the developer to access the application if something goes awry during testing. Some are used to bypass setup and authentication sequences, which can be considered cumbersome during program development. These remnants can become a huge risk when they are forgotten or left behind unintentionally.

Macros

A macro is a type of simple script used to automate routine tasks within spreadsheets or word-processing documents. Macro viruses have the ability to self-propagate locally as well as remotely. If the user shares a contaminated file via e-mail, USB flash drive, or other means, the contagious behaviors will continue. Macro viruses can be written by those with minimal skills and can spread to any platform on which the application is running. Chapter 5, "Office – Macros and ActiveX," from *Seven Deadliest Microsoft Attacks* (ISBN: 978-1-59749-551-6), covers these types of attacks in greater detail.

[H]http://rogueantispyware.blogspot.com/2009_07_01_archive.html
[I]www.eff.org/cases/sony-bmg-litigation-info

Boot Sector

These viruses target the boot sector of local hard or removable drives. They infect these devices by replacing part or all of the boot record. This record is the portion of the disk that tells the operating system how to load in memory. They will occasionally relocate these vital files, or in extreme cases, they will be overwritten. Boot sector viruses are very difficult to remove because they load into memory every time the computer is booted. Access to this level of a system is difficult to attain and has been historically transmitted by physical means.

Spyware

"Spyware" is a generic term used to describe software that is implicitly designed to collect data about the Internet search habits or other private information without the user's consent. Spyware is commonly associated with software used to display advertising. Typically, these programs get placed on a system during the installation of other software the user actually wants. Browser plug-ins, ActiveX updates, infected ads, or free shareware tools top a long list of distribution mechanisms.

Once installed on the computer, information can be secretly collected through a variety of techniques. These include keyloggers and Internet browsing history, as well as scanning files and registry entries on the hard drive. The purpose of these infections can vary greatly, but they are primarily used to track personal information for targeted marketing functions. Malicious forms of spyware can be used to collect sensitive information such as passwords, user accounts, or even bank-related information.

Metamorphic Code

Some viruses adapt and rewrite themselves completely each time they infect a new host computer or program. This type of program is said to be metamorphic. Metamorphic-based viruses are often very large and complex due to the programming required to support their functionality. They come complete with their own onboard metamorphic engine, which drives their ability to "morph" into new mutations of themselves. The engine can also undergo changes as it continues to spread and infect new files. This type of virus is programmed to avoid detection by common antivirus software, which often focuses on specific patterns or infected files.

Polymorphic Code

Polymorphic code is similar to metamorphic-based viruses in that it has the capability to rewrite itself after each new infection. These differ from metamorphic code in that they spread infected files and programs via an encrypted copy of themselves. A decryption module, also referred to as the *mutation engine*, is built into this program and is used to decrypt the required components so it can deliver the intended payload. In order for the program to actually work, the mutation engine must remain unencrypted. This is the characteristic that normally leads to detection and eventually the program's demise.

Variable Key Encryption

Similar to a polymorphic virus, this type of code also makes use of a decryption module. There are two distinct differences that separate this into its own classification. One of these differences is that the entire package is encrypted. The other dissimilarity is the utilization of a decryption module consisting of encryption keys instead of an algorithm for propagation decoding. These encryption keys resemble a password and are used to decode the payload as it transmits to new hosts. The newly infected files contain copies of the original, but the password to decrypt the code is changed.

Java Applets

Created by Sun, Java applets are a type of program developers add to Web pages to provide interactive components or enhanced functionality to the site. An Active Server Page or a Windows Scripting Host containing these modules can be extremely hazardous. These can allow unrestricted access to computer resources, which include the file system, registry, and applications.

While most are legit, some hostile applets exist, which can take command of the operating system, alter system files, or prevent the use of specific applications. Their popularity among Web developers is largely attributed to the cross-platform support of different operating systems and Web browsers. This also entices the hacking community because they have the ability to automatically execute when a user visits a Web site. In the time it takes a browser to render the page, the applet is loaded and the malicious code is run on the machine. These applets are sometimes planted by malicious authors, but taking control of existing applets is possible and is usually the result of poor coding. Since loading applets is a normal activity while surfing the Web, these attacks are rarely detected by standard security measures. Java applet attacks can deceive even the most savvy computer user.

ActiveX Controls

ActiveX is a collection of tools developed by Microsoft that enables Windows applications to have increased functionality across networked environments. An ActiveX control is a program built into a Web site to enhance the user's experience with other applications running within the site. It could be said that ActiveX is Microsoft's answer to Sun Java applets.

These controls can be written in many different languages, including C++, Visual Basic, Visual C++, Delphi, Powersoft, Java, C-Sharp (C#), and Visual J++ to name a few. They can be coded to run in different ways depending on the instructions passed to the program by the scripting language that interacts with it. Obviously, Windows Internet Explorer (IE) is a prime example of a browser where ActiveX controls are frequently developed. For instance, IE does not have the ability to display Adobe Portable Data Files or advertisements using flash programs exclusively. Instead, IE leverages an ActiveX control that enables significant versatility. This flexibility comes with a trade-off, as malicious code can be unintentionally downloaded from Web sites while the user is installing an ActiveX control.

Browser Plug-Ins

Browser plug-ins, also known as *snap-ins*, are small applications that extend the functionality of browsers for specific applications built into Web sites. They are very similar to ActiveX controls and Java applets except that they are explicitly designed to support the functionality of specific applications running within a Web page. Examples of plug-ins include Media Player, QuickTime Player, Shockwave Player, and Real One Player. Depending on how a Web page is designed, certain plug-ins may be required in order to view the content.

Introduction of security risks often occurs when these plug-ins are left stale due to lack of updates. In turn, this leaves the user's browser and entire system vulnerable to attack or exploit. Since these applications are running behind the scenes, they are frequently overlooked, as many users often forget to check for updated versions. It's important to remember that plug-ins are not automatically patched when the browser is updated. Be sure to update these on a regular basis to minimize the likelihood of exploitation.

Pushed Content

Push technology enables news and other content providers to automatically supply subscribers with information by downloading content directly to the user's desktop. This technology also provides a means by which software companies, oblivious to security, supply their users with automatic updates. These programs are activated when a user installs a small agent onto the system, which is called a *push-client*. The client constantly polls the provider's server and transports the latest news, stock quotes, sports scores, and so forth. Just as software developers (Sony) have inadvertently provided CD-ROMs to customers that included viruses, it is reasonable to assume that maliciously coded programs and viruses will continue to be inadvertently (and advertently) supplied along with the expected pushes.

Autorun

In the "Defending against This Attack" section of Chapter 1, "USB Hacksaw," we touched on autorun/autoplay, the default settings, and manual manipulation techniques. In this section, we will describe how autorun interacts with the Windows application program interface (API) in order to activate a program automatically. The primary purpose of autorun is to provide automation for software installations and multimedia applications. Nearly all data that is shipped on a CD/DVD has some type of autorun capabilities built into it.

A file named autorun.inf is responsible for the automagic that occurs when a CD/DVD is inserted into a computer. This file should be located in the root of the disk and can contain a number of customizable command-line options. These options will be covered in greater detail in the later sections of this chapter. In the meantime, it is important to understand that when the autorun feature in Windows is enabled, by either default or manual adjustments, Windows Explorer will read the contents of the autorun.inf file and automatically initiate any instructions it finds. This is the same concept the U3 creators intended to exploit when their drives are inserted.

Whenever removable media is inserted or detached from a computer, a *WM_DEVICECHANGE* message is sent to all running applications. This message is sent to all the top-level Windows according to their z-order. The z-order simply refers to the placement of Windows on the screen. So, in this case, the window at the topmost position receives the message first and then the remaining windows receive it in succession. To view this interaction, you can trap this message using the following API:

```
Public Declare Function CallWindowProc Lib "user32" Alias
    "CallWindowProcA" (ByVal lpPrevWndFunc As Long, _
ByVal hWnd As Long, _
ByVal Msg As Long, _
ByVal wParam As Long, _
ByVal lParam As Long) As Long
```

The ByVal wParam As Long, _ parameter of this message contains code that defines exactly what event occurred. Another event that is useful to us is DBT_DEVICEARRIVAL. This message is sent after a new device or a removable media has been inserted. Applications will receive this message when the newly inserted device is ready for use. At the same time, the Windows Explorer process will display the autoplay window that gives the user options for what to do with the inserted media.

The Windows shell then processes the *WM_DEVICECHANGE* messages and sends an interrupt request. It checks the registry to determine if the autorun function is enabled for the associated drive. If enabled, the Windows OS tries to locate the "autorun.inf" file in the root directory of the newly connected device. Once this file is located, the instructions contained in the file will be executed.

The instructions read from the autorun.inf file dictate what the Windows autorun feature will do whenever a removable media is inserted into the computer. This file instructs the Windows shell what to run and how to load the data contained on the device or drive with which it is associated. The following criteria are used in the determination process.

- Which applications or executable files will be run when the associated drive detects newly connected media
- The icon that will be displayed when the drive is viewed in Windows Explorer
- The menu options to be displayed to the user when he or she right-clicks the drive in Windows Explorer

Autorun.inf contains a series of instructions that the Windows shell executes when a drive or media (CD/DVD) has been inserted. The following five commands are available:

1. Defaulticon – This line specifies what the default icon will be for the drive. The user will see this icon when they right-click on the drive.
2. Icon – This line specifies the path and the file name of an application-specific icon for the drive.
3. Open – This line specifies the path and the file name of the application that will be launched when the drive is inserted.

4. Shell – This line identifies the default command in the shortcut menu of the drive.
5. Shell\verb – This line can be used to add options to the right-click shortcut menu of the drive.

Included below is a simple example of a typical CD/DVD autorun.inf file. The number of command options supported by the autorun.inf is not limited by the available programs on the computer hosting the device. USB flash drives can be customized to provide an alternate repository for transporting tools one might find useful to be called automatically.

```
[Autorun]
Open=reallycool.exe /argument1
Icon=\foldername\little.ico
```

The bullets below provide a brief explanation of the commands contained in a basic CD/DVD autorun.inf. The addition statements required to enable autorun specifically for a standard flash drive will be provided separately in this section.

- *[autorun]* – This tells Windows to read the file as an autorun.inf file.
- *open* = – This line tells Windows which application to launch.
- *reallycool.exe* – This is the value referring to the application that will be automatically started when the drive is detected. Windows will look for this file in the root directory of the inserted disk. If you need to access a file located in a specific folder or subdirectory, then you can choose to specify a path relative to the root. An example of this would be *open=%SystemRoot%\reallycool.exe.*
- */argument1* – This is the switch that is passed to the application as a command-line option. Any command-line parameter that is supported by the application you are calling can be used here as well.
- *icon* = *\foldername\little.ico* – This is specifying the path to where the icon associated for the drive can be found.

As stated earlier, the autorun feature was primarily designed to automatically launch applications distributed on CD/DVDs, but it can also be used on USB-based removable media for the same purpose. Per Microsoft, autorun only works on removable storage devices if all of the following rules are met.[J]

1. The device driver must notify the operating system that a disk has been inserted by sending a WM_DEVICECHANGE message.
2. An autorun.inf file must be found in the root directory of the inserted media.
3. Autorun must be enabled through control panel or the Windows registry.
4. No other foreground programs can be running on the system that will suppress the autorun feature.

In a typical scenario, when a USB device is connected to a machine, the driver will send a WM_DEVICECHANGE message to the Windows shell. This satisfies

---

[J]http://msdn.microsoft.com/en-us/library/cc144204%28VS.85%29.aspx

the first rule. If the USB device has an autorun.inf file in its root, the second rule is met. If the autorun feature is enabled in the Windows registry, this rule is also met. The fourth rule is not an issue so long as there are no third-party applications running, which will suppress the autorun feature.

Keeping the previous circumstances in mind, let's say a user wants to find out what is on the USB drive. He or she can double-click on the drive in Windows Explorer, double-click the drive in "My Computer," or right-click the drive and select **Open Folder** to view files. Once any of these options are initiated, the application that is being called in the autorun.inf file will be executed.

The autorun.inf file used on USB-based media drives requires a slightly different setup in order to get an application to launch automatically. The autorun feature for removable drives will likely be disabled by default, requiring user interaction. The information included below will walk you through how to set up autorun specifically for removable media.

```
[Autorun]
UseAutoPlay=1
ShellExecute=reallycool.exe
Shell\open\command=reallycool.exe
Icon=foldername\little.ico
Label=Click on me!
Action=Run Program to speed up your computer
```

Included below are descriptions of the command statements used in the above reference. Only new elements not previously covered in the CD/DVD autorun sample will be described here.

- *UseAutoPlay = 1* – This line enables the USB to provide the autoplay menu function.
- *ShellExecute = reallycool.exe* – This line tells the operating system what file to execute.
- *Shell\open\command = reallycool.exe* – This line tells the operating system to register the specified file as autorun, allowing the malware to load it when any of these files are called.
- *Label = Click on me!* – This line is used to specify the name of drive as it will be displayed to the user by autoplay and Explorer.
- *Action = Run Program* – This line adds a menu option to the autoplay menu displayed to the user when he or she right-clicks on the drive.

As you can see, there are additional statements required to enable the autorun feature from a removable drive. Once you have built your autorun.inf with the proper statements and parameters, your drive should display the options you have included. Figures 3.1 and 3.2 below illustrate an example of this autorun.inf.

By now, you should have a reasonable understanding of how autorun and autoplay interact with Windows depending on the type of media used. It is also important to understand specific examples of situations where these have been exploited. The next section will illustrate how to create an exploit that leverages removable media.

FIGURE 3.1

Autoplay Dialogue Presented upon Insertion of the Drive

FIGURE 3.2

Explorer View of the Inserted Drive (F: Drive)

How to Recreate the Attack

The most common deployment scenario, given in our previous discussions in Chapters 1 and 2, "USB Hacksaw" and "USB Switchblade," respectively, would be executing the payload of your choice by way of a U3-enabled flash drive. Using this method, you have the ability to craft a custom ISO enabling any program to run automatically simply by connecting a U3-compatible flash drive to a computer. Once again, this is assuming that autorun is enabled and working properly; otherwise, console access will be required to initiate via manual means.

This section will walk you through the creation of a custom ISO that can be used to automatically execute a program on a computer using a U3-compatible flash drive. Here is what you will need to recreate an attack of this sort.

- A scripting tool called *AutoIt*
- The U3 Universal Customizer tool
- A U3-supported flash drive
- A text editor program
- Icons to label your flash drive

This section will use the U3-enabled flash drive and Universal Customizer program applied in the previous chapters. Download and install the most recent version of AutoIt that is available on the Internet (www.autoitscript.com). Once you have downloaded the package, the following instructions will guide you through the installation process.

1. Run the AutoIt installation executable, then select **Next** when prompted, as shown in Figure 3.3.
2. Ensure you concur with the agreement presented (Figure 3.4) and click **I Agree**.
3. Select **Edit the script** when the dialogue box appears as seen in Figure 3.5, then click **Next**. This option will prevent accidental execution of the script on your workstation during testing.
4. There are some script examples that can be installed, as seen in Figure 3.6.

TIP

These are convenient for reference if you are having difficulty understanding the syntax. They are not required in order to complete the next section, but you may find them useful at a later time.

---

5. Click **Next** to continue the installation as seen in Figure 3.6.
6. Choose a custom location for installation or accept the default as indicated in Figure 3.7, and click **Install**.
7. Once the installation completes, click **Finish**, as illustrated in Figure 3.8.

FIGURE 3.3

AutoIt Installation Screenshot

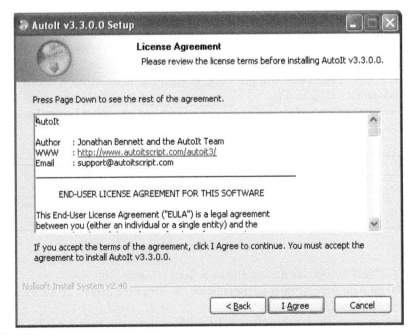

FIGURE 3.4

AutoIt Installation Screenshot

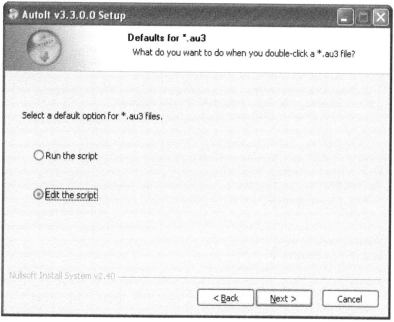

FIGURE 3.5

Autolt Installation Screenshot

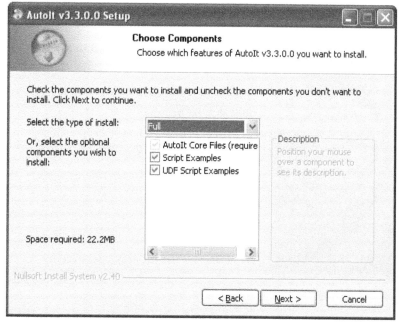

FIGURE 3.6

Autolt Installation Screenshot

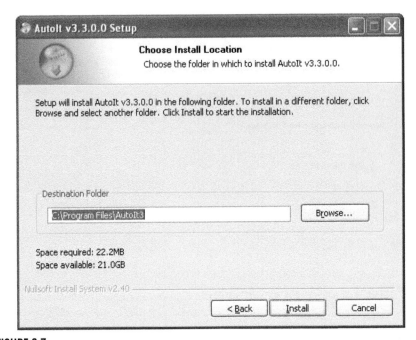

FIGURE 3.7

AutoIt Installation Screenshot

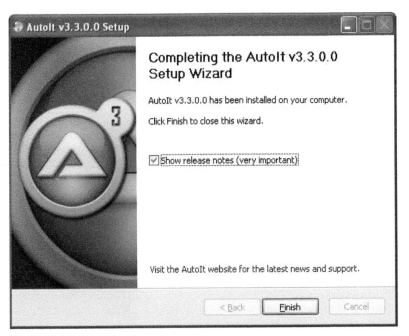

FIGURE 3.8

AutoIt Installation Screenshot

Now that the installation of AutoIt is completed, we will begin building the executable. In this example, we will send predefined text to Notepad, which will render it on the screen once activated via autorun.

1. Launch AutoIt.
2. Go to **File** and select **New File.**
3. On line one, enter **Run("notepad.exe")**
4. On line two, enter **Run WinWaitActive("Untitled - Notepad")**
5. On line three, enter **Send("YOU ARE NOW INFECTED WITH THE PINK SLIP VIRUS.{ENTER}NANNY NANNY BOO BOO{ENTER}")** or a phrase of your choice
6. On line four, enter **Sleep(500)**
7. On line five, enter **Send("+{UP 2}")**
8. On line six, enter **Sleep(500)**
9. Save the file using "hotfix" as the name.
10. Test the script to ensure it is working as intended by right-clicking the newly created file and selecting **Run Script**.
11. If there are any errors, the tool will let you know on what line the problem is located. The final script should look something like Figure 3.9.

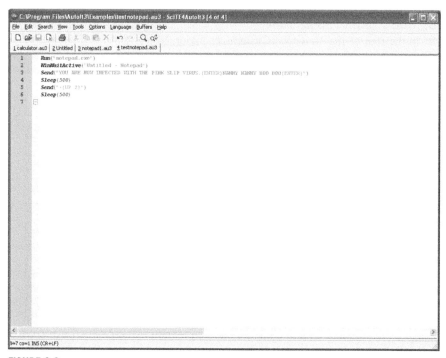

FIGURE 3.9

AutoIt Example Script

12. Next, we will compile the newly created script into an .exe file. To do this, simply right-click the **script** and select **Compile Script**. You should now see your file with an .exe extension in the same directory you originally created it.
13. Go to the directory where you extracted the Universal Customizer and copy the file you just created to the U3CUSTOM folder.
14. Download or choose a benign-looking icon. A good site to go to for this is www. freeiconsweb.com. This example used an icon called *MSN.ico*.
15. Next, we will create a custom autorun.inf file that will be used to run your payload. Open up a new text file and type in the following lines.

```
[Autorun]
open=HotFix.exe
icon=msn.ico
shell\Open\Command= HotFix.exe
shell\open\Default=1
shell\Explore\Command= HotFix.exe
shell\Autoplay\command= HotFix.exe
label=Microsoft HotFix
```

16. Save this file as autorun.inf and place it into the U3CUSTOM folder.
17. Next, run ISOCreate.cmd. This file can be found in the root of the Universal Customizer folder. Press any key to end the script when prompted. An example of the ISOCreate.cmd is included in Figure 3.10.
18. Insert your U3 USB flash drive.
19. In the root of the Universal Customizer folder, locate and run Universal Customizer.exe. Execute the program and follow the on-screen steps, accepting the default options provided in the installation dialogues. Steps 9 to 13 in the "How

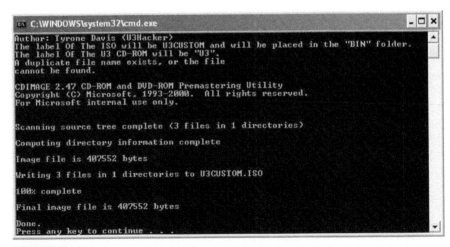

FIGURE 3.10

ISOCreate.cmd Example Script

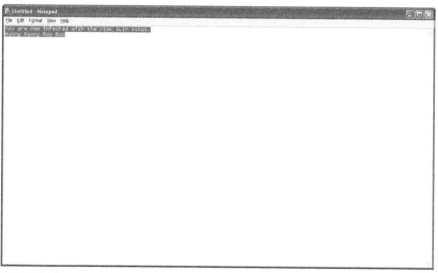

FIGURE 3.11

Intended Output of the AutoIt Script

to Recreate the Attack" section of Chapter 1, "USB Hacksaw," provides detailed directions and screenshot illustrations for these steps.

20. That's it! Now you're ready to rock and roll. Eject and insert your U3 drive into your computer. If everything is properly in place, you should see the image shown in Figure 3.11.

EVOLUTION OF THE ATTACK

Computer viruses have been a technological nuisance since the inception of the digital age. The first computer virus is a debatable subject, but some conclude it was known as the *Creeper*. This virus was authored by Bob Thomas in the early 1970s. Creeper was an experimental, self-replicating program that targeted the then-popular Tenex operating system. It was produced in a lab and was not written for malicious purposes. Its payload was fairly benign in nature, and infected systems displayed the message, "I'M THE CREEPER: CATCH ME IF YOU CAN."[K]

In 1981, the Rother J virus was one of the first to appear "in the wild." It attached itself to the Apple DOS 3.3 operating system. It was written by Richard Skrenta as a practical joke when he was still in high school. On its fiftieth use, the Elk Cloner virus would be activated, infecting the machine and displaying a short poem. Skrenta

---

[K]http://vx.netlux.org/lib/atc01.html

then decided that it would be funny to put a copy of his "code" on the school computers and rig it to copy itself onto floppy disks that other students used on the system. This was how the Elk Cloner virus was released into the wild.[L]

Agent.BTZ was mentioned previously in the "Invasive Species among Us" section and will be expanded upon here to exemplify the evolution of similar strains. This worm includes an additional payload known as a *Trojan dropper*. A dropper is recognized as a variety of Trojan that will look to download and execute other malware once it has infected a system. Upon insertion of the removable media, the virus will detect the newly recognized drive and then attempt self-replication to the device. If successful, it will then create an autorun.inf file in the root of the drive, which tells the system to run the associated malicious code. When the infected drive is inserted into a virgin host, the operating system will detect the autorun.inf file and run the payload contained within. Agent.BTZ can also spread through mapped network drives, but its primary means of propagation targets removable media.

Agent.BTZ is one of many viruses that have hijacked the removable-media bandwagon. A vast majority of these have two major concepts in common. These include the creation of an autorun.inf file and exploitation of the autorun feature built into the Windows operating system. W32/Agent.BTZ autorun.inf shown below is the content of the file that it creates. *[RANDOM]* represents the various names the worm can create for the *.dll file. This is used to evade automated detection and removal mechanisms.

```
[autorun]
open=
shell\open=Explore
shell\open\Command=rundll32.exe .\\[RANDOM].dll,InstallM
shell\open\Default=1
```

As has been previously discussed, this file is responsible for infecting new systems when the infected USB drive is plugged in. Opening the infected USB drive will automatically launch the rundll32.exe. Once this infected file is executed, it will copy itself to directories on the system included below.

```
%system%\muxbde40.dll
%system%\\winview.ocx
%temp%\6D73776D706461742E746C62FA.tmp
%system%\system32\mswmpdat.tlb
```

Winview.ocx, mswmpdat.tlb, and 6D73776D706461742E746C62FA.tmp are log files, and their contents are encrypted. Muxdbe40.dll is the virus itself, just with a different name. After these files are in place, the virus then modifies the following registry keys.

[L]www.smh.com.au/articles/2007/09/01/1188671795625.html

```
HKLM\Software\Classes\CLSID\{FBC38650-8B81-4BE2-B321-EEFF22D7DC62}
(default) = Java.Runtime.52
HKLM\Software\Classes\CLSID\{FBC38650-8B81-4BE2-B321-EEFF22D7DC62}\
    InprocServer32\
(default) = C:\WINDOWS\system32\muxbde40.dll
HKLM\Software\Classes\CLSID\{FBC38650-8B81-4BE2-B321-EEFF22D7DC62}\
    InprocServer32\
ThreadingModel = Apartment
HKLM\SOFTWARE\Microsoft\Windows\CurrentVersion\ShellService
    ObjectDelayLoad\
UpdateCheck = {FBC38650-8B81-4BE2-B321-EEFF22D7DC62}
HKLM\Software\Microsoft\Windows\CurrentVersion\StrtdCfg
HKLM\Software\Classes\CLSID\{FBC38650-8B81-4BE2-B321-EEFF22D7DC62}
HKLM\Software\Classes\CLSID\{FBC38650-8B81-4BE2-B321-EEFF22D7DC62}\
    InprocServer32\
```

Agent.BTZ is just one instance of many USB-focused viruses. The logic behind most of these is not complicated; in fact, Agent.BTZ is actually a variant of the W32/SillyFDC, which was first discovered back in 2005. Some of the other removable media viral variants are included in Table 3.1 for reference.[M]

Conficker is another worm whose variants' infectivity is extremely prevalent today. In fact, since it was first detected in November of 2008, the number of infections has already risen to 7 million.[N] "Conficker B copies itself as the autorun.inf to removable media drives in the system thereby forcing the executable to be launched every time a removable drive is inserted into a system. It combines this with a unique social engineering attack to great effect. It sets the "shell execute" keyword in the autorun.inf file to be the string "Open folder to view files" thereby tricking users into running the autorun program."[2] Conficker is considered a botnet and could easily call for reinforcing weaponry that can be used toward any attack the authors may deem necessary.

Table 3.1 Removable media viruses

Removable media viral variants	
Worm:W32/Conficker	Worm:Win32/Autorun.BO
Worm:VBS/SillyFDC.F	Worm:Win32/Autorun.RA
Worm:Win32/SillyShareCopy.AC	Worm:AutoIt/Renocide.gen!A
Worm:Win32/Autorun.A	Worm:Win32/SillyShareCopy.E
PWS:Win32/Wowsteal.ZE!inf	Worm:Win32/VB.CD
Worm:Win32/Nuj.A	Worm:Win32/Emold.B
Worm:Win32/Autorun.PH	Worm:Win32/Slenfbot.ACP

[M]www.microsoft.com/security/portal
[N]www.confickerworkinggroup.org/wiki/pmwiki.php/ANY/InfectionTracking

WHY ALL THE FUSS?

The risks that viruses can present cover a broad spectrum. Loss of data, resources, time, trade secrets, and personally identifiable data are just a few risks that can be introduced by malware. This section will highlight the most vicious viral concoction currently among us and how it might affect your network and data. Botnets are a recent threat example which exemplifies most of the viral hazards these entities can and do expose, often in an undetectable manner.

Botnets

A botnet is nothing more than an instrument cybercriminals use to carry out Internet-based crime. They closely resemble a Mafia hierarchy whose actions are controlled by a godfather. Listed below are a few of the possible activities botnets can be programmed to perform.

- Distributed denial-of-service attacks
- E-mail spamming
- Infecting new hosts
- Identity and credential theft
- Transporting illegal software
- Google AdSense and advertisement add-on abuse

Distributed Denial-of-Service Attacks

A distributed denial-of-service attack (DDoS) is an Internet-based assault that is delivered from multiple sources (botnet) to one destination. The goal of these attacks is to severely impair the victim's network or Web site in such a way that it can no longer service legitimate requests. During a large-scale attack, Internet service provider (ISP) networks can also be affected, resulting in degraded services to its customers. The botnet master can control a large number of bot computers from a remote location, leveraging their bandwidth and resources to send session requests to the intended victim. Botnets are frequently used to carry out these types of attacks because their sessions closely resemble normal Internet traffic patterns, just in excessive amounts. Depending on the nature of the attack, it can be hard to filter out what is and is not bad traffic. The most common tactics that attackers use in DDoS attacks are TCP SYN and UDP floods.

E-mail Spamming

In the past, whenever you were inundated by spam messages or phishing scams, you could report the incident to your ISP, who would then track down the source of the abuse and blacklist the Internet Protocol (IP). Spammers realized very quickly that these tactics were no longer effective. They are now operating their own botnets or renting existing infections to blast out spam messages. Losing one bot has little impact on the overall mission if there are thousands of other bots to keep up the pace. Botnets are an ideal platform for spammers. A single spam message can be sent to an individual bot and then redistributed to all others, which then relay the spam. This allows the individuals responsible for the operation to remain anonymous while all the blame gets transferred to the infected computers.

Infecting New Hosts

Botnets can enlist new recruits to join in the game through social engineering and the distribution of malicious phishing e-mail messages. These messages could have infected attachments or maybe an embedded link to a Web site that has a malicious ActiveX control. Just about everyone who has an e-mail account has seen a suspicious message in their inbox. The most important thing to remember is that if you do not know the person who sent the e-mail, it should be deleted, not opened.

Identity Theft

Identity theft is on the rise, and the trends are showing no signs of slowing down. Identities are bought and sold in online black markets every day throughout the world. Credit card numbers can be bought for as little as 50 cents while a full identity complete with social security number, mother's maiden name, account information, and passwords can be purchased for less than 20 bucks. Botnets are often used to gather the majority of this information.

Bots have also been found to use keyloggers and packet sniffers to collect confidential information being entered or transmitted in clear text. Social security numbers, credit cards, banking data, gaming valuables, or any other critical credentials can be easily collected using these tools. If the infected computer uses encrypted communication channels such as SSL, then sniffing traffic on the victim's machine is useless, since the appropriate key to decrypt the packets is not known. This is when keyloggers come into play. Using these tools, an attacker can collect every keystroke a user enters, making it very easy to gather sensitive information.

Transporting Illegal Software

Botnets can be used to transfer and store pirated software. They use these areas for temporary holding tanks that usually contain a slew of illegal material. Everything from pornography to full operating systems has been found on machines infected with bot programs.

Google AdSense and Advertisement Add-On Abuse

Google AdSense offers businesses the opportunity to earn revenue displaying Google advertisements on their own Web sites. Revenue is generated based on the number of clicks the ads receives. Botnets can and are used to artificially increment the click counters by scripting the process of site visits and viewing the advertisements.

The process can be further improved if the bot program hijacks the start page of the infected computer so that the clicks are executed each time the user opens his or her browser. Hosting companies often fall prey to this scam.

DEFENDING AGAINST THIS ATTACK

According to study done by brighthub, half of the top 10 viruses of 2009 were exploiting the Windows autorun feature.[o] When it comes to protection from USB-based malicious code, one may choose to tackle the problem from a few different angles. Each approach has beneficial and detrimental consequences, and these will be discussed in the remaining sections.

Malicious code currently has two preferred methods of transmission when it comes to removable media. The first is a technique that involves the infection of existing executables or files on the removable device. Propagation occurs when the tainted drive is introduced to a clean machine and the contaminated files are run from the media by the user. The more popular approach these programs take is to manipulate or create an autorun.inf file for auto-execution.

The most effective way to prevent USB-based malware from leveraging Windows autorun features is to prevent a computer from being able to run autorun.inf files completely. The only drawback of this method is that it will prevent the operating system from being able to read *all* autorun.inf files. This includes the convenient feature build into CDs and DVDs that makes them automagically run as soon as the operating system detects that they have been inserted. After making this change, a user of the system will have to navigate the removable media manually in order to initialize the appropriate program.

By following these steps, you can disable the usage of autorun.inf files completely from the system. This can be done by adding a key called autorun.inf in the registry paths included below.

```
HKEY_LOCAL_MACHINE\SOFTWARE\Microsoft\Windows NT\CurrentVersion\
    IniFileMapping
```

Add an entry under the newly created *autorun.inf* key called @. Next, set the value of the @ entry to "@SYS:DoesNotExist". Alternately, you can copy the below-mentioned text to a Notepad file and save it with a .reg extension. Once this file is created, browse to the saved location and double-click to add the registry value.

```
[HKEY_LOCAL_MACHINE\SOFTWARE\Microsoft\Windows NT\CurrentVersion\
    IniFileMapping\Autorun.inf]
@="@SYS:DoesNotExist"
```

This value tells Windows to treat autorun.inf as if it were a configuration file from a pre–Windows 95 application. The "IniFileMapping" is a key that tells Windows

---

[o]www.brighthub.com/computing/smb-security/articles/44811.aspx

how to handle the .inf files. In this case, it tells the operating system to parse the registry key included below for direction when it encounters an autorun.inf file. Since the "DoesNotExist" key is fictitious, the OS treats the autorun.inf as if it were empty, so the instructions mentioned in the autorun.inf are not executed.

Due to the inconsistencies you might encounter on different types of operating systems, you may decide that the best strategy for a particular situation would be to disable features on the USB device itself. Some USB flash drives include a read-only switch, but they make up the minority of what is on the market and in use today. The switch does no good if left unengaged, and most users don't understand its purpose or realize that it even exists.

If the flash drive is like most, which means having a file system formatted with FAT32, then there is a simple yet effective method to prevent propagation. If the drive uses an autorun.inf to provide a specific functionality you desire, do not apply this fix, as it will render the file and its functions useless. You will need access to a hex editor for the following steps. A good free hex editor called *HxD* can be found at the author's Web site (http://mh-nexus.de/en/downloads.php?product=HxD).

WARNING

You should test these procedures on an empty flash drive. If data exists on the drive, be sure you have a backup in case corruption occurs.

The following defensive technique must be accomplished on Windows XP or an alternate operating system due to recent updates with Vista and beyond. For Windows Vista and greater, a write on a volume handle will only succeed if the drive or volume is not mounted by a file system or if one of the following conditions is true:

1. Writing occurs on boot sectors.
2. There is any writing to sectors outside of the file system area.
3. *FSCTL_LOCK_VOLUME* or *FSCTL_DISMOUNT_VOLUME* has been used to lock or dismount the volume.
4. The volume or drive does not have a file system. (Mounted as a raw volume.)

The write for a particular disk handle needs only one of the following circumstances to be true for it to be successful.

1. The sectors that will be written to do not fall inside a volume's extents.
2. Sectors that will be written to fall inside a mounted volume, but something has explicitly locked or dismounted the volume by way of *FSCTL_LOCK_VOLUME* or *FSCTL_DISMOUNT_VOLUME*.
3. Sectors that will be written to fall inside a volume that is not unmounted or lacks a file system.[3] Sectors that will be written are within an unmounted or nonformatted volume.

The conditions listed above will likely prevent you from accomplishing a hex edit on a USB drive from a Vista system. If you have access to a machine running XP Professional, fortifying your USB autorun.inf file can be accomplished in a few steps. Download a hex editor and install it, if you have not done so already. Next, you will need to insert the USB flash drive and create an empty autorun.inf on the root of this drive. Once you have done this, follow the instructions below to complete the process. These instructions were built using the HxD hex editor from an XP system, so if you are using another editor or operating system, the instructions will be slightly off, but the concept is still the same.

1. Open the HxD hex editor, then go to the Extra menu, and select **Open disk**.

> **NOTE**
> Close all other programs or applications that are accessing the USB flash drive.

2. Uncheck the Open as Read-only box, then select your flash drive.
3. Go to the Search menu and select **Find**, then type **AUTORUN** in the Search for window and select **OK**. Figure 3.12 illustrates what should be found.
4. Ensure you have the value highlighted as seen in Figure 3.12, then select **Edit**, then **Fill selection**. In the Fill selection dialogue, you will find a section called *Hex-values*. Change the 20 to 40 in the box provided. The dialogue should now look like Figure 3.13.
5. Select **OK**, then **Save**, and click **Yes** to the Warning.
6. Close HxD and remove your flash drive.

The value of 20 indicated the archive bit setting, and the change to 40 changed to the device bit. Now, when you browse to the disk, the autorun.inf file can be seen, but it cannot be deleted, opened, edited, overwritten, or have its attributes changed.[P]

For those of you without XP or an alternate operating system, there are tools that some vendors provide to inoculate your USB flash drive autorun.inf. Panda produces a free utility called *USB Vaccine* that creates an unwritable autorun.inf file on the drive. The software and user guides are available on their Web site. They have also just released a NTFS beta version for USB flash drives that are formatted in this manner.[Q]

Antimalware

The anti-malicious code market has been steadily growing for well over a decade. Anti-virus, Trojan, spyware, adware, and rootkit products are abundant, and most provide an adequate amount of protection. Many new players have entered this game, often finding their niche when these new threats arise. Most established AV vendors

---

[P]https://security-shell.ws/showthread.php?t=26372
[Q]http://research.pandasecurity.com/archive/Panda-USB-Vaccine-with-NTFS-Support.aspx

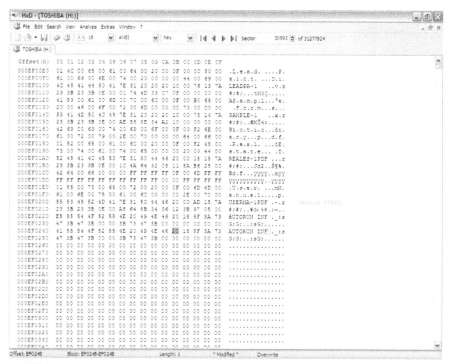

FIGURE 3.12

HxD AUTORUN Search Results with Applicable Bytes Highlighted

deem spyware, adware, and rootkits as separate entities, thus requiring additional cleaning engines or components. These existing vendors are often slow acknowledging fresh adaptations, leaving room for these startups to become viable players in the market. Lately, many of the top vendors such as Trend Micro, Symantec, and McAfee now include features to fight against these updated threats. You can visit the Anti-Spyware Coalition[R] Web site to validate standards, participating members, and updated developments in the area of spyware prevention.

EPIC FAIL

Reliance on AV alone can leave you susceptible to USB and other attacks as demonstrated in Chapter 2, "USB Switchblade." Use of a firewall, heuristic-based engines,[S] and adherence to security best practices[T] will significantly minimize the risk from these threats.

[R]www.antispywarecoalition.org/

[S]www.securityfocus.com/infocus/1542

[T]www.sans.org/reading_room/whitepapers/bestprac/system_administrator_security_best_practice_657

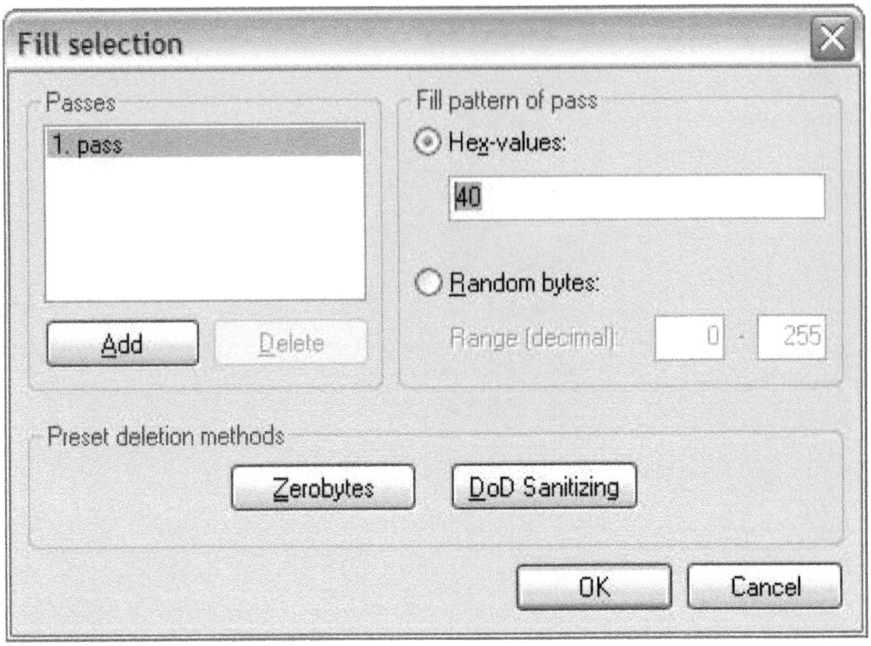

FIGURE 3.13

HxD Fill Selection Dialogue with Modified Value

There are numerous vendors who supply free versions of their products for home and personal use. Many of these can provide ample protection, but only when combined with additional tools, which compensate for areas where these free versions are lacking. Examples of this would be to use the free version of Avast[U] (AV) with MalwareBytes[V] (anti-spyware) or AVG[W] (AV) along with Spybot[X] (anti-spyware).

Those inclined to use free protection products should consider alternating these tools on a regular basis to ensure you have eradicated the highest majority of pesky programs. Free versions often fail to update the engines and filter drivers, which may leave you vulnerable to new forms of attacks. They will still provide updated signatures or definitions, but this may not be enough to fight off the most current viral variants. If you choose to alternate or update AV programs, uninstalling the one being replaced is usually the best option. Some of these programs can conflict, detect, and inadvertently remove the other, rendering corruption or a system crash depending on the specific functionality enabled.

[U]www.avast.com/eng/avast_4_home.html

[V]www.malwarebytes.org/

[W]http://free.avg.com/us-en/homepage

[X]www.safer-networking.org/en/home/index.html

Whether you are using a free product or have purchased a licensed copy of the latest and greatest, it is always a good idea to keep up with comparative analyses in the anti-malware realm. At minimum, annual checkups are recommended on these products to ensure they continue to meet updated quality and performance criteria. There are several independent organizations that provide this data for consumer consumption. Included below are some of these organizations and certification bodies that can be referenced when the need arises.

- AV-Comparatives,[Y] an Austrian nonprofit organization, provides independent antivirus software tests that are free to the public. To be included in these standard tests, vendors must fulfill various conditions and a minimum set of requirements.
- AV-Test[Z] includes testing against the latest proficiency and development standards. This company is one of the leading global providers of test scenarios that analyze the effectiveness and behavioral aspects of these security solutions.
- Antimalware[AA] provides free public testing results. The choices of test scope and vendor participants are established by a panel of experts who are not affiliated with vendors tested against. Paid services are also provided for nonpublic testing and research.
- ICSA Labs[BB] is an accredited certification body that performs cryptographic and security testing and works with security product vendors to help them understand and meet requirements mandated by the United States and Canadian governments in order to participate in government markets.
- WestCoastLabs[CC] is another certification body that provides operational testing in areas that are structured to satisfy the needs of both clients and the regulatory authorities to aid operation of the international standards (ISO/IEC 17025:2005).

If you are planning to purchase an AV product or a security suite of tools, be sure to evaluate their additional features independently. Most vendors are now including bundled products containing firewalls, HIPS, antispam, and other components, which can sometimes lack in luster. Some of these products features can also have interoperability issues that can complicate normal operation and individual user compatibility.

Be mindful of illegitimate or rogue products and services in this market.[DD] The saturation of software in this industry has left much room for fraudulent folks who peddle their products to unsuspecting victims. These fake healers are often driven by spam or deceptive advertising and usually masquerade as genuine or well-known vendors. They commonly deploy invalid detection techniques and produce false positives, even on clean systems.

[Y] www.av-comparatives.org/comparativesreviews/main-tests
[Z] www.av-test.org/publications
[AA] www.anti-malware-test.com/
[BB] www.icsalabs.com/
[CC] www.westcoastlabs.com/productTestReports/
[DD] www.2-spyware.com/corrupt-anti-spyware

SUMMARY

The days of malicious code isolation on Windows systems is nearly gone. These developers are beginning to code their creations to infect cross or multiplatform systems. New strains are being cultivated to perform joint task force operations on Windows, Solaris, Linux, and OS X, and some are now even targeting networking equipment. Mobile phone–based malware types are another growing trend and will likely continue to be a major issue moving forward.

Malicious code will continue to keep security vendors and professionals fighting on their heels into the new decade. Removable media appears to be one of the many favorite avenues for propagation and shows no signs of slacking off. Proper precautions must be exercised with removable media on foreign and known systems alike.

Endnotes

1. www.wired.com/threatlevel/2008/08/virus-infects-s/. Accessed October 2009.
2. http://mtc.sri.com/Conficker/. Accessed October 2009.
3. http://msdn.microsoft.com/en-us/library/aa365748%28VS.85%29.aspx. Accessed November 2009.

Printed and bound by CPI Group (UK) Ltd, Croydon, CR0 4YY

03/10/2024

01040345-0001